AF522395

MANBENDRA NATH ROY

MANBENDRA NATH ROY

Edited by
M.K. SINGH

ANMOL PUBLICATIONS PVT. LTD.
NEW DELHI - 110 002 (INDIA)

ANMOL PUBLICATIONS PVT. LTD.
H.O.: 4374/4B, Ansari Road, Darya Ganj,
New Delhi-110 002 (India)
Ph.: 23278000, 23261597
B.O.: No. 1015, Ist Main Road, BSK IIIrd Stage
IIIrd Phase, IIIrd Block,
Bangalore - 560 085 (India)
Visit us at: www.anmolpublications.com

Manbendra Nath Roy

© Reserved

First Published, 2008

ISBN 978-81-261-3519-6

PRINTED IN INDIA

Printed at Mehra Offset Press, Delhi.

CONTENTS

PREFACE

M.N. Roy was a great Marxist philosopher and Indian freedom fighter. He was one of the extremists in the struggle of Indian national freedom. For quite sometime he remained under the influence of Communism, but subsequently he changed his ideology and struggled even from the platform of Indian National Congress. His approach to the problem was absolutely different and quite untraditional. He had deep faith in individual freedom. He was a rationalist and wanted to test every philosophy by the yardstick of reason and rationality. He very strongly believed in the concept of freedom and placed that above everything else. For him state and society should come latter and the individual first in all social, economic and political arrangements. About human nature he said that it must be governed by the same principles as physical universe. His significant contribution, however, is his concept of organized democracy which was quite different from indirect democracies in the East and the West.

In his philosophy organized democracy provided more freedom to the individual than indirect democracy. To a large extent he was indebted to Marx for his political ideas but with the passage of time he tried to interpret that in a way which was quite different from that of Marx. He even challenged his basic concepts of dialectical materialism and theory of surplus value. For the first time he gave it a very logical way, the concept of decolonisation. His ideas were also defective in many ways but all the more he is still studied seriously.

The book covers up the detail about M.N. Roy comprising his Life Sketch, His Concept of Philosophy, A Communist Leader and Revolutionary, As Fugitive, Jail Life and Reaction to policies, Theses on Chinese Problem, Concept of Radical Humanism and an Overview.

The book is of tremendous significance for the students, teachers, scholars and researchers etc.

Preface

In March 1919, he also became close to Michael Borodin, Comintern's emissary to Mexico and founded the Communist Party of Mexico. In May 1920, he went to Moscow at the invitation of Lenin to attend the second congress of Comintern. There he presented a Supplementary Thesis to Lenin's Theses on The National and Colonial Question. Though initially created a stir, his supplementary thesis was accepted along with the main thesis presented by Lenin. Roy rose to occupy the highest offices of the Communist International and led the Commintern's delegation to China (1927). At the same time he authored such Marxist classics as India in Transition (1922), The Future of Indian Politics (1926) and Revolution and Counter-revolution in China (1930); and founded the organ of the emigre Communist Party of India, The Vanguard (and later The Masses) and edited it for seven years (1922-28).

Denouncing Communism

Roy broke with the Communist International in 1929 having publicly opposed the Stalinist line adopted by the Comintern at its Sixth Congress. Returning to India he spent six years in various prisons during which he wrote a 3000-page draft manuscript provisionally titled The Philosophical Consequence of Modern Science. On his release he campaigned against every variety of authoritarianism, supported the anti-fascist war, drew up a Draft Constitution for free India and the outlines of a decentralist people's plan for economic development.

Radical Humanism

Disillusioned with both bourgeois democracy and communism, he devoted the last years of his life to the formulation of an alternative philosophy which he called Radical Humanism and of which he wrote a detailed exposition in Reason, Romanticism and Revolution. In his monumental biography, Sibnarayan Ray writes: "If Nehru had his problems, so had Roy.

From early life his sharp intellect was matched by a strong will and extra-ordinary self-confidence. It would seem that in his long political career there were only two persons and a half who, in his estimate, qualified to be his mentors. The first was Jatin Mukherji (or Bagha Jatin) from his revolutionary nationalist period; the second was Lenin (...) The half was Josef Stalin..."

Roy and Second World War

On the onset of the Second World War he asked the people to stand behind the British to fight against fascism. His line was clearly different from the of the mainstream of the national liberation movement, that was launching the Quit India movement at that juncture. According to Roy, a victory for the Germany and the Axis powers would have resulted in the end of democracy worldwide and India would never be independent. In his view to him India was to win her freedom in a free world only. He foresaw that India would attain independence following the defeat of the Axis powers and weakening of the economic base of the British Imperialism.

IHEU World Communist Congress

The 14th IHEU World Humanist Congress which attracted 600 delegates from 24 countries took place in the partially-built M.N. Roy Memorial Human Development Campus at Mumbai in Jan '99. But who was M.N. Roy and why is the world's largest humanist campus being built in his name? Over-view of the life of a founder Vice-President of IHEU. Humanist philosopher and activist with rare intellectual gifts and vast practical experience, M.N. Roy was a leading participant in revolutionary movements in four countries spread-out in three continents. A school dropout, Roy joined the ranks of the Bengal militants as a teenager, and soon became a leader of the revolutionary movement which aimed to overthrow British colonialism by means of an armed insurrection. Roy's clandestine travels in search of German and Japanese arms to achieve this purpose began in 1915. In the course of the next 15 years, Roy realised that the Japanese and the Germans had their own designs on India, discovered Karl Marx in a New York library, established in Mexico in 1917 the first communist party outside the Soviet Union, disagreed at the Second Communist International in 1920 with Lenin on the National and Colonial Question, was soon elected to the highest decision making bodies of the Communist International, travelled to China as sole emissary of the Communist International with a brief to transform the Right Wing Kuomintang into a revolutionary instrument in the hands of the proletariat, befriended Gramsci and Einstein, inspired and influenced Nehru, earned universal respect for his courage of convictions, and was expelled in 1929 from the Communist International for his heretical and non-doctrinaire views. Even though much is now known about this phase of Roy's life, one of his biographers despaired that the story of his early life may never be fully told: official documents and his notes relating to China and Russia were suppressed or destroyed because he fell out with Stalin, the manuscript of a magnum opus. The Rise and Fall of the British Empire written in 1929 and predicting the fall of the Empire was destroyed by the Nazis, to complicate matters further, Roy wrote in several languages - Bengali, English, Spanish, French, German and Russian - and often in proscribed journals and used over 15 noms de plume... Indeed, M.N. Roy is itself the most permanent of the several pseudonyms that Narendranath Bhattacharya (1887 - 1954) adopted in 1917 to escape from the American police when he jumped bail! Roy's clandestine return to India in 1930 after spending 15 years in 17 countries finally led to his arrest, in camera trial and imprisonment by the British. Despite the difficult conditions of his imprisonment as an ordinary criminal and not as a political prisoner, Roy continued with his prolific writing, and produced 9000 pages of writings, some of which have later been published as Fascism; Historical Role of Islam; Heresies of the 20th Century; Nationalism: An Antiquated Cult; Science and Philosophy etc. As a tribute to his sole companion in prison, Roy also wrote an amusing best selling critique of Hinduism: Memoirs of a Cat! On release from prison in 1936, Roy formally announced his break with Marxism by rejecting historical determinism and class war, and declared that without a cultural and philosophical revolution no social, political and economic revolution was possible. Terming this desired cultural transformation a 20th century renaissance, Roy later founded in 1946, along with his second wife Ellen Gottschalk and other colleagues, the Indian Renaissance Institute for 'spreading the spirit of Enlightenment, Humanism and the Search for Truth'. Roy formulated his materialistic approach in 22 thesis where he attempted to restore to 19th century Radicalism its humanist essence, and hence called his philosophy Radical Humanism.

Roy's approach integrates the scientific attitude and the democratic spirit - democracy is not merely a process, it is a system of values. For the Radical Humanist, the quest for freedom and search for truth constitute the basic urge of human progress. The quest for freedom is the continuation, on a higher level - of intelligence and emotion - of the biological struggle for existence. The method and programme of a social revolution must therefore be based on a reassertion of the basic principle of social progress. Hence, the programme of the humanist revolution will be based on the principles of freedom, reason and social harmony. In this way, Radicalism gives to freedom a moral-intellectual as well as social content; and it also offers a comprehensive theory of social progress in which both the dialectics of economic determinism and dynamics of ideas find their due recognition; and it deduces from the same a method and programme of social revolution in our time. Radical Humanism provides an approach to the reconstruction of the world as a commonwealth and fraternity of free men, by the collective endeavour of spiritually emancipated moral men. In 1944 Roy prepared a draft Constitution for India where he proposed an alternative system of political economy emphasising decentralisation and devolution of power, which would be in tune with his humanistic approach of restoring sovereignty to the individual in society. Roy soon rejected political parties themselves as legitimate instruments for the spread of democratic values, and in 1948 dissolved his own Radical Democratic Party which he had founded in 1940 to promote a humanist approach to politics and (most unpopularly) to support Britain's anti-fascist war efforts.

Roy's alternative proposal for a humanist society was a partyless but organised democracy with a network of people's committees as its base. His ideas are elaborated in a collection of speeches: People, Power and Parties. After dissolution of the political party, Roy spent the rest of his life working for his cherished Renaissance, and the Radical Humanist Movement joined hands with similar groups in Europe and America to found in 1952 IHEU. Roy was closely involved in the establishment of the IHEU, but could not attend due to an accident to which he finally succumbed. He was elected a founder Vice-President in absentia. A revolutionary at heart, and fired by the ideal of Human Freedom, Roy finally became a philosopher of the modern renaissance and that of the humanist revolution. Roy's approach is summarised by Justice Tarkunde: "A humanist revolution, which is designed to achieve the ideal of comprehensive democracy, must necessarily partake of the character of the ideal. A humanist revolution is also a path to be traversed rather than a goal to be achieved. A Radical Humanist who traverses the way to a humanist revolution is, therefore, succeeding all the time". And Roy's life is summarised in the eloquent tribute paid by the late Prof. G.D. Parikh: "Beginning as a nationalist worshipping geography, he could make any land his own.

Appearing to swear by a dogma, he could struggle as a rationalist; seeming to believe in ideologies, he retained an indomitable interest in ideas. Founder of a political party, he never became partisan. A politician universally respected for honesty and integrity, a man of action hailed as a philosopher. He did not strive for greatness, he strove to lead a good life and to bring such living within the reach of all those who live". One may not agree with Roy's ideas or thoughts, but a fitting memorial for this symbol of the indomitable human spirit has long been overdue.

2

M.N. Roy : Conception of Philosophy

M. N. Roy (1887-1954) is one of the greatest, if not the greatest, Indian philosopher of twentieth century. Unlike some other Indian thinkers of twentieth century, Roy has made a clear distinction between philosophy and religion in his thought. This alone, I think, entitles him to be recognized as the foremost Indian philosopher of twentieth century. According to Roy, no philosophical advancement is possible unless we get rid of orthodox religious ideas and theological dogmas. On the other hand, Roy has envisaged a very close relationship between philosophy and science. Roy has discussed the nature of philosophy and its relationship with religion and science in his books Materialism and Science and Philosophy. Philosophy, says Roy, quoting Pythagoras, in his book Materialism, is "contemplation, study and knowledge of the nature". Its function is "to know things as they are, and to find the common origin of the diverse phenomena of nature, in nature itself." "Philosophy", according to Roy, "begins when man's spiritual needs are no longer satisfied by primitive natural religion which imagines and worships a variety of gods as personification of the diverse phenomena of nature. The grown-up man discredits the nursery-tales, with which he was impressed in his spiritual childhood ... Intellectual growth impels and emboldens him to seek in nature itself the causes of all natural phenomena; to find in nature a unity behind its diversity." In his book Science and Philosophy Roy defines philosophy as "the theory of life". The function of philosophy, in words of Roy, "is to solve the riddle of the Universe". Elaborating on his definition of philosophy, Roy says:

Philosophy is the theory of life, because it was born of the efforts of man to explain nature and to understand his own being in relation to its surroundings; to solve the actual problems of life in the light of past experience, so that the solution will give him an encouraging glimpse into the future.

Philosophy and Metaphysics

Roy has made a distinction between philosophy and metaphysics. According to him, metaphysics, too, begins with the desire to discover unity behind the diversity. But it leaves the ground of Philosophy in quest of a noumenon above and beyond nature, something which is distinct from the phenomena. Thus, it abandons the inquiry into what really exists with the object of acquiring knowledge about it, and plunges into the wilderness of speculation. It takes up the absurd task of knowing the intangible as the condition for the knowledge of the tangible. It is obvious that Roy was opposed to speculative philosophy, which set for itself the impossible task of prying into the transcendental being above and behind the physical universe - of acquiring the knowledge of the reality behind the appearance.

In words of Roy: Speculative philosophy is the attempt to explain the concrete realities of existence in the light of a hypothetical absolute. It is the way not to truth, but to dream; not to knowledge but to illusion. Instead of trying to understand the world, the only reality given to man, speculative philosophy ends in denying of the existence of the only reality and declaring it to be a figment of man's imagination. An inquiry, which denies the very existence of the object to be enquired, is bound to end in idle dreams and hopeless confusion.

Philosophy and Religion

Roy is opposed not only to speculative philosophy but also to the identification of philosophy with theology and religion. As he says in Science and Philosophy: For the average educated man, the term philosophy has a very vague meaning, but sweeping application; it stands not only for speculative thought, but also for poetic fancy. In India, particularly, this vague, all-embracing sense is generally prevalent. Philosophy is not distinguished from religion and theology. Indeed, what is believed to be the distinctive feature of Indian philosophy is that it has not broken away from the medieval tradition, as modern Western philosophy did in the seventeenth century. According to Roy, "Faith in the super-natural does not permit the search for the causes of natural phenomena in nature itself. Therefore, rejection of orthodox religious ideas and theological dogmas is the condition for philosophy". With the assumption that the phenomena of nature are determined by the will of some supernatural being or beings," says Roy, "philosophy must make room for faith". What is supernatural, points out Roy, must be always beyond the understanding of man, who is himself a product of nature, and is, therefore, limited by the laws of nature.

In this way, according to Roy, "as soon as the cause of the phenomenal world is thus placed beyond the realm of human knowledge, the world itself becomes incomprehensible." Roy is of the view that, "religion is bound to be liquidated by science, because scientific knowledge enables mankind to answer questions, confronted by which in its childhood, it was compelled to assume super-natural forces or agencies." Therefore, according to Roy, in order to perform its function, "philosophy must break away from religion" and start from the reality of the physical universe.

Philosophy and Science

On the one hand, Roy regards rejection of orthodox religious ideas and theological dogmas as the essential condition of philosophy, and on the other, he envisages a very intimate relationship between philosophy and science. In fact, according to Roy, the philosophical significance of modern scientific theory is to "render the old division of labor between science and philosophy untenable". Science is, says Roy, "stepping over the old boundary line. Digging deeper and deeper into the secrets of nature, science has come up against problems, the solution of which was previously left to philosophy. Scientific inquiry has pushed into what is traditionally regarded as the 'metaphysical' realm." The problems of philosophy - cosmological, ontological and epistemological - can all be progressively solved, according to Roy, in the light of scientific knowledge. The function of philosophy is, points out Roy, to explain existence as a whole. An explanation of existence requires knowledge of existence; knowledge about the different phases of existence is gathered by the various branches of science. Therefore, in words of Roy: The function of philosophy is to coordinate the entire body of scientific knowledge into a comprehensive theory of nature and life... Therefore, philosophy is called the science of sciences. Even in his Scientific Politics, which is more in the nature of a popular lecture than a philosophical treatise, Roy says, "having thus yielded position to science, philosophy can now exist only as the science of sciences - a systematic coordination, a synthesis of all positive knowledge, continuously readjusting itself to the progressive enlargement of the store of human knowledge." Such a philosophy, according to Roy, has "nothing in common with what is traditionally known, particularly in this country, as philosophy. A mystic metaphysical conception of the world is no longer to be accorded the distinction of philosophy." In Reason, Romanticism and Revolution, too, Roy repeats his conception of philosophy as a logical coordination of all the branches of positive knowledge in a system of thought to explain the world rationally and to serve as a reliable guide for life. Thus, Roy has given a secular and modern definition of philosophy. In twentieth century the academic Indian philosophy, as taught and studied in Indian universities, has been dominated by Hindu religion, particularly advaita vedanta, owing to the pervasive influence of Radhakrishnan. At least, in twenty first century Indian "philosophy" must make a clean break from religion, and stop masquerading "religion" as "philosophy". Otherwise, the future of "Indian philosophy" will remain bleak and it will be liquidated along with religion.

The Revolt of 1857 was born out of various features ranging from the British policy of conquest and expansion to the colonial exploitation of India. Geographically speaking, it affected north-western, north and central India. The 'Sepoy Mutiny'- as it was labelled initially by the colonial official writings, focused on the 'Mutiny' theme. To colonial officials and writers it was the handiwork of a set of discontented sipahis who were unhappy with the introduction, in 1857, of the new Enfield rifle, with its distinct ammunition, which required the bullet to be bitten before loading. Rumours that the grease used on the bullets was either from the fat of cattle or pigs had symbolic implications. Thus, whereas cows were considered 'sacred' by the Hindus, the Muslims considered pigs to be 'polluting'. This created strong animosities and was located as an attack on Hindu and Muslim religious beliefs. As can be expected, this understanding gave primacy to the religious factor and reinforced a line of thinking which saw the Revolt as a 'Muslim conspiracy', that gained acceptance among contemporary officials. Syed Ahmad Khan (1817 - 1898) wrote a tract (Asbab-e-Baghawat-e-Hind viz. 'The Causes of the Indian Revolt') to counter this allegation, where he sought to examine the underlying features that determined the nature of 1857. And taken together these seem to be the basis for formulations like the 'clash of civilisations', echoes of which are heard even today in the post-9/11 context. Contemporary writings in the mid-nineteenth century generated political hysteria and racism, which legitimised the barbaric image of the 'Indian'. Nevertheless, the 1857 Revolt demonstrated the way English opinion itself was divided at home.

Thus, Chartists like Ernest Jones hailed the Revolt and unmasked the colonial exploitation of India (The Revolt of Hindoostan; or, The New World, London, 1857). Of course the most serious dissenting voice was that of Karl Marx who linked the colonial exploitation of India to the anger that was displayed by the people during the Revolt. Marx and Engels hailed the unity displayed by the different religious communities who opposed British colonialism (Marx and Engels, The First War of Independence, 1857-1859, Moscow, 1975). Interestingly, the Indian National Congress after its formation (1885) actually denounced the 1857 Revolt, given the social background of most of the leaders who were pro-British in their thinking. However, by the end of the nineteenth century the Revolt attracted and inspired the first generation of the Indian nationalists. Thus, V.D. Savarkar, who was perhaps the first Indian to write about the Revolt in 1909, called it The Indian War of Independence of 1857. His pro-nationalist stance made Savarkar reject the colonial assertion that linked the Revolt with the greased cartridges.

As he put it, if this had been the issue it would be difficult to explain how it could attract Nana Sahib, the Emperor of Delhi, the Queen of Jhansi and Khan Bahadur Khan to join it. Besides, he also focused on the fact that the Revolt continued even after the English Governor General had issued a proclamation to withdraw the offending greased bullets. Savarkar went ahead and connected the Revolt to the 'atrocities' committed by the British. At the same time, the importance he gave to religion illustrates the influence of the imperialist writers on him. From the 1920s, efforts were made to analyse the Revolt from a Marxist position by pioneers like M.N. Roy (M.N. Roy in collaboration with Abani Mukherji, India in Transition, 1922) and Rajni Palme Dutt (India Today, 1940). Roy was rather dismissive about 1857 and saw in its failure the shattering of the last vestiges of feudal power. He was emphatic about the 'revolution of 1857' being a struggle between the worn out feudal system and the newly introduced commercial capitalism, that aimed to achieve political supremacy.

In contrast, Palme Dutt saw 1857 as a major peasant revolt, even though it had been led by the decaying feudal forces, fighting to get back their privileges and turn back the tide of foreign domination. Consequently, one witnesses the beginnings of a process that interrogated and critiqued the internal feudal order, even while lauding the popular basis of the Revolt. The access to sources after the independence of India saw interesting developments related to the studies on the 1857 Revolt. What developed was a rather sophisticated Nationalist historiography that harped on the complexities of the Revolt. It included Nationalist historians like R.C. Majumdar, S.B. Chaudhuri, S.N. Sen, and K.K. Datta, (viz. R.C. Majumdar, The Sepoy Mutiny and the Revolt of 1857, 1957; S.B. Chaudhuri, Civil Revolt in the Indian Mutinies, 1857-59, 1957 and Theories of the Indian Mutiny, 1965; S.N. Sen,

Eighteen Fifty-Seven, 1957; and, K.K. Datta, Reflections on the Mutiny, 1967).

These historians were not uniformly comfortable with the idea that the 1857 Revolt was the 'First War of Indian Independence'. Moreover, they referred to ideas like nationalism that were supposedly witnessed during 1857 or saw the very inception of the national movement contained in the Revolt. Nevertheless, they went very clearly beyond the simple categorisations that had seen two dominant and opposing narratives - lauding the British, the victors who had 'won' the war and the claims of the 'rebellious Indians', who had been 'defeated'. This meant a shift in focus, with efforts being made to locate the internal contradictions (viz. the Indian 'rich', which included the moneylenders and buniyas) and the popular basis of 1857 and not concentrate merely on the influential classes which had been the focus of contemporary British officials. It is here that Nationalist historiography worked on and developed the legacy of the Marxists, even as some Nationalist historians inscribed their disapproval of seeing it as the 'First War of Independence'. In this sense at least, the Nationalist historians accorded a space - howsoever limited - to the popular basis of the Revolt. Since peasants did not/do not write their histories, they did not document their interaction with the 1857 Revolt. But, is it possible to ignore the folklore and traditions of resistance associated with the 1857 Revolt?

Moreover, can one afford to ignore the connections between 1857 and the peasant revolts of the preceding phase, or those outside the northern region of India? One can for example refer here to the Revolts of the Bhills in 1852 (in Khandesh, Dhar and Malwa), the Santals in 1855-6 (in Rajmahal, Bhagalpur, Birbhum), the Mapillas over the 1836-1854 period in Malabar, the Kandhas in Ghumsar and Baudh

(1855-60), the Savaras of Parliakhemedi (1856-57), or, for that matter, the Indigo Revolt in Bengal (that began in 1859 and was directed against white planters) - inspite of being told repeatedly about the role of the Permanent Settlement and the bhadraloks, that supposedly left Bengal as a 'zone of peace' in this phase. Unless one locates historical processes in a narrow, factual manner, it would be indeed almost impossible to assume that peasants cannot think or incorporate components from the past while struggling against colonial rule as well as their immediate oppressors. In this sense at least, it is difficult to study the Revolt unless one takes into account the social history of peasant protest prior to 1857 and in the phase after it. This would show the peasants in a bitter anti-imperialist political struggle, where the internal exploiter in the form of the sahukar or buniya was not spared. It would also undermine a point that has almost got frozen as common sense - viz. that the impact of the 1857 Revolt was not felt outside the Indo-Gangetic plain. With the passage of time the development of other historical approaches generated a lot of debates on the nature of 1857 among historians. The first exhaustive work on the Revolt was published in 1957 to commemorate the 100th anniversary of the event. Edited by P.C. Joshi (1857: A Symposium, 1957), it focussed on both the diversities and the specificities of the 1857 Revolt . This included assessing 1857 against the colonial backdrop, examining aspects of participation and focusing in a major way on the internal contradictions. This volume also sought to highlight dimensions of popular culture by incorporating folk poems that have survived. One has in mind here the contributions especially of P.C.Joshi and Talmiz Khaldun. In many ways this work inspired a serious spell of writings on the Revolt. Here mention must be made of Eric Stokes who examined issues ranging from the way the nature of 1857 was conditioned by the background, the demographic and ecological features to the social composition and the role of the peasants, especially the 'rich' peasants' (viz. Peasant and the Raj: Studies in Peasant Society and Agrarian Revolt in Colonial India, 1978; and his The Peasant Armed: The India Revolt of 1857, 1986). Interestingly, his research guided Stokes to reassess his position. Thus, whereas in his first work he had focused on the 'rich' peasant leadership and mobilisation, in Peasant Armed Stokes enlarged the social basis of peasant participation in the Revolt. However, it was left to historians like Rudrangshu Mukherjee (Awadh in Revolt, 1857-58: A Study of Popular Resistance, 1984) and Tapti Roy (The Politics of a Popular Uprising: Bundelkhand in 1857, 1994) to enrich our understanding of the Revolt by their focus on the popular level of the Revolt.

Their effort was based on specific area studies - viz. Awadh and Bundelkhand - that brought to light fascinating complexities of popular militancy that had remained ignored. Alongside, historians likes Iqtidar Alam Khan have studied questions related to organisation ('The Gwalior Contingent in 1857-58: A Study of the Organisation and Ideology of the Sepoy Rebels,' Social Scientist, January-April 1998, pgs. 53-75; hereafter S. Sct.), Gautam Bhadra and Saiyid Zaheer Husain Jafri have focused on the middle level leadership ('Four Rebels of Eighteen Fifty Seven', in Ranajit Guha, ed. Subaltern Studies IV, 1985, pgs. 229-75; and 'Profile of a Saintly Rebel - Maulavi Ahmadullah Shah' in S.Sct., respectively). Scholars like Khaldun (in P.C.Joshi, pgs. 1-70) and E.I. Brodkin ('The Struggle for Succession: Rebels and Loyalists in the Indian Mutiny of 1857', in Modern Asian Studies, 1972, pages 277-90) have focused on activities in the areas where British authority had been subverted, and if 1857 was indeed a restorative Revolt. What needs to be emphasised is that the 1857 Revolt represents possibly one of the most powerful and dramatic anti-colonial movements which united the peasants and the landed sections against the ruthless imperialist onslaught over the first half of the nineteenth century. At the same time, it also questioned the internal exploiters like the moneylenders and buniyas. What has been delineated illustrates the evolution of the historiography on the 1857 Revolt.

As seen, historians have shifted their focus from the mutinous 'sepoys', and seeing in it the origins of Indian nationalism to studying the diversities of the Revolt both in terms of popular participation and regions affected by it as also highlighting the internal contradictions. Presently some historians are engaged in researching gender-related issues, which would undoubtedly enrich our understanding of the Revolt of 1857.

3

M.N. Roy : Communist Leader and a Revolutionary

Manbendra Nath Roy's father Dinabandhu Bhattacharjee was a Sanskrit teacher in a minor English school in Arbelia village of 24 Parganas of West Bengal. Born on 21 March 1887, his early name was Narendra Nath Bhattacharjee and was known in this name till 1916. Though he adopted different names such as C Martin, Hari Sing, Mr White, D Garcia, Dr Mahmood, Mr Banerjee etc. at different times in conducting revolutionary activities, he was known as Manbendra Nath Roy (MN Roy), the name he adopted at San Francisco to evade arrest. Naren had his early schooling at Arbelia. The family shifted to Kodalia in 1898. He studied in Harinavi Anglo-Sanskrit School until 1905. Keen in social service, he organised a volunteer group to nurse the sick, particularly those suffering from epidemics and famines. He was inspired by the writings of Bankimchandra Chattopadhyay and swami Viveknanda. At the wake of the partition of Bengal he came in contact with the militant nationalists. In 1905 Naren and some of his friends were rusticated from the school for attending a meeting addressed by Surendranath Banerjea and joining the procession, in violation of the order of the Headmaster. Later on he was introduced to the Anushilan Samiti of Aurobindo Ghosh. Naren passed the Entrance Examination from the newly started National University (started by Aurobindo) and then he studied Engineering and Chemistry in the Bengal Technical Institute. He was actually a self-taught person. At this time, with his underground group, he experimented in bomb making and practised shooting in the Sundarbans. The group collected money by robbery for revolutionary purposes. For sometime he worked with Bagha Jatin (Jatindra Nath Mukhopadhyay) in the Jugantar of the Anushilan Samiti.

Naren and his group were involved in underground activities in Howrah-Sibpur area and were arrested in 1910 to face the 'Howrah-Sibpur Conspiracy Case, 1910-11'. During the trial period that lasted for more than a year, Jatin and Naren, in confinement, planned to arrange armed insurrection all over India. On release, Naren travelled in the garb of a sanyasi until 1914. The revolutionary organisations were extended to Far East, West America, and Germany where Indian revolutionary committees were formed. They approached the German government for help and, at the outbreak of the First World War, an emissary from Berlin came to Calcutta and assured them of German military and financial help.

Accordingly, Naren, under the pseudonym of Charles Martin, was sent to Batavia to negotiate the deal with the German Consul General. It was arranged that a shipment of arms and ammunition would be delivered in the Sundarban area. Naren took Jatin to Balasore to keep him in hiding. However, the cargo did not arrive. Naren went back to Batavia, this time under the name of Hari Sing, and found the German diplomats non-cooperating. He resolved not to return to India without arms. So, he pursued his mission by contacting the revolutionaries in Malaysia, Indonesia, Indo-China, the Philippines, Korea and Japan. Naren went to Japan as Mr White to meet Rashbehari Bose in Tokyo. There he met the exiled Chinese President Dr Sun Yat-Sen. It was arranged with him that Naren would receive ammunitions from two Chinese governors near the Assam border on payment of a sum to be paid by Germany. He went to China and the German Ambassador in Peking decided to send Naren to Berlin to sign the contract with German authority. He arranged a passport for Naren showing him as Father Charles Martin who would go to France via USA to study theology in Notre Dame University. Naren arrived in San Francisco on 14 June 1916. Next morning newspapers carried the news in banner headline 'a dangerous Hindu revolutionary, German spy, lands in USA'. Naren quickly left his hotel and went to Stanford University to meet Professor Dhanagopal Mukherjee, the younger brother of a co-revolutionary, who changed Naren's name to Manbendra Nath Roy. Dhanagopal introduced him as Manbendra Nath Roy to Dr David Jordan, the progressive minded President of the University. In Dr Jordan's house, Roy met Evelyn Trent whom he later married in New York where Roys took shelter in the house of Lala Lajpat Rai. There he met American 'slackers' and studied Marxism in the New York Public Library. USA declared war against Germany in April 1917, and the police began to round up Indian revolutionaries in USA as German spies. To escape arrest Roy fled to Mexico with an introductory letter from Dr Jordan. Through Dr Jordan's letter, Roy got the opportunity to be introduced to the War Minister and the President of the Republic who arranged to make Roy's acquainted with the top ranking officials and leading intelligentsia of Mexico.

The President assured him safety and provided a respectable residence. Roy delivered series of lectures and published articles on India and Monro Doctrine that created sensation. During this time, he learnt Spanish, French and German. In the anti-US stand of the President, Roy became his non-official advisor. By August 1918, he organised Socialist Party Conference in a grand style. During this time, many American slackers (journalists, artists, poets, scientists and philosophers) fled to Mexico to avoid conscription. President Carranza was delighted at Roy's popularity. Virtually Roy was in power by proxy, so much so that the President asked him to nominate a labour minister as the representative of the socialist party. Meanwhile, Michael Borodin, an emissary of Lenin, was sent to the Americas. He contacted the Roys who introduced him to the Mexican President. This resulted in the diplomatic relations between Mexico and the USSR. Consequently, Borodin could communicate with Moscow and briefed Lenin, in detail, about the activities of Roy.

Lenin invited Roy to participate in the Second World Congress of the Communist International (CI), to be held in Moscow during July-August 1920. Roy reached Berlin on his way to Moscow and during his stay in Berlin he gained valuable experience, particularly about the conflicts within the ideology of Marxism. He saw the defeat of German Communist Party and the rise of militarism. In Moscow, Roy met Lenin and disagreed with his point of view in his thesis titled, 'On National and Colonial Question'. Lenin asked him to write his own thesis. Both the theses were debated intensively and presented to the Congress.

The Congress accepted both the theses. After the Congress Session was over, Roy was placed in charge of Asian bureau of CI, with headquarters at Tashkent. He drove out British contingents from Masha of Khorashan in Iran by guerilla warfare. He established Bokhara Soviet through a bloodless revolution. He rehabilitated Indian Mohajerin of the Khilafat Movement, converted the educated section to Communism and established schools. Communist Party of India was formed in Tashkent on 17 October 1920. Roy joined Third World Congress of CI in August 1921. CI published his India in Transition in four languages in 1922. He founded Toiler's University in Moscow. He shifted his headquarter to Berlin in 1923 and started a pen-revolution for India. He published periodicals titled The Vanguard of Indian Independence and sent copies to India which the Indian government immediately banned. He published it under a different title Advanced Guard which also was banned. Next, he published The Masses, which also suffered the same fate. During the lifetime of Lenin, Roy attained all the top positions of the CI. This was maintained for three years after Lenin's death in 1924. As a joint-secretary of Chinese Commission of CI he was sent to China to settle a dispute between the Communists and Kuo Minh Tung. Roy had differences of opinion with Borodin and the Chinese Communist party in settling the dispute. Ultimately, Chiang Kai Sheik ruthlessly suppressed the Communist movement. On his return to Moscow, Roy fell ill and was taken to Berlin for treatment. In December 1929, in his absence, he was placed outside CI, for contributing to Communist Opposition Newspaper. While in Berlin, he wrote Revolution and Counter-Revolution in China and Decline and Fall of British Empire in German. MN Roy came to India in 1930 as Dr Mahmud. He was captured in July 1931 in Bombay, tried in Kanpur Jail on the charge of sedition and sentenced to transportation for 12 years, which, on appeal, was reduced to 6 years hard labour in jail. During the period from 1932 to 1936, he compiled a monumental volume under the title Philosophical Consequences of Modern Science in several volumes. The following books were published during 1937 to 1945 from his jail volumes under the titles: Materialism, The Historical Role of Islam, Heresies of 20th Century, Science and Superstition, Man and Nature, From Savagery to Civilization, Nationalism: An Antiquated Cult, The Philosophy of Fascism, The Ideal of Indian Womanhood, Letters from Jail, Memoir of a Cat, Science and Philosophy and India's Message. On his release in November 1936, Roy joined the Indian national congress and organised the league of Radical Congressman.

He supported Subhas Chandra Bose to become the President of INC. His differences on war policy with the Congress High Command made him and his followers resign from Congress and form the Radical Democratic Party. He supported the Allied Powers in World War II and vigorously supported war efforts because he considered declining imperialism a lesser evil to Fascism, which to him was a menace to mankind. MN Roy wrote several books between 1940 and 1946: India and War, Alphabet of Fascist Economy, Draft Constitution of Free India, People's Freedom, Poverty or Plenty, The Problems of Freedom, INA and the August Revolution, Jawaharlal Nehru: The Last Battle for Freedom. He conducted study camps at Dehradun in 1940 and wrote The Scientific Politics. In 1946, after another study camp, he wrote New Orientation. He advocated election to be held on non-party basis to form Constituent Assembly, which would frame the constitution of Independent India on a federal basis and recognise the rights of the minority communities and the regions. He advocated complete decentralisation of power and the prevention of corruption. In 1947, Roy critically analysed the events of USSR since 1917, in his monumental volume named The Russian Revolution. In 1948, he revised Marxism in his two books Beyond Marxism and New Humanism. In 1948, he abolished Radical Democratic Party and founded Radical Humanist Association. He founded Indian Renaissance Institute and edited the quarterly journal The Humanist Way which was originally named as The Marxian Way. He wrote another significant book titled Reason, Romanticism and Revolution. He attempted to write his memoirs that he could not complete. Roy succumbed to a severe attack of coronary thrombosis at midnight of 24-25 January 1954 in Dehradun. He married Ellen Gottsechalk in 1937 after his first wife Evelyn had left him in 1925. He had no children. The Amrita Bazaar Patrika depicted him as the 'lonely lion who roamed about the world'.

4

M.N. Roy : As Fugitive

As fugitive Roy went to Mexico having jumped jail in the United States of America where he was wanted for his part in the Hindu-German conspiracy case. He was also a fugitive from British justice for his part in the effort to import arms for the armed insurrection that he and his colleagues had planned under the leadership of Jatindranath Mukherji. For these offences the British police were on the lookout for him even during his stay in Mexico. A plan was hatched once, it seems, to kidnap him. Roy mentions in the Memoirs the hint to that effect dropped by the Mexican Minister of Defence and the reported secret visit to Mexico of Denham, "the chief of the British Indian C. 1. D." For that reason Roy had to take some precautions and also avoid going to areas under the control of America or England and travelling on ships which touched American or British ports. When Roy went to Mexico, General Venustiano Carranza had established his supremacy over the two other contenders for power, Emiliano Zapata and Pancho Villa. It was established after a bitter civil war extending over a period of about five years. The civil war was in the hundred years old tradition of the country. After winning its independence from Spain in 1820 and even after promulgating two constitutions, once in 1824 and then again in 1857, the country had not been able to develop a satisfactory procedure for finding who should rule it as President.

There was a provision for election, but contenders for the post of the President were usually averse to accepting the verdict as it could be easily manipulated by the person or group in power. The history of Mexico, since independence, was therefore full of civil wars, revolutions and anarchy. From time to time heroic leaders like Hidalgo, Monaloss, Jaurez and Madero appeared on the scene, to accomplish the social revolution of establishing racial equality, of abolishing clerical and military privileges and of restoring land to Indians. They did not succeed even in laying down a strong ground for a stable democratic regime. The tradition continued even after Carranza's rise to power and, when the time came for the next election of the President, there was a conflict in which he lost his life. That happened after Roy had left Mexico.

The civil war had subsided by the time Roy reached Mexico, though both Zapata and Villa held power in some parts of the country and continued to disturb peace and dislocate communications from time to time. In the course of the civil war Carranza, who was himself a pretty rich landlord, a hacendado in Mexican terms had to make a bid for popular support. He issued a proclamation listing the necessary reforms and early in 1915 he issued a decree for agrarian reform according to which lands illegally taken from Indian villages were to be restored to them and where these were inadequate, the Indian villagers were to be given additional lands expropriated from the landlords. To workers, he promised help in unionisation and settlement of disputes with employers. These and other measures made Carranza "the spokesman of the revolutionary upsurge of the Mexican masses. "In appearance, it is stated; "he was the personification of philosophic wisdom and dignity." It is also stated that "he had substantial virtues; he was financially honest and he had no love for bloodshed." He was, however, no statesman and failed in providing a stable and peaceful administration. Towards the end of 1916 Carranza convened a constituent assembly which drafted, a new constitution. It came to be known as the Quertaro Constitution of 1917.

From the social point of view, two Articles of the Constitution Article 27 and Article 123 were important. Article 27 established common ownership of the gifts of nature. It was not liked by landlords and the Church which owned extensive lands. Article 123 protected the rights of wage-earners, industrial and agricultural. It granted them an eight-hour day, minimum wage, the right to organise unions and the right to strike. These Articles marked an advance as stated by Parkes. He writes : "The constitution of 1917, like most Mexican constitutions, was a statement of aspirations rather than of facts; but unlike its predecessors of 1824 and 1857, what it promised was not only a system of democratic government and of guarantees of civil liberty, such as was still in Mexico, meaningless and impossible, but also concrete economic reforms which actually corresponded to the needs of the Mexican people. Mexico had passed through several violent revolutions and several bloody civil wars. There were several advances and also several reverses. One may be tempted to think that all this effort was futile. But a historian's verdict is : "Yet in spite of all appearances the Mexican revolution had not been futile. It had profoundly changed, in however intangible a fashion, the spirit of the nation; it had awakened new hopes and new aspirations which could no longer permanently be frustrated. Never again, however often it might be betrayed by corrupt leadership, would Indian

Mexico reconcile itself to the supremacy of the Creole and the foreigner. Agrarian reforms as against the landowners, protection for the working classes as against the industrialists and national sovereignty as against foreign capitalism these were the needs of Mexico, and only a government which recognised them could hope to remain in power. "It is this situation in which the government of President Carranza found itself which made it possible for Roy to stay in Mexico and help the progress of the revolution. The States of the Republic were only partially amenable to the control of the Centre. They were ruled by military Governors who carried on the government according to their own policies. One of the States, the State of Yucatan was under the control of General Alvarado who was reputed to have established a socialist regime in the State. The reputation travelled to the United States and attracted several socialist and leftist Americans to go to the State to watch the experiment. Roy had the same idea in view when he decided in favour of Mexico.

Later he realised that socialism in Yucatan consisted only of state monopoly of foreign trade. Another State was ruled by General Obregon who followed an entirely different policy. He was in close touch with the American Government and desired active collaboration with it in opposition to the anti-American and pro-German attitude of the Carranza Government. President Carranza had established a constitutional regime where laws enacted by Parliament were gradually taking the place of decrees promulgated by a military government. Under the constitution there was an elected Chamber of Deputies. But it did not enjoy much power. However, under General Carranza "the government was significantly demilitarised, several distinguished civilians having been appointed to important ministries. "All the same the Government did not enjoy much active public support. At a fateful moment in its career Roy was able to mobilise that support behind the Government, which carried him its confidence and gratitude. Roy landed in Mexico without any money and without any friends. The only credential he had was a letter of introduction to General Alvarado, the Governor of the State of Yucatan which was far away from Mexico City and practically inaccessible from that place. That letter enabled him to find an entry into the higher ruling circles of Mexico, and contacts with officers of the German military machine established in Java enabled him to get hold of large amounts of money. These were the two assets with which be began his life in Mexico without the least idea of the big role that he was to play with their help in the political life of the country. The role that he played was big by any standard and it was unique because it was played by an utter stranger who had arrived in the country as a political fugitive. In less than a week after his arrival in Mexico, Roy was spotted by the German agents. Mexico was a neutral country; several Germans lived there as officials and also as private citizens. There was a good deal of sympathy for Germany in official as well as non-official quarters, mainly as an expression of anti-American sentiment.

The German agents put Roy in touch with the two German officers whom he had met in Java. They were in Java "to arrange for the transport of arms to India. "They introduced Roy to the host at whose place the meeting took place. He was "Commander Von Konig of the Deutschland" the famous German submarine which had broken the British blockade and made two trips across the Atlantic carrying valuable cargo to American ports. The talk then turned to the plan which Roy, as Naren, had proposed for purchasing arms in China and transporting them overland to India. The reason given for asking about the plan was as follows : "Geheimrat (the Kaiser's Privy Councillor) von so and so was soon coming to Mexico with plenipotentiary powers for an overall review of the activities of the diplomatic and secret agents in the American cities and the Far East. The supreme authorities in Berlin would then issue orders for the execution of the recommendations in his report." Roy outlined the plan though he was no longer much interested in it.

The Germans were outraged by the report that "agencies in China had failed to appreciate the importance" of the plan and had not rendered the necessary help "which they thought was paltry." This meeting was followed by a number of meetings in the office of the German legation. Roy was introduced to the German society in the city and was also provided with ample funds for preliminary expenses. A few weeks later the Geheimrat arrived. He approved the plan after a couple of meetings with Roy. It was decided that Roy should go back to China in order to pursue the plan. Again a large amount of money was placed at his disposal for his travel expenses and also for sending emissaries to re-establish contacts in China, Japan and India. The receipt of these large amounts of money from the Germans posed "a moral problem" before Roy. "Should I accept more money than I could spend for the purpose for which it was offered His answer to the was as follows : The memory of the callous behaviour of the Germans quietened my conscience. In China I had personally experienced that behaviour. They refused financial help when I could purchase a large quantity of arms practically on the frontier of India. Why should I not provide for the future when the opportunity to do so might not again come my way ? Moreover, I might make another serious effort to carry out the plan, now that the Germans appeared to be ready to play their part. In that case, I should not place myself again completely at their mercy. It would be wise to provide myself with a sufficient fund before returning to China, if it came to that. The chance to do so was there, and it should not be missed. In India, we used to commit dacoities, often resulting in the murder of innocent people, in order to get money. The end justified the means : the money was to be spent to promote the cause of revolution and freedom. I was still pursuing the same cause. So, the decision was made." As it turned out later, Roy could not go to China and pursue the plan. The money remained with Roy. It was eventually used for socialist propaganda and organisation in Mexico and for advancing the cause of the Russian Revolution through timely help to Borodin and other Bolshevik leaders. Roy undertook to go back to China for securing arms with mixed feelings. His heart was not in the mission; "It was undertaken under the force of habit." It was arranged that Roy should travel on a Japanese ship from a Mexican port on the pacific. He had to reach the port of Manzanillo. It was a hazardous train journey as it had to pass through some territory under the control of the Zapatistas. The train could travel only under military escort. After reaching Manzanillo it was found that there was no certainty of a Japanese ship calling at that port. Roy, therefore, decided to take his chance at the bigger port of Salina Cruz, three hundred miles south of Manzanillo. He waited there several days for the ship. Ultimately it was learnt that the ship would not call at that port as she had taken a full load in Chile and was already on her way to Honolulu. The next ship was due only after a month. Roy had then to decide whether to wait there for a month or give up the mission and return to Mexico City. He chose the latter course. Justifying his choice he wrote later in the Memoirs : "It suddenly dawned on me that I really did not want to go again on the wild-goose chase. Mexico called me back; there I had made new friends, found new interests and planned to begin a new political career. On the other hand, the way back to old adventures was practically closed. The difficulties of going ahead and the predisposition to return contributed to the resolution to go back." The return train journey to Puerto Mexico was hazardous. The bandits attacked the train at one place but the, escort repulsed them.

From Puerto Mexico he went in a small steamer to Veracruz and from there to Mexico City by train. It was like homecoming" he states in the Memoirs. The mission was a wild-goose chase, but it gave Roy the first opportunity to see several distant parts of the country and acquire knowledge about them which stood him in good stead in his subsequent political activities. Roy had undertaken this mission to China with the knowledge and approval of the President of arranged his first meeting with the assured all facilities for the Mexico.

The Geheimrat had President. The President had journey. He was further assured that, in case he returned to Mexico, his services would be utilised for the work of the Latin American Union. It was the Geheimrat who had broached the idea of a Latin American Union. In the course of a talk with Roy he had said : "In order to hold the Western front yet for a time, we must attack America in the rear. Mexico must be the bast of operation. President Carranza must be incited and helped to lead a Latin American revolt against Monroe doctrine. In the U. S. A. and Canada we must organise extensive sabotage." Roy found "the idea of helping the formation of a Latin American Union against Yankee Imperialism attractive. So when he abandoned the plan of going to China and returned to Mexico City he knew he would be welcome and would have something worthwhile to do. Later when he organised the Socialist Party of Mexico he made use of the idea of a Latin American Union to serve as a centre for the development of socialist parties in Latin American countries. Roy's first contact with political personalities in Mexico was with the Minister of Defence who was also the son-in-law of the President.

The Minister granted him an interview in response to an inquiry about how to reach General Alvarado with his letter of introduction. Roy was informed that General Alvarado was shortly expected in the capi..l and that the Ministry would inform him of the latter's arrival. To his surprise, Roy learnt at the interview that the Government knew about him and his arrival in the country. He was assured that he was welcome and would be free and safe in Mexico. His next meeting was with the Editor of a leading daily El Pueblo (the people) which was known as "the non-official mouthpiece of 'the Government." The Editor, an elderly man, took kindly to Roy and, after knowing his antecedents and views, invited him to write for his paper a series of articles about British rule in India. The observations that he made while making the request explain why he felt such a regard for Roy. He said, "You know ours was also a colonial country: our forefathers revolted and the Mexican people overthrew the Spanish rule. Unfortunately' even after a century, Mexico is not yet really free. We are still waging the war of independence. Therefore, Mexicans sympathise with you, and would be benefited by a knowledge of your country and the struggle of its people for freedom. We are also Indians, you know, I am of the pure blood." Roy expressed his inability to write in Spanish.

A young man was immediately assigned to translate the articles. Roy wrote and the articles were immediately translated and published. Later Roy learnt Spanish and also German. At the Editor's place and through him Roy met several Mexicans prominent in the political and social life of the country. Eventually he also me,' the socialists. Roy had by this time become not only a socialist but also a communist. As stated in the Memoirs, "The Bolsheviks had just captured power in Russia, and a faint echo of the revolution reached across the Atlantic. All left-wing socialists were in an exuberant mood, and lived in an atmosphere surcharged with great expectations. They were all would be Communists. I was sucked up in that electrified atmosphere. In my case, it was not a few degrees rise of the revolutionary temperature. It was a mutation in my political evolution : a sudden jump from die-hard Nationalism to Communism.... It was an emotional satisfaction to profess the most revolutionary faith. Culturally, I was still a nationalist and cultural nationalism is a prejudice that dies very hard.

Socialism appealed to me because of its anti-imperialist connotations... The anti-imperialist connotation of left-wing socialism was emphasised in Communism. Therefore, my stay in the halfway house was brief. The road from revolutionary anti-imperialist Nationalism to Communism was short." Socialism with its emphasis on social justice was in the air in Mexico and transition to communism was quick as the Russian Revolution had just proclaimed the dawn of a new society of freedom and equality. It was years later that Roy and several others discovered the deceptive nature of that proclamation. The socialists were impressed by Roy's articles published in El Pueblo and were anxious to meet him. In the articles Roy had not painted the picture of la India Mysteriose which might have delighted middle class intellectuals. He portrayed on the contrary a realistic picture of poverty and exploitation. "I outlined the picture of India, past and present, as a picture of class struggle. The poverty of the Indian masses was the result of economic exploitation by British imperialism and native feudalism. The liberation of the Indian masses, therefore, needed not only the overthrow of British imperialism but subversion of the feudal-patriarchal order which constituted the social foundation of the foreign political rule. The corollary was that India required a social revolution and not mere national independence." This plea for a social revolution struck a sympathetic chord in the hearts of the socialists. And yet because the articles appeared in a bourgeois paper they would not make the first move to meet the author. Roy had to go out and search the socialists which he did after picking up enough Spanish to carry on ordinary conversation. He met the leader of the Socialist Party, Ignazio Santibanez, in whom he found a kindred spirit. Later he was invited to a meeting of the Executive Committee where he met half a dozen other prominent members of the party. They called themselves socialists but most of them were more anarcho-syndicalists than socialists. They had no concern for the independence of their country; they had no faith in political action; and they had a terrible distrust of all non-proletarians including members of the educated middle class.

The Socialist Party was, therefore, a small group without any influence in politics or social life. Roy had to fight against these prejudices, of the party and establish an alliance between the workers and the middle class in order to develop it into a significant political force. This battle for Marxism and against anarcho-syndicalism began on the day that he first met the members of the executive committee. A number of American pacifists, anarcho-syndicalists and socialists of a variety of shades had by then gathered together in Mexico City. They had come away in order to evade compulsory military service which was introduced as soon as America joined the war. "They were derogatively called the slackers." Some amongst them became good personal friends and colleagues of Roy. Prominent amongst them were Charlie Philips who later attended the second congress of the Communist International along with Roy, and who still later as Manuel Gomez became a prominent member of the Communist Party of the U. S. A. and Irvin Granwich who later, as Michael Gold, became famous as a novelist. They worked together as a group for broadening and strengthening the socialist movement. Later, at Roy's suggestion, they joined the Socialist Party and took a prominent part in organising the socialist conference. One of them, Charlie Philips, accepted the editorship of the English section of a new paper El Heraldo. It was accepted as the collective responsibility of the group. Roy contributed to the journal a series of articles on the Monroe Doctrine. In the course of his stay in Mexico he also published two books in Spanish. They were La India su pasado, su presente y su pervenier a book on India and The Way to Durable Peace. The books were nationalist in content which shows that, even after his acquaintance with socialism in U. S. A., he continued to be a nationalist in the first part of his stay in Mexico. A scholar has given the following description of Roy's writings of that period. : "Roy's writings in 1916-1917, mostly in Spanish (and perhaps done with the assistance of an anonymous native Spanish writer) present a black and white view of India and her past.

The pamphlets and letters are frankly written as political propaganda to counteract views of India which Roy said were completely incorrect. But his lengthy book, La India, is a little more scholarly and factual, although it gives inevitably the same vision of India's glorious past and her bondage under British rule. Pre-British India, according to Roy, was a thriving nation with all its young men at schools and universities and with commerce and industry growing apace. Although the Mughal emperors were despots, they were more benevolent than their contemporaries in Europe. And India was the land of great cultural achievements with writers greater than Tagore.

With the British came the end of that happy and bounteous age. The British came to power by trickery and deceit, and under their rule the country fell from its previous state. By Roy's time, it had become a land of famines and uneducated men, a land whose commerce and agriculture benefitted only the men of another nation. India, said Roy, was a land of beggars. He mentioned the drain of resources from India and claimed that there had been no benefits from British rule. Even the railways were not constructed to benefit

India, but only to suit British military convenience. Roy asserted that the reforms granted to give the beginnings of self-government were a sham and that the men elected were toadies of the rulers, not representatives of the people. "Roy went to some lengths to defend the nationalists and revolutionaries, especially in his letter to President Woodrow Wilson. He compared the Indian revolutionaries to the American revolutionaries of the eighteenth century and equated German assistance to the Indians with French assistance to the Americans during their war for indeper nce. "Liberty ", wrote Roy,-is the innate right of every human being. "If Wilson supported "the noble ideal of liberating the Balsams, the Serbs, the Poles, the Slavs, the Bohemians, the Magyars, "why should he not also Support the liberation of Indians from the British yoke? Roy even listed the betrayals of despotic Indian princes by the British as a mark of Britain's bad faith, it is as if all that is Indian is good, all that is British evil." Mexico was facing at this time the threat of an invasion by the United States. The conflict between the two countries centred on the nationalisation clause of the new constitution promulgated under the Carranza regime. The contention of the Mexican Government was that the clause nullified the concessions granted earlier ıor the exploitation of petroleum and other mineral deposits. It was prepared to grant new leases, but the American concerns who held old leases were not agreeable to it. The Government then threatened to prohibit the export of petroleum.

The American Government regarded it as ail invasion of property rights and declared its intention to land troops, to protect the property of the American concerns. The dispute assumed serious proportions because the American Government suspected German hand behind the firm stand of the Mexican Government. Mexican neutrality was already under a heavy cloud of suspicion. It was believed to be weighed in favour of Germany. This placed the Government of President Carranza in a very difficult position. On the one hand, it could not compromise on the issue of sovereignty involved in the nationalisation clause of the constitution; on the other hand, it did not have the strength to resist the pressure of the American Government. Even the Army was not a reliable factor as some Generals were opposed to a confrontation against the mighty Army of the United States. There was a good deal of anti-American sentiment in the country, but there was no organised popular force to stand behind the Government. Roy created that force and helped President Carranza to survive the crisis. The force that was created was the broadened Socialist Party of Mexico. The tiny group of socialists whom Roy had met was persuaded to throw its door open to middle class intellectuals, lawyers, doctors, teachers and others. It was also persuaded to abandon its anarcho syndicalist attitude of indifference to politics and accept the necessity of resisting foreign aggression. Roy succeeded in accomplishing this with the assistance of his American friends who were named "Red Slackers". Roy was appointed about this time the propaganda secretary of the party. In that capacity he published a number of pamphlets about socialism and its tasks in Mexico. Many of them were written by him.

The broadened party was inaugurated at a socialist conference held in Mexico City in December 1918. The conference was a great success. It was attended by a large number of delegates from Mexico and a few fraternal delegates from other countries of Latin America. A number of prominent citizens of Mexico City also attended the conference and gave it weight and respectability. The proletarians in the party were opposed to their participation. They eventually agreed to it only out of consideration for al companero Indio (the Indian Comrade). The conference unanimously elected Roy the

General Secretary of the party, a unique honour for a pennyless foreigner who had landed in the country only about a year back. Roy was also elected the secretary of the international committee that was set up to convene as soon as possible a Regional Conference to set up the Latin American League. Before organising the socialist conference and undertaking other antiaggression activities, Roy, had talks with his friends in high government circles. They resulted in an interview with the President, General Carranza. Roy had already outlined a plan which he put before the President. The plan was as follows : "The Socialist Party would hold a public meeting to protest against the threatened American intervention; the meeting would pass a resolution calling for a mass demonstration of protest and appealing to the democratic middle class to join hands with the toiling masses in a mighty defence of the sovereignty of the Republic and its Constitution; democratic leaders like Don Manuel should publicly endorse the protest in one form or another; students and teachers should join the demonstration; and finally, there should be no interference by the police or the military-After the demonstration in the capital, emissaries of the Socialist Party would go to organise a strike of the petroleum workers to hold up the pumping, refining and export of oil, should the foreign companies defy the law of the land. The working class initiative to develop a popular resistance to foreign intervention should encourage the Government to take a stronger attitude. At the same time, the Government should encourage the working class by supporting the latter's economic demands." The President liked the plan not so much because he was a liberal by conviction but as a matter of Practical politics. He also talked about a Latin American League and suggested to Roy a tour of Latin American countries in order to canvass support for the League. Roy liked the idea and Promised to consider it after the socialist conference was held.

The President assured the assistance of diplomatic agencies in Central and South America for contacting socialist leaders in those countries and arranging their participation in the socialist conference. He spoke of his plan of appointing a Labour Minister in his government and asked for Roy's suggestion. Later a leader of the Socialist Party, Plutaro Elias Calles was appointed to that post. With this interview Roy's relations with the President became closer; he met him several times, formally and informally; and very soon he acquired the reputation of being an unofficial adviser to the President. After the socialist conference several circumstances combined to push the Socialist Party into prominence. General Obregon, the Governor of the State of Sonara situated on the northern boundary of the country, was one of the contenders for power against President Carranza. He disliked the foreign policy of the President and desired friendly relations with the United States. It was reported that he was increasing his military strength with support from the Americans. President Carranza decided to remove him from the post on the pretext that he should be free to conduct his campaign for the presidential election and that the post should be filled by election according to the constitution.

The idea originated with Calles, one of the leaders of the Socialist Party who hailed from that Stale, and was conveyed to the President through Roy. As soon as the election was announced, the Socialist Party decided to contest it. Roy was asked to go to the State and select the candidate after consultations with the local people. Calles was the obvious choice. He was put up as a candidate and was elected without a contest. Thus within a few months of its formation, the Socialist Party found itself-in control of the governorship of an important State in the country. That raised the stock of the party. Calles later became Labour Minister in the Federal Government and still later the President of the Republic. The latter event took place after Roy left the country. The Labour Ministership of Calles put additional responsibility on Roy. As stated in the Memoirs :

"A programme of legislation for the protection of labour, particularly against exploitation by foreign imperialist capital, was drawn up, of course, by the Minister in consultation with the head of the legislative branch of the State. The principles having been approved by the President and the full Cabinet, I was asked to draft the bills with the co-operation of trade union and socialist leaders. The texts were then to be finalised by the legal experts and law officers of the Republic. One of the proposed measures was to legalise strikes to enforce the workers' demand for collective bargaining." As news about the projected legislation leaked out there was a spate of strikes. More ominous were the strikes in petroleum industry and ports. They might have led to intervention by the United States, as in the last decisive stage of the war, petrol and other products were badly required. It was, therefore, essential to stop the outbreak of strikes. Roy suggested that the Labour Minister should go to various places to pacify workers. The suggestion, was accepted but Roy was asked to go along with him. Roy was to see that the interests of workers were protected but without endangering the safety of the Republic." The visits of Roy and Calles were useful. They were able to settle some strikes and avoid others.

Roy relates as follows what happened at the port of Tampico : "In a hurriedly convened meeting of local workers' leaders, I pointed out the danger of any rash action. The counsel of caution convinced them, because the workers really had no legitimate grievances, wages being higher than elsewhere in the country. I pleaded that a representative of the revolutionary proletariat was in power; he should not be embarrassed. It was just the beginning. We must not gamble.

The point went home." The danger of strikes and consequent foreign intervention was thus averted. The prestige and influence of the Socialist Party increased as an outcome of this statesman like handling of an explosive situation. It may be noted, however, that it is on the same plea that in later years communist regimes in several countries outlawed strikes and prevented the growth of free trade unions. While engaged in this work of building up the Socialist Party, editing the English section of El Heraldo and generally helping the Carranza Government in broadening its social base, Roy came across a mysterious visitor to the Mexico City in the spring of 1919. It was reported that he was a Bolshevik and was worry to meet "Hindu" General Secretary of the Socialist Party. Ultimately he turned out to be Michael Borodin, one of the leaders of the Communist Party of Russia on a secret mission to the New World. Borodin landed in Mexico City without any money. He was sent from Moscow with crown jewels worth a million roubles with instruction to sell them and utilise the sale proceeds for the upkeep of the stranded Trade Mission in Washington and the development of the communist movement in the Americas. On the journey on a Danish ship Borodin had to entrust the two suitcases in which the jewels were sown to an Austrian army officer, when the ship was halted in Haitee and searched by the American police.

Fearing arrest, Borodin left New York after landing there and escaped to Mexico. In Mexico City he was daily expecting news from his wife in Chicago about the receipt of the suitcases as the Austrian officer was instructed to deliver them, at that address. His wife and family were in straightened situation since Borodin left them in 1919 to return to Moscow after the revolution.

The loss of the suitcases and the plight of his family in Chicago and of the Trade Mission in Washington were weighting on Borodin's mind when he met Roy. Roy relieved him of a large part of his worry. He invited Borodin to stay at his place and remitted substantial amounts of money to Borodin's wife in Chicago and to the Trade Mission in Washington. Referring to the remittances of money Roy wrote : "And presently it did turn out that my relation with the Bolsheviks began by helping them financially, instead of receiving the legendary Russian roubles as reward for the revolutionary profession." At another place he wrote : "Since the Bolsheviks captured power ' Russian gold went to all the corners of the world, far and near, to promote the communist movement. At least once the traffic, was reversed." Roy also spent a good deal of money for the recovery of the suitcases containing the crown jewels. A couple of years later they were recovered and Borodin's life was saved. That Roy regarded as his "second contribution to the cause of revolution." Borodin stayed with Roy all the time that he was in Mexico. The two became very good friends and the friendship continued, in spit, of differences, till Roy left Moscow for good in 1928. Borodin completed Roy's conversion to communism. Borodin was a very learned and cultured individual and Roy was a willing pupil. Roy learnt from him not only the intricacies of dialectical materialism but also the greatness of European civilization and the appreciation of art and culture. Roy also learnt from him the imperative need of a worldwide social revolution and the tactics and policy of organising it. What jarred on his mind was Borodin's insistence on unquestioned party discipline. He attributed it to the "religious fervour of the revolutionary faith of Bolshevism "and found it difficult to harmonise it with "its materialist philosophy. "Years later he found it difficult to harmonise his convictions with party discipline and had to part company with the Communist International. The news of the Russian Revolution had travelled all over the world and electrified the atmosphere in several countries.

There was a demand in the Socialist Party for declaration of its support to the Russian Revolution and of its affiliation with the Communist International established thereafter. The demand became more insistent when the news of the presence of a Bolshevik emissary in the city as the guest of the General Secretary leaked out. A suggestion was made that an extraordinary conference of the party should be held to convert it into a communist party. Roy was in sympathy with the demand and the suggestion. He had, however, to consider the pros and cons, consider the effect that the change of name would have upon the Government and especially on the middle class intellectuals who had joined the party since the conference. He met the President and some Ministers ; he also met some leading intellectuals; he was assured that there would be no change in their attitude as long as the programme remained the same and as long as the party followed the same statesmanlike policy. It was then decided to hold an extraordinary conference. The conference met under the chairmanship of Roy. It passed two resolutions, one endorsing the manifesto issued by the first congress of the Communist International and the other changing the name of the party. Thus the first Communist Party outside Russia was born. The Memoirs state: "Both the resolutions were passed with acclamation; nevertheless, nothing more than a change in the name of the party took place.

The Communist Party remained committed to the revolutionary democratic programme of the defunct Socialist Party. The conference decided to send a delegation to attend the second congress of the Communist International to which it had decided to affiliate itself. The names of the delegates were not mentioned. It was understood, however, that Roy would lead the delegation. His plea to be relieved of the General Secretaryship was, therefore, accepted and a new Acting General Secretary was appointed to be initiated into the work by Roy before he left for Moscow. Borodin had already prepared the ground for Roy's visit to Moscow. He had been sending reports to the Communist International in which he had highly praised Roy's work. Roy had secured for him facility to send his reports through Mexican diplomatic channels. He had also arranged for Borodin to meet President Carrarnza, the Foreign Minister, and others.

At the meeting Borodin had conveyed communist Russia's feelings of sympathy and solidarity with the struggles against imperialism of the peoples of Latin America. He had also broached the idea of a Latin American Bureau of the Communist International to be located in Mexico in charge of Roy. The idea appealed to President Carranza as he regarded it as the realisation in a different form of his plan of a Latin American League. The meeting went off very well and resulted practically in a de facto recognition by Mexico of the new regime in Russia. Borodin was happy at these developments, formation of the first Communist Party outside Russia and de facto recognition of the new Russian regime. He had not recovered the lost suitcases, but these achievements were sufficient to counterbalance that loss. He gave Roy due credit for them and was anxious that he should attend the second congress and begin to work in a bigger field. On his recommendation, an invitation soon arrived asking Roy to go to Russia to attend the congress and to meet the leaders of the Russian Revolution. The invitation opened out a new hope before Roy, the hope of working for social revolution in a bigger field in the company of leaders of world revolution. The hope was fascinating and it attracted him. Borodin had also reminded him that Moscow was on the way to India; so that there was also the hope of going back to India not only with arms, but also with a revolutionary philosophy. And yet it was not an easy decision to make. Mexico had-been very kind and hospitable to him. It had given him an opportunity to be politically and socially influential. He had made several friends and he knew that they would be unhappy at his decision to leave them. And yet he knew that he could do nothing more than what he had already done, and that whatever he bad done would remain even after he went away. He decided to accept the invitation and leave Mexico. Before he took the decision, however, he consulted the President and other influential friends and secured their approval. In the Memoirs there is an eloquent description of the rich experiences that he had in Mexico and of the new wisdom that he learnt. It deserves to be quoted. It says : "As the day of my departure drew nearer, the feeling of loss became keener. I had been in Mexico for only two years and a half. But it seemed as if I had lived there since my childhood. I never made several personal friends. Mexican exuberance, heavily tinged with conventionality, though not always hypocritical, was incompatible with my temperament. Nevertheless, I could not possibly help being moved by the facts that it was an extremely hospitable country, the government friendly beyond expectation, out of proportion to the little service that I could render out of gratitude, and a large number of highly developed individuals treated me with kindness, consideration and affection. On the whole, it was a rich and gratifying experience. In a sense, Mexico was the land of my rebirth. It is true that before coming there I had begun to feel dissatisfied with ideas and ideals of my earlier life. But it was during my stay in Mexico that the now vision became clear and the dissatisfaction with a sterile past was replaced by conviction to guide me in a more promising future. It was more than a change of political ideas and revolutionary ideals. I acquired a new outlook on life; there was a revolution in my mind—a philosophical revolution which knew no finality.

The fundamental change in the outlook on life enabled me to overcome the emotional attachment to the land of my rebirth." Continuing Roy wrote : "I left the land of rebirth an intellectually free man, though with a new faith. But the philosophical solvent of the faith was inherent in itself. I no longer believed in political freedom without the content of economic liberation and social justice. But I had also realized that intellectual freedom-freedom from the bondage of all tradition and authority was the condition for any effective struggle for social emancipation." The Foreign Minister arranged a diplomatic passport for Roy, of course, in a different name and also arranged passage on a ship going to Spain. Diplomatic representatives in European countries were advised to render Roy any assistance that he might need.

Moscow Journey

M.N. Roy was not the only one who had that feeling about Moscow in those days. There were hundreds in Europe and America who had the same attraction for that centre of the first socialist revolution in the world. All of them were noble souls distressed by the poverty, misery and inequality that they saw around them and eager to see the rise of a new social order of liberty and equality. Many of them rushed to Moscow to place their services at the disposal of the Revolution and to watch its unfoldment. What they saw disappointed and disillusioned many. But that was a painful process extending over years and depending upon an individual's reaction to what happened in the course of the Revolution. Disappointment and disillusionment came to Roy also, but that happened much later, after about two decades. After the Revolution in Russia and after the defeat of Germany, several Indian patriots also turned towards Moscow. Some of them went there and met the leaders of the Revolution, including Lenin. But as they were inevitably nationalists, they could not establish a proper relationship with them. One leader of the Indian patriotic groups of those days, Bhupendranath Dutta has in a history of the period described the trend as follows : "There was a stir in the minds of the emigrant revolutionaries in Europe after the Russian revolution. Some of them held left wing socialist opinions even earlier. Indian revolutionaries in their stay abroad received sympathy for the struggle for the country's independence only from the left-wing Europeans.

From England's socialist leader Hyndman to the anarchist leader Peter Kropotkin and the Bolshevik leader Lenin-all of them wished to see India independent. Hence when one of these parties made a revolution and established their own state, all leftwingers should turn to it. All revolutionaries therefore turned to Moscow. Moscow became the "New Mecca" for them." Dutta visited Moscow later in 1921 along with Virendranath Chattopadhyaya and others of the Berlin Independence of India Committee. However, Roy was the first committed Indian communist to visit Moscow and establish relations with the leaders of the Russian Revolution. In spite of his eagerness to reach Moscow as early as possible, it took Roy months to reach that place. In that postwar period of instability and disorganisation travel was not easy in Europe.

For communists particularly, it was extremely difficult as they were regarded as dangerous and disruptive. Russia had not yet secured international recognition and a war of intervention was being actually fought on her soil. Few channels of communication were open and Russia had to be reached through Scandinavian countries. About the difficulties of travel in those days, Alfred Rosmer, who was also a delegate at the second congress writes in Lenin's Moscow : "Travel across Europe in the post-war period was very complicated. The new nations established with the help of Wilsonian ideology were barricading themselves behind their frontiers. They were defending themselves against Bolshevik penetration, and also against illicit traders of the social type thrown up in periods of upheaval. To get into them you required entry visas; and then exit permits to leave again. You had to put up with meticulous customs inspections, with endless and intolerable formalities, and you were glad enough if you got away unscathed. Finally—the last and the most serious obstacle the bordering states, which had seceded after being part of Tsarist Russia, did not allow travel through their territory." The diplomatic passport that was issued to him in Mexico helped Roy to some extent, but for entry into Russia he had to depend entirely on arrangements made from Moscow for the transport of delegates to the second congress of the Communist International. Roy left Mexico in November 1919 on a ship which took him to Spain. It was a Spanish ship. He had to avoid a British or American ship and also a ship which touched British or American ports.

The journey on Alfonso XIII was pleasant as, with his diplomatic passport, he was treated as a high dignitary by all on board the ship. By this time, having lived in the United States for a year and in Mexico for over two years, Roy had learnt to enjoy the pleasures of the European way of living. He had, as said by him, "lived through a couple of centuries of cultural history." The ship had to call at Havana, the capital of Cuba which was then an American protectorate. "The wartime practice of searching neutral ships, at the port of Havana, was still in force." That posed a grave danger to Roy as, if found, he might be taken off the ship by American authorities.

The Master of the ship was, therefore, asked to "keep me out of sight as long as the ship stopped at Havana." But when the ship called, there was a strike of port and dock workers which might have delayed it indefinitely in Havana. Roy found a way out of the difficulty. He sent word to the Secretary of the Cuban Federation of Labour who was a socialist and had met Roy many times in Mexico. On learning of the danger that Roy faced, the Secretary agreed to withdraw pickets and allow the ship to sail. The ship sailed the next day. The passengers were surprised at this special treatment accorded to their ship, but apart from the Master and a couple of others, none knew the part that Roy had played in securing it. Roy left the ship at Santander and then went by train to Madrid, the capital of Spain. Roy had a mission to perform in Spain. Borodin had entrusted it to him. The mission was to persuade the leading socialists and anarchists to attend the second congress of the Communist International. The International was founded in April 1919, but the first congress which founded it was attended only by a few socialists from countries other than Russia. It was essential to make the second congress more representative. But the terror which began in Russia after the effort on Lenin's life alienated several European socialists. They started to regard the October Revolution as a manifestation of Russian despotism. It was essential to check this trend and to win over as several socialists as possible. Roy was asked to contact Iglesias, the veteran leader of the Socialist Party of, Spain, and persuade him to attend the second congress. Iglasias had a big name amongst European socialists and liberals. His agreement to attend the second congress would silence and undermine the liberal and socialist opposition to the Russian Revolution. Roy met him but failed to convince him. As stated in the Memoirs, 'But he proved to be too hard a nut to crack by my youthful enthusiasm. The fervent faith of a new convert could not move the mountain of classical rationalism". Roy then met some left-wing socialists and also some anarcho-syndicalists. He had to go to Barcelona to meet the latter. He succeeded in persuading both to send their representatives to the second congress. Having completed this, he left Spain and made his way to Berlin. Roy reached Berlin towards the end of 1919. It was with the intention of reaching Berlin that he left Asia in the middle of 1916. It took him over three years to reach his destination, but by the time he reached it, it had ceased to be his destination; it was only a stop on the way. His destination was further east, Moscow, the seat of the victorious Russian Revolution. But he could go to Moscow only through Berlin. That was the arrangement that Borodin had made for him. Delegates to the second congress were to assemble in Berlin and then arrangements were to be made to transport them to Moscow.

Russia was then passing through very' difficult times and it took some time for the arrangements to be made. That enabled Roy to stay in Berlin for a few months. He used the time for studying the German political situation, for meeting the leading figures of the German socialist movement and for visiting a few places in the country. That short period of about four months proved very fruitful in advancing Roy's political education and in securing for him a couple of life-long friends and wide contacts amongst the communist leaders of Germany. When Roy arrived, the imperial regime of the Kaiser had given place to a republican regime set up under the Weimar Constitution. The imperial regime had been overthrown by the rebellious sailors and soldiers after the military defeat in November 1918. A Soviet Republic on the Russian model was proclaimed but it had a very short life. The heroic effort of the Spartakus League led by Karl Liebknecht and Rosa Luxemburg to save the Soviet Republic was drowned in blood. "A few days later, Luxemburg and Liebknecht were seized by a band of young officers and taken to the military head-quarters. They were brutally treated and literally slaughtered. Their mutilated bodies, almost beyond recognition, were found floating in a canal the next day. The verdict of the Military Tribunal set up to investigate the crime was that the prisoners were shot while they tried to escape." For a few months there was civil war, terror and anarchy, but ultimately power passed into the hands of the Social Democratic Party. The Social Democratic Party of Germany was the strongest and best organised of the socialist parties of Europe. It had the powerful backing of a strong and well-knit trade union movement, "the number of thoroughly indoctrinated ideologically class conscious industrial workers was much larger in Germany than in other country." It had in its leadership many experienced and mature socialist thinkers. They were all Marxists, but their interpretation of the teachings of Karl Marx was different from that of Bolshevik's who had captured power in Russia.

As Marxists, they believed in he essentially of social revolution and cherished the ideal of the liberation of workers and the establishment of a new social order of freedom and equality. They believed in essential but gradual development towards socialism and disapproved violent activities and armed insurrection. In power, they tried to steer the country in the direction of socialism. But they had to contend against powerful forces, on the one side, the force of the militarists which desired the reestablishment of the imperial rule and, on the other side, the force of the communists and others who desired a clean sweep of a established institutions and selfish interests and forced march towards socialism. A needed debate between all these forces, on the theoretical as well as the practical plane, was taking place in Germany during Roy's stay. His sympathies were clearly with the communist side but he had the wisdom of listening to all and that enabled him to get a deeper understanding of the Marxism that he had learnt in Mexico. Roy was struck by the "humanness" of the socialist leaders. He writes about them and their relations with communists the following in the Memoirs. "An intellectual brotherhood, they cherished as common ideal social liberation of the working class. Learned men of high culture and refined taste they kept their personal relations and social intercourse on the intellectual and humanist plane, untarnished by party politics. A goodhumoured reciprocal tolerance held them together even when conflicting loyalties were pulling them apart." He met several of them during his stay in Berlin. Prominent amongst them were Bernstein, Kautsky and Hilfferding. The tragedy of the German revolution was that, despite of the defeat, the Army did not disintegrate. It kept itself together, more especially the officer corps. It was hostile to the Republic established by the Social Democratic Party. In the starting it made several efforts to destroy it. Roy has given in the Memoirs a graphic account of one such effort, which has gone down in history as the Knapp Putch. The account is as under:

"Early in March 1920, a section of the old German army made an almost successful effort to overthrow the newly established Weimar Republic. One fine morning, it marched into the capital and without any resistance occupied all the strategic positions. The Social Democratic President, Ebert, with his Cabinet left Berlin in panic to avoid arrest. That was one of the most dramatic moments of the history of post-war Europe. From the window of my hotel in the heart of Berlin (the Postdamer Platz), I watched a typical Prussian army fanning out in different directions. People of all classes stood by listlessly, as if paralysed by a sudden blow. The huge city was plunged into confusion. "But overnight, there appeared a bold leadership to take the situation in hand, and deal a counterblow. Something utterly unexpected had happened.

The call to resist the counter-revolution had been issued by Carl Legien, President of the powerful German Federation of Labour, whom the Communists together with the entire left wing of the Social Democratic Party had for years denounced as a rank reactionary. He had decided to call a political general strike to be declared from the dawn....... "For four days, the big city was dead, shops closed, factories idle, streets deserted in the day, everything enveloped in complete darkness in the night. On the fifth morning, from the same hotel window, I watched the mass of steel-helmeted soldiers marching in the opposite direction, in sullen silence. The might of organised labour had triumphed over brut force. For days, there was not a soul in the streets; the insurgent army did not have the chance of firing a single shot. It was great luck to have had that experience. Naturally, it made an indelible impression on my mind." Later the Army changed its attitude when it found that the Socialist Republic was not going too far. Roy was in Berlin according to the arrangement made by Borodin. But for so many weeks he could not get hold of Borodin; nor could he get hold of the intermediary through whom the contact was to be established. The intermediary was a distinguished academician but because of his close relations with communist leaders, he was required to go into hiding in those days of disorder and terror.

The communist leaders, whom Roy knew by name like Wilhelm Pieck, Ernst Meyer, August Thalheimer, Klara Zetkin and Paul Levi were also in jail or underground. After some weeks Borodin contacted Roy and put him in touch with all communist leaders. By this time Roy had already made friends with socialist leaders. Then started his lively discussions with both about the existing political situation in Germany and other European countries and the prospects of revolution in Europe and elsewhere. By and by communist leaders started inviting Roy even to their secret meetings where they planned their tactics and strategy. Participation in these meetings gave him advantage inmensely. Amongst communist leaders he struck special friendship with August Thalheimer and Heinrich Brandler. Brandler was the leader of a revolutionary outbreak in central Germany which took place immediately after the news of the Knapp Putch spread in the country. Later he became the leader of the Communist Party of Germany. He and Thalheimer were some years later thrown out of the Communist International. Roy evolved deep liking and respect for both which continued even after their expulsion. In the closing years of the decade he collaborated with them for the rectification of the wrong policies that the International had adopted then. In 1920, the Communist Party of Germany was not a, well-knit, disciplined organisation. The Spartacus League out of which it grew was "a losely organised propagandist group." The party had yet to build for itself a strong mass base. It was looking for allies both on the right and the left and both tendencies were strongly represented in the party.

On the right was the Independent Social Democratic Party which was a breakaway from the ruling Social Democratic Party. Attempts were then being made to persuade the Independent S. D. Party to send delegates to the second congress. On the left was the Communist Workers' Party which supported immediate armed insurrection for the capture of power. According to Roy, they were mostly young people; they respected the memory of the martyred Rosa Luxemburg, but disapproved of her opposition to Bolshevism, they were bitterly opposed to Paul Levi, the leader of the Communist Party, who according to them, was a reformist parliamentarian and not a revolutionary. He attached, according to them, greater importance to a reformist organisation than to the revolutionary mass movement, they claimed large support to themselves in the Communist Party in Berlin, Hamburg and. Rhineland. Left Communism of the period produced a curious offshoot, National Bolshevism. That school of thought advised communists to establish alliance with ultra-nationalists in order' to overthrow the established Social Democratic Government and bring about a revolution. The established Government had earned the hostility of ultra-nationalists and of the officer corps of the Army by signing the Versailles Treaty which demanded the disbandment of a large part of the Army. Roy describes the rise of the curious cult. "The ultra-nationalist German youth conceived the bold idea of an alliance with Russia in the war against the Entente Powers for the liberation of Germany and vindication of her honour. Overthrow of the Social Democratic Government and subversion of the bourgeois democratic republic being also the objectives of the German Communists, the alliance could begin at home to be international in the course of time. Young army officers sought the alliance of the revolutionary proletariat to put a resistance against the enslavement of Germany under the flag of National-Bolshvism. The curious cult gained numerous adherents in the ranks of the Spartakus League." Karl Radek, the Russian communist leader who was then in Germany, in prison for sometime and then-outside, was the main supporter of National Bolshevism. His support led to its becoming wide spread amongst rank and file communist activists. Radek's reasoning was : "In Russia, the Bolsheviks were in a precarious position. If the Entente Powers were engaged by a mass resistance in Germany they would not be in a position to rush reinforcements to the White' Russian armies marching on Petrograd and Moscow. A Russo-German alliance in a revolutionary war could possibly liberate the whole of Europe. He was of the view that Lenin would like and support the idea. But Lenin rejected it unceremoniously and denounced it in his pamphlet Left-wing Communism, An Infantile Disorder published about the time of the second congress. National Bolshevism did not survive that attack." To Roy, National-Bolshevism appeared to be a "fantastic idea". His own experience had taught him that "nationalist revolution was an equivocal ideal." He met Radek after his release from jail and before he left for Moscow to place his idea before Lenin. Radek, according to Roy, was "bubbling with enthusiasm about the great possibilities of an alliance with the demobilised army officers." One day, Roy relates : "By way of driving his point home with an illustration, he

(Radek) walked upto, placed his hand on my shoulder, which happened to be higher than his head and said : 'The Indian Comrade is a personification of National Bolshevism, which will not only conquer Germany, but win the whole of the East for Communism.' At that time I did not realise how prophetic his opinion was. I disowned the dubious distinction, and said that at least in my case the nationalist had to fade out before Communism could be an honest conviction." Roy believed that his scepticism about NationalBolshevism played some part in persuading the Communist Party of Germany to reject it. Roy and Radek were to work together later in a number of activities. Germany for the first few years of the Russian revolution played a crucial role in the calculations and thinking of Bolshevik leaders. They had captured power in Russia but they believed that they would not be able to retain it unless the revolution in Russia was followed by revolutions in Germany and other industrially advanced European countries. Amongst them Lenin was most emphatically of that view. About him Roy has written : "Lenin was the most Orthodox Marxist. His faith in the Master's prophecy was unbounded. He did not believe that in a backward country like Russia the proletariat could hold power for any length of time. Yet he stubbornly advocated an apparently adventurist policy with the firm conviction that it would help revolution in Germany which, in its turn, would enable the Russian Bolsheviks to consolidate themselves in power. But even then, the leadership would pass on to the German proletariat, the capital of the Communist World would shift from Moscow to Berlin.

"Defending his policy of capturing power prematurely in Russia, Lenin argued : We know that Karl Liebknecht will be victorious; we know that he will come to our assistance, and that revolution in Germany will come to our assistance, and that revolution in Germany will liberate us from all international difficulties and from the necessity of revolutionary war. But the German revolution needs time. It needs preparations, propaganda, fraternisation in the trenches, a period of development. That is why the Bolsheviks paid particular attention to Germany and were all along awaiting the outbreak of a revolution in that country. The situation was, no doubt, revolutionary, but the expected country-wide and successful revolution did not take place. The effort made in 1918, and another effort in 1923-both ended in grievous failure. During the period the German question was elaborately discussed several times in the various bodies of the Communist International as well as in the committees and conferences of the Communist Party of Germany. Roy had the unique opportunity of participating in several of those discussions and also in the planning of some revolutionary activities. Those discussions and his conversations with leading German communists contributed substantially to his training as a communist theoretician and tactician. That is why he wrote in the Memoirs : "The stay in Berlin was useful. I learned much and made several new friends and acquaintances."

Besides German communists, Roy also met some Dutch communists associated with the West European Bureau of the Communist International. The Bureau was in charge of getting delegates for the second congress and arranging for their journey to Moscow. Those communists were leftists in their views but were at that time held in high esteem in Moscow-Prominent amongst them was H. Sneevliet. He is described by Roy as "the first to bring the message of Socialism to Asia." Through him Roy "came to know several leaders of the Indonesian revolutionary movement such as Samaoer Sudarshana, Tan Malaka, Alimin Hatta, Sjahrir, to mention only the best known few." They were then students in Dutch Universities. Sneevliet attended the second congress as a delegate. Later he became "an important lieutenant of Trotsky." Political differences did not, however, come in the way of personal friendship. Sneevliet and J. Rutger, who was another important member of the group, met Roy in Berlin. Both were keen on the liberation of the subject peoples and desired that the Communist International should pay special attention to !ha' problem. They suggested to Roy that he should raise the issue in the second congress. He was already thinking on those lines. He thought of that course after listening to the reports made by delegates from various countries at conferences that were held in Berlin prior to their departure to Moscow. He has recorded in the Memoirs what he thought at that time:

"Having personally experienced the debacle of the German revolution, I could not share the optimism that the proletariat in a number of other countries would capture power as soon as the World Congress meeting in Moscow sounded the tocsin. What I learned during my several months' stay in Germany about the conditions in Europe and their immediate perspective fostered in me the feeling that the proletariat in the metropolitan countries would not succeed in their heroic endeavour to capture power unless Imperialism was weakened by the revolt of the colonial peoples. To be defeated, it must be attacked on two fronts. I suspected nationalist atavism in the feeling, but at the same time wag exasperated by the insularism of the average proletarian revolutionary, who sympathised with the struggle of the colonial peoples for national liberation, but did not believe that would succeed before Socialism was established in Europe. I wondered why the revolution should not spread eastward, and resolved to rush to the exciting task of opening the second front of the World Revolution." That sumps up in a few words the role that Roy was to play in the second congress. Though he had no sympathy now with the work that the Indian Revolutionary Committee carried on during war years; Roy did not neglect to meet its members during his stay in Berlin' Virendranath

Chattopadhyaya, the pillar of the Committee, was not then in the city. He was away in Stokholm where a branch of the Berlin Committee bad been established. The only person Roy could meet was Bhupendranath Datta. Datta had participated in the revolutionary movement in India and was a brother of Swami Vivekananda. After leaving India he was for some time in America and had gone to Berlin and become an important member of the Revolutionary Committee.

Later he returned to India. Roy has written the following about him in the Memoirs : "As a youngster at home, I had admired him as a martyred national hero. Years of mysterious revolutionary activities abroad had added to the original glamour. But the man I met in Berlin early in 1920 was disappointing—a sort of Rip van Winkle, who was still enjoying his blissful slumber." Roy met him again in Moscow in 1921 along with other members of the Revolutionary Committee including Virendranath Chattopadhyaya. Another Indian of consequence that he met during those days in Berlin was Abani Mukherji. J. Rutgers of the West European Bureau of the International had sent him to meet Roy. Mukherji had also, it was supposed, played a part in the revolutionary movement in India. Later he became a communist and Roy has stated. "He was the first Indian Communist I met." Roy was not keen on his going further to Moscow. So he sent him back to Rutgers. But Rutgers was of a different opinion and eventually Mukherji attended the second congress as a delegate from India. For a year or two thereafter he collaborated with Roy in a number of activities, but subsequently there were suspicious about him and Roy bad to terminate his association with him. By the time Roy reached Berlin he had well-defined views about the hope of revolution in India. They are stated as follows in the Memoirs :

"According to my new faith, revolutions took place of necessity. No individual was indispensable. They were brought about by the operation of new social forces. The maturity of the latter was the objective condition for a revolution. Until that basic condition was created, no armed uprising should be undertaken because it was sure to fail. Social forces antagonistic to the established order must, in the first place, be politically mobilised and recruited in the army of revolution. Only then would arise the question of arming the soldiers ready to fight for liberation.

"Our old idea of revolution put the cart before the horse, it attached the decisive importance to arms, and when the opportunity of getting them appeared to present itself, we believed that revolution was round the corner. We did not stop to consider the problem of recruiting men to carry arms. The number of members of an underground party was too small to compose an army of revolution.

"The new idea of revolution and the mental picture of how it should take place made me feel that there was no sense in my going back to India in a hurry."

He was also convinced that to build up a communist party was the immediate task. He, was further convinced that the communist parties of various countries must be welded together in a strong international organisation. It was to help in the building up of such an organisation that he was going to Moscow. While in Berlin Roy had already prepared a manifesto putting forward the communist position on the national and social struggle in India and calling upon workers of all countries "especially Great Britain" to help the cause of social revolution in India. It was published in Glasgow Socialist in June or July 1920. it is to be found in the National Archives, New Delhi and is reproduced in Documents of the History of the Communist Party of India, Vol. I (Pages 151 to 155). Apart from Roy, it is signed by, Abani Mukherji and Santi Devi, the penname of Evelyn Roy. It is not, however, mentioned in the

Memoirs. Roy left Berlin for Moscow some time in the latter half of April 1920. Special arrangements were made for his journey. Other delegates followed a few weeks later. He travelled by sea as far as Reval and then by train to Leningrad. Roy would have liked to spend some days in the city, "the cradle of the Revolution." But the representative of the International who accompanied him had orders to take him straight to Moscow. The train was in the night. The day was spent visiting a few places in the city and the next day by about noon Roy was in Moscow to begin his work as an officer in the international army of the world revolution.

5

M.N. Roy : Jail Life and Reaction to Policies

During the period he was first in Kanpur Jail, as an undertrial prisoner, and then in Bareilly, Almora and Dehra Dun Jails, all in Uttar Pradesh. At the time of his appeal he was taken to Allahabad, but that was for a few days. During the years of Roy's imprisonment so many significant developments took place in the country and abroad. The Civil Disobedience Movement which was restarted in January 1932 petered out in about a year. After its failure, rightwing tendencies became very prominent in the Congress. They secured approval of their programme of council-entry first at the AICC meeting in Patna in May 1934 and then at the Congress session in Bombay in October 1934. Next year, British Parliament passed the Government of India Act of 1935 granting a wider franchise and provincial autonomy and holding Out the hope of a Federation and some sharing of power at the Centre. The Congress was opposed to the Federal part of Act, but not to the transfer of power in the Provinces, though it continued to talk regarding wrecking the Reforms.

The failure of the C. D. movement and the drift towards the right led to the growth of leftist trends in the Congress, the most significantly expression of which was the organisation of the Congress Socialist Party. To counteract these trends the Congress tightened its organisation by adopting at its Bombay session amendments to the constitution suggested by Gandhiji.

From 1934 onwards there was a revival of trade union and communist activity. The Government answered to it by banning the Communist Party and some organisations under its influence and by imprisonment of several trade union leaders. In 1936 there wag a revival of Congress activities. Jawaharlal Nehru was elected the President. He started to popularise socialism and the demand for Constituent Assembly. The Congress was getting radicalised and at that moment Roy joined it after his release in November 1936. In the international field the most significant and tragic development was Hitler's rise to power in Germany. He destroyed socialist and communist parties and trade unions and all other independent organisations and established a reign of terror. He started preparations for war, and ail alliance for war developed between Germany, Italy and Japan. The three States had pronounced anti-communist character and the alliance seemed to be directed against the communist State of Soviet Russia. Western Democracies adopted a tolerant attitude towards Hitler and the alliance and followed a policy of appeasement with the intention of avoiding war. But amongst the people there was a revulsion against Hitler as a result of the cruelties and repression practised by him. A People's Front arose in France and similar movements developed in other countries. Revising its earlier policy of ultra-leftism, the CI gave a call in 1935 for a broad united front against Nazism and Fascism. It did not, however, re-establish unity in communist ranks as expected by Roy.

Another crucial event was the outbreak of civil war in Spain early in 1936. Cooped up in his prison cell Roy took note of all these developments. Occasionally he gave expression to his reactions to them in his letters and other writings. As an undertrial prisoner Roy was placed in A Class. After conviction the Sessions Judge gave him B Class, a classification that was not changed despite of several representations from him and from his friends in the country and abroad and despite of alarming deterioration in his physical condition. In a footnote to a letter written from jail, published in 1943, Roy writes : "All the representations made by myself personally and by friends in, India and abroad failed to convince the authorities that, according to their own standards, I was obviously qualified for A class. I was made to forfeit legitimate privileges on the ground that as an A Class prisoner I should be kept in a District Jail, where the essential "watch and ward" could not be arranged." As a B Class prisoner, Roy could get and write only one letter a month. There was also a good deal of difficulty in getting books as well as writing materials. In another footnote he writes : "There was a good deal of difficulty about writing material; after conviction I was placed in the B Class, and therefore was not entitled to have any. Eventually, special permission was given, but I was allowed to have only one note-book at a time; once that was used up I could get another only by depositing the old one in the jail office. Consequently, notes made during months of study could not be used for writing later on. Although friends kept me supplied with plenty of books, I could not make free use of them, because I was not allowed to have more than three at a time with me. Consequently, there was almost insuperable difficulty for carrying on any systematic research or use of reference material." Another handicap from which Roy suffered was the inability of any of his co-workers from Bombay and other places to meet him. Their applications to interview him were rejected on the ground that only relatives could be permitted to meet a prisoner in jail. The only person who was permitted to meet him was. Brajesh Singh and that too in connection with his appeal in High Court. In 1932 Brajesh Singh met Roy many times. But early in 1933 he went away to Europe. He went away without making any arrangements for the appeal and without informing any of his political associates. His sudden going away disorganised the arrangements for the appeal and also dislocated for a time Roy's channels of communication. They were repaired in a short period, but the hearing of the appeal was delayed. In his letters Roy characterised it as "desertion". It turned out to be political desertion as well. A few months later, while still abroad. Brajesh Singh joined the official communists. After his going away nobody was permitted to meet Roy during the rest of his period in jail baring for legal port. As a prisoner, Roy was well-behaved. He never failed to perform his allotted work. In one of the letters that he was permitted to write he has stated : "My jail record is entirely favourable." For some time he was made to ply the Charka which brought forth the following comment from him : "I am learning to ply the divine spinning wheel, with which, Gandhi proposes to save the world. It is an irony of fate that I should have to do this! The Mahatma has finally scored a point on me. If he only knew it !" The work was not heavy and left him a good amount of time to do his reading and writing. He obeyed all rules and regulations except one of not maintaining unauthorised contacts with the outside world. He was determined to break that rule from his first day in jail and succeeded in breaking it constantly throughout his term. Roy had an immense capacity to make friends and to retain their respect and affection. He won friends amongst his fellow convicts and also amongst warders and other jail officers.

They supported him smuggle out his messages, letters and other manuscripts of which there was a constant flow from all places of his confinement. Political prisoners who happened to be in the same jail were always keen to help him. The earliest to meet him, though for a short period, were the two Pandey brothers, Surendranath and Birendranath of Lahore conspiracy case fame. Both became later active workers of the Roy Group. Rajendra Dutt Nigam remained with Roy for a long time and was of immense help. He was in jail for his part in the Delhi conspiracy case. He became an ardent Royist and worked with Roy after his release until his death which was hastened by tuberculosis contacted in jail. He copied several of Roy's manuscripts and sent them out in his own handwriting so that, even it detected, they might not be traced to Roy. On most occasions the materials that were sent out reached the addressees safe. Superintendents of jails and other high officers of the Government tried their best to stop the flow. Extra restrictions used to be placed; warders used to be changed; convicts used to be threatened; for a time the flow would cease; but it would start again after a short while. The jail officers did not succeed in putting a stop to the clandestine political activities of Roy. They went on throughout his period of imprisonment. Years later Ellen Roy wrote about these secret contacts of Roy with the outside world. The occasion was the first anniversary, after his death, of 20th November, the day of his release from jail. The day used to be celebrated each year at their place in Dehra Dun in the company of friends and coworkers. She wrote : "The fact of his secret contact with outside could of course not remain hidden, and caused his jailors much embarrassment with their superiors. But they would never find out the channels of the secret traffic. One— when he was directly challenged by a Superintendent of one of the jails, he replied that, if there was anything of the kind happening, it was the jailor's job to find out, and it was none of the duties of a prisoner to do the job of his jailors, for that he should go to his subordinates, Who ought to know. Upon that the frustrated official burst out : "That is the whole trouble, the damned lot is all in league with you!"-That is your worry, was the reply, and none of my business. Nothing happened, barring that even more passages were struck out in the next letter I got, perhaps out of spite. When once things became too hot, an ingenious sweeper manufactured an air-tight cylinder, in which he smuggled out letters hidden in the conservancy drum." About these "secret allies" or Roy she wrote: "But what would he have done without those men who enabled him to be in touch with his friends and colleagues in the country, who required him for guidance and advice in those initial days of his political work in the Country. He always retained a great gratitude for these secret allies of his in jail. We came across a few of them in later years, who had been transferred to other places or retired; and suddenly turned up, furtively, in the midst of a conference or at a meeting hall,, and always it was like a cordial reunion of friends or relations, and they all knew me and I looked at them as old intimate friends. He used to tell the stories of the clandestine goings on with great gusto." Once when Roy was in Almora jail, the punishment of withdrawal of writing facilities was imposed upon him. It might have been as a result of the detection of some unauthorised writing that he might have efforted to smuggle out. He made all application to the Inspector General of Prisons for the restoration of those facilities. A couple of extracts from the application will be of interest as they throw light on the conditions that were imposed on the use of writing materials. The application stated inter alia : "Limited facilities for doing some literary work- were granted to, me from the very beginning of my imprisonment. This is proved by the fact that a number of duty paged and certified note-books were issued to me on various dates over the whole period of my imprisonment by the Supdt. Dist. Jail Cawnpur, as well as Supdt. C.P.B. These note-books bearing the signatures of the issuing officers and used by myself are among my properties deposited in jail.

The grant of the concession is also regularly recorded in my history ticket." Stating that there could be no "reasonable objection" to his doing some literary, work, it urged in support the following three considerations: "Firstly, it is of purely scientific philosophical nature and being always open to examination by the jail authorities cannot contain an-objectionable matter. Secondly, it does not interfere with my duties as a prisoner. All along, I have performed the full prescribed prison task as much as done by any ordinary prisoner and shall to do in future. "Thirdly a rigid restriction of intellectual life is not part of the punishment to which I have been condemned by the Court of Law and I attach neater value to my intellectual life than to the physical. Subject to the loss of freedom and the rigour of jail life, I may be allowed what some prisoners are accorded, special treatment in consideration of the higher standard of living they are used to. It is but logical that the intellectual as well as physical standard should be taken into consideration in prescribing the special treatment.

On flits grounds I pray that I shall not be deprived of the use at least of the strictly limited amount of writing materials as hitherto granted. At the same time, I hope you will give a clear order, to keel) the written books in my possession. Because these contain the notes, the result of two years research work, which are to be basis of any future writing I may be fortunate to he allowed to do." Under the rules Roy was allowed to write one letter a month. The letter was restricted to one sheet and had to pass the scrutiny of jail officials. Sometimes many sentences were blacked out. The same rule applied to the incoming mail which was also restricted to one letter a month. Books were permitted more liberally, but after strict scrutiny which led several a time to exasperating delays. Roy wrote his letters to Ellen Gotschalk who was for the first part in Berlin and later after Hitler's rise to power in Paris. As he could not write to others the letters to Ellen took the form sometimes of "circulars". Olen preserved all those letters. They were published in 1943 in book form under the title Letters from Jail with a few footnotes by Roy. They are the chief source of information on Roy's life in jail, his literary activity and his reactions to events happening in the world and India, the Letters is a fascinating document throwing a flood of light on the personality of the writer and on the working of his mind. There will be several quotations from the Letters in this chapter in so far as they give information about the author's life in jail and his reactions to political events. The information was given in a guarded manner as it had to pass the scrutiny of jail officers. The first letter in the series was written on August 11, 1931 from Kanpur Jail, twenty-one days after the arrest which is described as-It has happened as expected by me, at any rate." It is further pointed out : "It (imprisonment) is a stage in the process. It must be gone through. No matter whatever may come out of it. To work in India one must be an Indian, having regard for the Indian mentality." This was with reference to Brandler's and Thalheimer's, opposition to his plan to return to India. Roy then declares his intention to utilise his time "to improve his mind" and urges Ellen to send him "intellectual food". Ellen complied with the request immediately and continued to send him intellectual food for the next five years. She sent him all the books that he ordered from time to time. They were books on science and philosophy and history and sometimes novels.

Roy was a voracious reader and he took pains to "improve his mind". Nothing pained him more than the delay in getting books occasioned by bureaucratic procedure. It was more difficult to get books in German or French. Sometimes they were returned to the sender who had to pay postage, charges. Roy's Indian friends also kept him supplied with the books that he required and were available in India. The last letter from Kanpur was written on January 6, 1932 in which he complains : "The day of judgment is still hanging on my accursed head." The judgment was delivered three days later imposing a sentence of twelve years', transportation. It was an "unexpectedly heavy blow', he states, in the first letter from his new address, Central Prison, Bareilly. In the same letter he writes about the appeal : "There will be an appeal to the High Court. And I have sufficient reason to expect a substantial reduction of the sentence, if not acquittal. Eight years ago, for the same evidence, others were given four years. There is no reason why I would get so much more. As there is little likelihood of my getting the permission, to argue the case myself in the High Court, we shall secure the services of one of the first rate lawyers in the country. It may be another three or four months before the final settlement is made." The appeal was filed in the Allahabad High Court. Roy was taken to Allahabad when it came up for hearing. He wanted to conduct it himself. But he was advised against it. In the end it was argued by the famous lawyer, K. N. Katju who later became the Defence Minister of India and still later the Chief Minister of Madhya Pradesh. The conviction was confirmed but the sentence was reduced to six years' rigorous imprisonment. Despite of reduction, it was longer by two years than the sentence imposed on Muzafar Ahmad, Dange and others in the earlier case. Roy's petition to the High Court requesting permission to be present in court at the time of the hearing of the appeal is available in the volumes of his Jail Notes. The following extracts will give an idea of the requests that were made and why it was essential to make them : "That the Counsel, engaged to represent Your petitioner in the High Court, had not been present (in) the Lower Court, and required to be duty instructed by the appellant as well as by the lawyers who had been in charge of the defence in the Lower Court, but that owing to his being detained in a jail so far away the petitioner had until now no opportunity of any interview with the Counsel who is to argue his appeal. "That it is practically impossible, and financially very burdensome for the petitioner to have his Counsel (who is a member of the Calcutta Bar) come to this great distance and stay here for the time required to receive from the appellant adequate instructions without which he will not be able to represent the appellant satisfactorily. "That placed in these circumstances, the petitioner apprehends, that his case will not be properly placed before the High Court."

"Therefore your petitioner prays:

That the High Court be pleased to order his transfer to the Dist. Jail Allahabad or any other prison where he may be in the position to be in closer touch with his Counsel and legal advisers before and during the hearing of the appeal; and

That he be granted the permission to be present in the Court during the hearing of his appeal in order to assist the Counsel to represent him correctly, and to argue the appeal personally in case he finds the Counsel, lacking adequate instructions, not fully prepared to do so satisfactorily." After the appeal in the High Court an effort was made to file a further appeal in the Privy Council. Katju took the papers along with him to London. Roy wrote about it to Fenner Brockway, H. N. Brailsford and Stafford Cripps. For some time he was also thinking of asking his German lawyer friend, Rosenfeld to London to argue the appeal. But he was arrested by the Hitlerite regime. Ultimately the idea of the appeal was dropped on Cripps' advice. In a letter from Bareilly prison of December 23, 1933 Roy writes the following about the advice. "Please communicate the following to Sir Stafford. I have given careful consideration to the point raised by him, and fully appreciate its gravity. Having done so, I feel that there will be no particular harm, whatever may be the verdict of the

Privy Council. As far as India is concerned, the situation will be hardly affected by an adverse decision, whereas a favourable verdict may be advantageous. The extension of the possible evil to Britain is a very remote possibility, too remote to counterbalance the immediate advantages of a favourable verdict. The precedence of the Meerut case is not quite relevant in view of the practical uselessness of an appeal to the Privy Council. On that occasion, the appeal was to be exclusively on principle-for establishing a possibly favourable legal precedence. Therefore, the decision to appeal or not had to be determined exclusively on the point raised by Sir Stafford. For these reasons, I am in favour of proceeding with the appeal. But there is one condition. The gravity of the point raised by Cripps had to be measured by the legal merit of the case. On this point, the lawyer is the best judge. If from the merit of the case it seems to Sir Stafford and other competent legal authorities that there is a fair chance of a favourable verdict, then the risk-taken becomes almost negligible. So, while giving my answer to the question put to me, 1, in my turn, request Sir Stafford to be guided by the merit of the case. Personally, I think that on the merit of the case the Privy Council is not likely to uphold the judgement of the Indian court. But I may be mistaken or optimistic. That is for the lawyer to judge." Roy kept himself remarkably well-informed about political developments in the country and abroad. For the former he must have relied on the newspapers he got and on talks with political prisoners that he came across in the jails. The second Civil Disobedience Movement started early in 1932 and it brought several Congressmen to jails.

Trade union and peasant workers and revolutionaries were also arrested from time to time. They must have talked to Roy about the political happenings that they knew. Foreign political developments he came to know from newspapers and magazines and also from Ellen's letters. In his letters he provide only a guarded expression to his views on the developments. On developments in India he had to be very circumspect. And yet on occasions one comes across passages like this : "But it seems their (old Congress leaders') days are numbered; of course, in an old country like ours, days may be numbered in terms of the year of other mortal lands. Yet they are numbered;" or "There are weighty reasons for satisfaction. It may not be long before things will appear in a clear perspective. They are bound to and are shaping that way slowly but surely';' or "I am full of confidence in so far as my special zone is concerned. And our success there will tell upon the general situation." On developments in Germany and France and the world as a whole he could express himself more frankly. He took note of Hitter's rise to power and was alarmed by the disastrous effect it would have on his friends. In one letter he wrote : "In comparison with the terrible ordeal of you all living in the Dritte Reich, my personal troubles are so insignificant that now the less said about them, the better. I shudder to think what might be happening to several even now. What a terrible price shall have to be paid for mistakes which could be so easily avoided" This refers to the mistakes of refusing to unite with Social Democrate and of uniting with Nazis on some occasions committed by official communists in pursuance of the ultra-left line of the sixth CI congress. From time to time he made anxious enquiries about the welfare of "our family" consisting of Opposition communists and some leaders of the Social Democratic Patty. Roy saw the growing danger of war. In April 1935 he was happy that the Stress a Conference and the Extraordinary Meeting of the Council of the League of Nations "have cleared away the war cloud which recently hung so ominously over Europe."

However a year later, he is needed to write : "The political atmosphere of Europe seems to be getting more and more charged. Adolf's last move might have precipitated the fatal blow to the shaken fabric of peace. But the crisis seems to be over, for the moment. How long will it continue in this precarious way? That is the question. It seems that "Western stability" is going to be secured, by throwing Russia to the wolves. Germany has made her demand clear. "Drang nach Westen". Something more than Abyssinia is to be looted. Can the Western Powers and America sanction that loot, and save Western civilisation ? Nazi paganism and Japanese feudalism together will surely throw the "achievements of the nineteenth century" into the flames of neo-barbarism" A month later he writes again : "These must be extremely exciting, hectic days in France-having a general election under the ominous shadows of Prussian militarism reborn. But if they would stop to think, the shadow is cast on the opposite direction. France is not menaced. I believe the rulers of the glorious Third Republic are not blind to the reality of the foreign policy of the triumphant Third Reich. There will be no war on the Rhine, not in the near future at any rate. Of course, there always remains the possibility of some contingent event putting the fat on fire. But the premeditated plan is to make a Western combination against the East.

The success of the diplomatic moves made from Wilhelmstrasse will depend to a great extent on the outcome of the French general election. It appears practically certain that the Front Populates will win: That will be some guarantee against the immediate execution of the nefarious scheme. But the question is : How long will the front last? The Japan on the other side, seem to be confident of definite developments in Europe in the near future. They must have got the tip from their Western ally. Well, it is a critical moment. In Europe, people are sitting on the top of a power magazine." Roy's prophecy that there would be no war on the Rhine proved wrong; for Hitter first moved west and east against Russia about two years later, which Roy was amongst the first to foretell long before the event. Roy watched anxiously the developments in the communist movement, both official as well as oppositional. In an early letter he writes : "The Big Hèads (leaders of the CI) are simply crazy. They feed themselves on mere imagination. What they talk about simply does not exist but in their feverish dream" he wrote in several letters about their inability to see things as they were, about their stupidities and meanness. All the same he was against setting up a "new shop". In one letter he writes : "I hope experience has taught them the correctness or my attitude-no new shop, but flood line with new share-holders enlisted by us. That is the only way to the much required amalgamation, and recovery from the crisis." In a footnote to the letter appended at the time of the publication of the Letters Roy states : "I was opposed, to the Communists, opposed to the then official policy of the Communist International, and consequently expelled, establishing a separate Organisation. I advocated the policy of their working just like members of the Communist Party, carrying on propaganda according to their views, and advising the supporters of those views to join the official Communist Party. I was of the opinion that, pursuing that policy, opposition Communists expelled from the official parties would thus be able to extend their influence in the rank and file of the parties, and eventually change their policy." He repeated the same advice in the next letter. The advice is a little strange as in India he had-himself to setup a "new shop". Conditions in India were, of course, materially different from those in Germany. In one the Communist Party hardly existed while in the other it counted its members in lakhs and had large influence in the country as a whole.

However, it was utopian to hope to influence a highly centralised party through enrolment of individual members at the bòttom. The organisation was moreover so constituted that the leaders at the top could effect drastic changes in policy and still exercise those who had urged them. What happened after the seventh CI congress bears out the truth of this observation. Roy was keen on unity of socialists and communists. The triumphal march of Fascism practically throughout Europe "would, he hoped, persuade both to "close up their ranks, so that a powerful resistance could be put up against the menace." Roy was hopeful about the seventh congress of the CI, that it would hear the breach between the CI and the Opposition Communists.

The latter had applied for permission to attend the congress in order to effect reconciliation. Permission was not granted and reconciliation was not effected. That hurt Roy and he writes : "It is really distressing how mean the people are-to take hated enemies in brotherly embrace, and treat old friends and tried treasures as untouchable. I am afraid there will be more bitter experience before the lesson is learned." Despite of this, he welcomed on the whole the new line that was chalked out by the congress. The letters are full of Roy's plans of writing books. He did a lot of writing in jail. Writing on political matters, which was unauthorised will be mentioned separately. The other writing was on philosophical, scientific and sociological matters which had to be done under the close supervision of jail officials. It had to be done on bound foolscape size volumes of about 1000 pages each. He was never allowed to keep more than one volume with him.

When he was released he brought out with him nine closely written volumes. A good part of what was written is published. It comprised of such books as Fascism, Historical Role of Islam, Materialism, Hersies of Twentieth Century, Ideal of Indian Womanhood and others. A part remains unpublished. It consists mainly of Roy's thoughts on philosophical consequences of modern science. In jail, Roy devoted a good deal of thought to the discoveries of modern science and their effect on philosophical demands. Every letter comprises a list of books on the subject that he would like to have and some of them contain discussion of the problems that he was efforting to tackle. The deep study that he carried on helped him later to write his outstanding book, Reason, Romanticism and Revolution. Towards the end of his term in jail, Roy started to plan his future. The plan was of devoting himself to the study of various scientific and social problems. "I have developed the mood for scientific work", he wrote once. On June 20, 1936, four months before his release, he wrote : "If some stable arrangement could be made (about the publication of my book), I would be almost prepared to spend the next five years in pure scientific work to finish what I have begun; and that programme would naturally include a more or less prolonged visit to Europe.

There is an inducement for Heinz and August 1 If they really want to have me there in the near future, let them go after Weil. I can give the assurance that it would be a very useful undertaking, and I shall put in some solid work probably that would be my lasting contribution! The rest seems to be so evanescent, Nor will there be anything more pressing or practical to do in the near future. I am reconciled to a long perspective. Heinz was quite correct in his judgement of the situation in this country. The judgement still holds. The situation is indeed very immature. No useful objective will be served by my joining hallu-balloo or paying over and over again a fancy price for moral assets of dubious value." Two years earlier, he had broached the plan of a publishing house and a book shop. He wrote : "The plan I wanted you to consider is more than of a book shop. It is to found a publishing house which will grow into an intellectual centre. The object is promotion of modern scientific literature, and to encourage young intellectuals on that line. Of course, the plan necessarily comprises a book shop as well. The things I am working on will not be taken up by any big publisher in this country.

Nationalist publishers would not touch things which are not in the order of ch ap platitudes, the usual claptrap about India's world mission, spiritual genius and glorification of the past. On the other hand, books published abroad necessarily have a restricted circulation in this country. Therefore, one of the conditions for a progressive intellectual movement is some serious arrangement for the production and circulation of proper scientific literature. Hence the need for a publishing house which will not be bound by purely business considerations, or nationalist prejudices and reactionary views." In March 1936 he wrote to Ellen to explore the possibility of persuading the Frankfurt Institute to establish a branch in India to develop as the "centre of an intellectual movement" which, he stated, would be "the main thing I shall undertake on my release". These plans that Roy made did not materialise, for soon after his release, he was drawn into the vortex of the political movement from which he could free himself only a few years before his death. It is owing to that involvement in politics that the two institutions, Renaissance Publishers and the Indian Renaissance Institute, established some years after his release did not grow into the vital institutions that Roy would have liked them to be. Roy's keenness about renaissance is to be seen in several of his letters. He attributed most of the ills of the Indian society to the absence of the renaissance which the European society went through in the fifteenth and sixteenth centuries. In one letter he stated : "Indian Society is still living in the fifteenth century. All our problems are bred in that cesspool of social stagnation." In another letter he wrote : "But I am a realist and to a realist eye this country is overburdened with filth, poverty and ignorance. It is really a depressing problem and the worst of it is that there are a blessed few among our would-be, saviours who realise the magnitude and nature of the problem." Much earlier expressing his distaste of a companion forced upon him a companion whom he called "a typical son of India"—he had expressed the requirement of a Kemal Pasha to change several habits and customs prevalent in the country. Thoughts like these which found expression in several letters eventually led to the development of the renaissance movement which became a distinguishing feature of Royist politics. Life in jail shattered Roy's health. He was proud of his "iron constitution", but it Could not stand the rigours of jail life that were imposed upon him. The most oppressive was the summer heat. He had to stand it for the first three years in Kanpur and Bareilly. Despite of several representations, his own and those of his friends in India, Europe and America, he was not removed to a cooler place in the hills. In 1934 he became so alarmingly ill that during summer months he was removed to Almora and brought back again to Bareilly after the summer was over.

The next year he was taken to Dehra Dun when the weather became hot and kept there until his release. In that latter part he did not have to stand the gruelling heat of the plains, but the damage had been already done. He suffered from dilatation of heart and pain in chest and slow fever from time to time. These made him very weak and for days together he had to be in hospital under constant medical supervision. He could not write much about his health in his letters to Ellen, in the first place, because he did not want to alarm her, and in the next place, he was not allowed to write much about it.

In a footnote to a letter of July 11, 1932 Roy writes : "As a matter of fact, all references to my health and conditions of life in jail were struck out from my letters. At the time of writing this letter, I was seriously ill, having been removed to the hospital. The following note from Jail Superintendent was enclosed in the letter : "Mr. Roy has not been keeping very fit the past week or two owing to the heat and other causes. He has been advised to confine his mental food to light reading matter only and to completely give up for the-present political and allied subjects. I would ask you to confine your letters to light and domestic matters only. I ask this in the interest of Mr. Roy, who is in my charge, executive and medical." Many eminent persons in India and the world, including Albert Einstein, the famous scientist, made representations to the Government in India and England for humane treatment to Roy. But they had no effect. In 1936, Jawaharlal Nehru wrote the following letter on the state of Roy's health to the Congress leader, Govind Ballabh Pant, who later became the Chief Minister of U. P. and still later the Home Minister of the Government of India :

August 29, 1936

"My dear Pantji,

I enclose two letters which will speak for themselves. One is from Khurshed Lal and the other from M. N. Roy's wife who is in Paris now. Both refer to Roy's state of health. I wonder if it is possible for you or anyone else to do anything in the matter in the Assembly or outside it. I am myself sure that Roy is seriously unwell. Whether he has any serious internal trouble or not I cannot of course say, but there can be little doubt that five years solitary confinement has injured him greatly, as it would injure any person. And Roy is a very sensitive person who reacts to his surroundings more than the average person might. "I do not suppose you can do much in the matter. Still an effort should be made. 'Even if his release cannot be hastened, he ought at least to be examined thoroughly by competent outside doctors. He is being kept, and he has been there a long time now, in the female ward of the Dehra Gaol. You know well what an awful hole this is. I could not survive this place for several weeks. The government have not even had the decency to keep him in the new barrack outside the main goal where they kept me, although that was depressing enough." It is clear from the letter that Roy was treated worse than several Congress leaders.

On the same day Nehru wrote the following letter to Ellen Gottschalk in reply to her anxious inquiries about Roy's health

"Dear Miss Gottschalk,

On return from Bombay yesterday I received your letter of the 3rd Aug. I have myself been receiving unsatisfactory reports about Roy's health in prison and have been distressed about it. A friend of mine in Dehra Dun had an interview with him in the jail on the 19th July and he wrote to say that Roy complained of severe internal pains. He issued a statement to the press to this effect but subsequently it was stated, perhaps on behalf of the Government, that Roy was keeping good health. I should very much like to be of service to Roy in this matter but we are so helpless in it. Quite apart from any internal trouble that he may have, I can well understand the terribly depressing effect of long solitary confinement. Five years of it for a sensitive individual ! From what I could find out, the place where he is kept in the Dehra Dun jail is highly unsatisfactory and depressing. I am told that Roy's release is due on Nov. 20th. Personally I doubt if the Government will give him any further remission. They are peculiarly callous in such matters. But I am writing to friends in the legislative assembly and asking them to do what they can in the matters. Apart from the prejudice which induce Government to act in such a way towards those who are their political opponents, the government is a terribly slow moving machine. At every step there is red tape and references from one department to another. Probably these references will take several weeks and we shall be on the eve of November before the final answer is forthcoming. In any event we shall try to press that a competent outside doctor should examine him." Roy had all along entertained the hope that he would not be needed to spend more than four years in jail. Prisoners are usually granted some remissions and a Revision Board reviews sentences after half the term is served. He was hopefully looking forward to a favourable decision from the Revision Board. After solving nearly half his sentence, Roy sent a memorial to the Governor requesting that his case might be placed before the Revision Board. It was sent from Almora jail and it stated inter alia : "That the memorialist should have the benefit of-the judgement of the Hon. Chief Justice of the High Court in the Meerut Conspiracy Case. In the light of this judgement the sentence of the memorialist has remained excessively severe even after the reduction ordered by the High Court. The charge in both the cases was identical, and the evidence was certainly not stronger in the case of the memorialist than in the Meerut Case. On the contrary, white in the Meerut case the evidence proved some acts committed by the accused which were interpreted as overt acts proving the charge, no overt act whatsoever was proved in the case of the memorialist. This is admitted by the Hon. High Court which held that the lower court had relied too much upon hypothetical evidence (had the accused been successful in what he desired to do the consequences might have been dangerous). The Hon. High Court held that the effects of the memorialist's acts as proved by the prosecution evidence were negligible, and was pleased even to ridicule the alleged pretensions of the memorialist.

"That while in the Meerut case, the comparatively light sentences were justified on the ground of long period of under-trial confinement in the case of the memorialist the antiquated nature of the evidence offers an equally justifiable if not weightier ground. The memorialist was convicted in 1932 for acts committed between 192124. The acts, according to prosecution evidence, were purely propagandist-propagation of social-political views and effort to organize a political party. The principal witness for the Crown, Col. Sir Cecil Kaye, admitted in the Magistrate's Court that owing to the great change in the political situation of the country what would be considered rank sedition several years ago was common political opinion at the time of the trial of the memorialist.

"That the imprisonment of the memorialist has been much more rigorous than it ought to be for those convicted on purely political charges. Disregarding the well-known facts qualifying him for it in every respect and disregarding the fact that the Dist. Magistrate concerned on his own initiative gave a written order placing the memorialist in the "A" class, the memorialist on his conviction was reduced to the "B" class, was obliged to live on a standard much lower than he is accustomed to.

"The rigour of living in conditions so much below the standard. He is accustomed to has adversely told upon his health which was perfect at the time of his conviction. Having lived for the best part of his life in cold countries the memorialist naturally found the summer heat at Bareilly intolerable. But for two years he had to live under that intolerable condition. The cumulative effect has impaired his health (loss of weight to the extent of 40 lbs., heart was affected, low temperature, constant pain in chest and back etc. etc.). Nevertheless, he was made to perform the full prescribed jail task (manual tabour) as much as done by any ordinary prisoner all the time except when he was actually confined to bed. Although since his transfer here this summer the memorialist feels much better, complete restoration of his health is not possible in the conditions of life in jail. He still suffers from constant pain in the pectoral region, fits of severe headache, sleeplessness, cough, general debility etc. The causes of these complaints have not been properly diagnosed. Specialised medical aid essential for the purpose is not available to a prisoner. For such treatment it might be essential to go abroad. But it might be too late, should the memorialist be obliged to serve the full term of the extremely severe sentence under conditions of exaggerated rigour. That would be sentencing the memorialist to punishment not sanctioned by law.

"That the law under which the memorialist is sentenced is the same as in Britain, but there one has never, in modern times, been given more than 2 years for the identical offence. In other countries people are seldom punished so severely as the memorialist even for participating in actual armed struggle against the established state." The memorial concluded with the request that he might be released after completing half his sentence on the grounds mentioned in it. The request was not considered and Roy had to spend over five years in jail. The memorial it will be seen was made according to rules and the main ground that was urged was the much lighter sentences imposed in the Meerut Case which was more recent and based on more concrete proof. It will be appropriate now to cast a glance at the unlawful and unauthorised political activities of Roy. They started soon after his arrest and continued throughout his period of imprisonment. Roy's associates in Bombay and other places were bewildered by his arrest and did not know]low to react. For some days they kept up the pretence that a so-called Roy was arrested. Roy cleared their doubts by admitting that he was Roy and by making no effort to hide his identity. In a few days after he was taken to Kanpur, he established contact with the Bombay Group. He established similar contacts with others and all of them remained alive for the better part of his term in jail., Strangely enough, it was the prisoner in jail and not his associates outside who arranged the contacts and channels of communication; their only merit was that they did not fail to respond which in itself was not a small thing in those day of severe repression. Roy's arrest did not kill the Roy Group, but it brought ii its wake some great setbacks. Sunder Kabadi, one of the two early organisers of the Group, left the country a few weeks after the arrest. J. K. Banerji, an associate from Calcutta, followed him a couple of months later. Brajesh Singh left after a year. His going away isolated Roy entirely for some time. Being in Lucknow and with his contacts in higher circles in U. P., he was the main channel of communication and was also entrusted with the liability of legal defence, in the lower courts. Tayab Shaikh was prosecuted and remained underground for quite some time. Some members of the Group in Bombay, Lucknow and Calcutta became inactive when they percepted that it was not safe to related to it. Arrests and searches took place from time to time and even normal political activity became full of hazards. Those were the days of Emergency Powers and arbitrary rule-!

Despite of those difficulties, the Roy Group continued its work. It expanded to cover new cassettes like Ahmedabad and Poona. In the older centres of Bombay and Calcutta it recruited new members and extended the sphere of its activities. Love and admiration for Roy and conviction that the programme and policy enunciated by him were the only road to revolution, to which they were passionately attached, kept the Royists together and gave them the strength to light governmental repression and official communists opposition and harassment. The latter took several ugly forms. Starting with vile abuse of Roy as renegade, traitor, lackey of imperialism and what not, it went to the extent of physical assaults on Royists and breaking up their meetings and raiding their offices. Official communists could not tolerate the rise and growth of another communist group.

The Royists were then called as a communist group; they were functioning as such and were claiming to be "better communists". Official communists regarded them as a serious challenge to their monopoly and were afraid that, if the Royists grew in strength and influence, they would lose their credibility in the eyes of the CI and lose its support which enabled them to exist. To them, the Royists were, therefore, their worst enemies worse even than imperialism and capitalism. Those were the days of ultra-leftism which condemned socialists as social-fascists and regarded them as worse enemies than avowed fascists. That mad course dictated by the sixth congress and subsequent plenums was followed as zealously in India as in other countries. A few instances of this insane propaganda of anger and hate can be mentioned. It was high-level propaganda from Moscow which was dutifully echoed by its agents in India. It went along with the propaganda against the Congress and its left wing. In a letter to Indian communists CP of Great Britain, Germany and China, published in the May 19, 1932 issue of International Press Correspondence, it was stated : "The prerequisite for a correct policy for communists in the anti-imperialist movement is a definite sharp clear and uncompromising struggle and exposure of the National Congress and specialty the 'Left' national reformist first of all its special variety the group of Roy and Kandalkar At another place it was said : "The Roy-Kandalkar-Joshi, group in deeds are the worst enemies of the international revolutionary proletariat and the Indian anti-imperialist and agrarian revolution." The Roy Group was regarded as "foremost detachment" of Left" national reformism.

A year and half later a letter of the CP of China published in the same journal on November 4, 1933 poured the following abuse on the Roy Group : "The group of renegade Roy, who by 'Left' phrases and half criticism of the policy of the National Congress, came out in practice against the development of mass revolutionary struggle of the workers, and peasants."

In pursuance of this line laid down by the CI and its influential sections like the CP a of Germany, Great Britain and China, the CPI put it down in its constitution adopted in 1934 : The following are expelled from the party : (1) open or concealed Supporters of Gandhism, of the Roy group and other political trends condemned by the C.I. as enemies of Communism and a,; disorganisers and betrayers of the struggle for national independence." In 1943 it went a step further and made the following provision in Section 10 of Article IV of its constitution : "No party member shall have personal or political relationship with Fifth Columnists, Trotskyists and Royists or other known enemies of the Party, of the working class and of the nation." The enmity which started in 1931 was expressed again in 1943 long after the Royists had ceased to challenge the communists as communists. By that time Roy and Royists had travelled beyond communism. Royists survived these attacks of official communists and also the repression of the Government and grew into an influential group all over the country. They did not make much progress, in the Congress. After the defeat of the second Civil Disobedience, it was mostly inactive. However, they were recognised in the political field as a distinct group with a new outlook and a new policy. They were not several in numbers and yet the contributions that they made to political thought and action were regarded as significant. Some of them took a notable part In the establishment and development of the Congress. Socialist Party (The CSP and the Royists' role in it will be considered later). Some others rose to prominence in the Youth and other auxiliary movements. Royists were more successful in the trade union movement. They rescued the All India Trade Union Congress out of the hands, of Communists and saved it from extinction. It became soon the powerful central organisation of the trade union movement. They initiated the process of trade union unity on the ground of the Platform of Unity drafted by Roy. They participated in several trade union struggles and secured valuable concessions for workers. The present writer has described as follows the work of the Roy Group in his history of the Indian trade union movement : "The Roy Group entered the trade union movement in Bombay through the Congress Labour Committee which had been formed to spread and popularize the message of the national movement amongst industrial workers. The attitude towards the National Congress was one of its differences with the communists who came to be known in those days as official communists, as there were others, like members of the Roy Group, who were dissident communists. The Royists regarded the Congress as a national movement which was to be broadened and deepened; while to the official, communists it was a counter-revolutionary party of the upper classes which was to be opposed and exposed in every possible manner. Gradually, the Royists established contacts with trade unions and their non-communist leaders, and helped them to revive their activities. That was another basic difference between the Royists and the official communists. While the communists talked and thought of only the revolution, the Royists; emphasized the day-today demands of workers and endeavoured to build up trade unions for their satisfaction. Through the efforts of the Royists a number of trade unions in Bombay, which had been all but destroyed as a result of communist tactics, were revived and started to function as genuine workers' organisations. Similar activities were developed in other cities also, more particularly in Calcutta." That the work of the Roy Group was proving effective can be easily seen from the following assessment of the Intelligence Bureau of the Government of India "The Comintern's apprehension that Roy would put to good use his political sagacity, organisational ability, capacity for leadership and above all his remarkable personality and would attract leftists to himself thus weakening the "official" communist movement proved correct. Almost all the agents he had raised in India from Europe had remained loyal to the Comintern abandoning Roy. Yet, by the end of 1934 Roy's new followers had shown excellent outcomes. They had consolidated their position in the A.I.T.U.C., secured the affiliation to it of over 40 labour organisations and had set up a permanent office in. Calcutta. The A.I.T.U.C. was gradually resuming the former position as leader and organiser of the trade union movement in the country." Continuing it paid the following tribute to Roy : "It was only the genius of Roy, that could have accomplished so much single-handed in the short time that he had spent in India since his return.

He inspired and guided his followers even from jail. The progress of the communist movement in India in subsequent years has shown how right were the tactics that Roy advocated". Official communists were fighting against the Roy Group and pouring all manner of vile abuse upon it. But the Government regarded both groups as communists and equally dangerous from their point of view. The following paragraph records the judgement of the Intelligence Bureau formed after a close study of the situation : "In short, therefore, the ultimate objective of both 'the Indian parties in question is the same, namely, the establishment of the rule of the proletariat on the lines of a Soviet Republic. Both are more or less agreed, too, on the expediency of an appeal to nationalist fervour and racial hatred in colonial countries such as India, where undisguised Communist sentiments may make little appeal by themselves, or may even antagonize public feeling. They differ only in their methods. The "Official" communists prefer the direct route and scorn to make a secret of the fact that they propose to seize political power by mean of an armed uprising, for which the fomenting of strikes and intensive agrarian agitation are to prepare the way. Roy's programme, on the other hand, is more gradual and more insidious. Its basic aim is to make the fullest use of whatever advantages existing organisations offer in building up, step by step, strong groups of workers and peasants. His message to the masses of India is less harsh and less Utopian, more in consonance with their everyday surroundings, than that of his one-time colleagues. But let no one misunderstand Roy.

He is no more averse to the use of mass violence than the very Comintern itself." Roy was watching all these developments from jail. He was happy at the progress that was being made by his associates. Occasionally he was sending them instructions about day-today work and they proved useful several a time. But his horizon was wider, it was not restricted to the small group that was working in his name. He desired to influence the entire political situation in the country. Sometimes he sent direct messages to important political leaders and organisations. He is known to have sent a couple of letters to Jawaharlal Nehru and his Letters to C.S.P. are well known.

Besides his desire to build up a left wing in the national movement, he was also keen on building up a revolutionary party of the working class. "Organise a Communist Party" was the clarion call with which he had started his arrival. It was to be a better party than the one passing by that name. It would accept the general guidance of the CI but would have the courage to point out its errors when they were committed. It would take a realistic approach of the situation in the country and adopt a course of action that was according to it. It would not indulge in romantic dreams nor would it follow an adventurist line of action. Roy was anxious to develop such a party. The attempts that he started soon after his arrival continued even after his imprisonment. Roy prepared for the party, named the Revolutionary Working Class Party, the Communist Party of India, two basic documents. One was the programme which after adoption, was publicised as Our Task in India and the other was the less known Statement of Policy the Central Committee of the Party adopted a couple of years later.

Both are important documents setting out Roy's views on long-term as well as short-term tasks to be performed in the country. They also set out his views on some of the then current problems. The earliest document to be Smuggled out of jail was the booklet published as China in Revolt, by S. K. Vidyarthi. It was immediately proscribed by the Government of Bombay under the Press (Emergency) Powers Act of 1931. It was later published as experiences in China, the first edition in 1938 and the second in 1946. The object of the booklet was to draw lessons from Chinese developments for application to the situation in India. The author stated in the Foreword : "And there certainly are Indian Nationalists who reckon those facts as parts of the victory of the Oriental Soul of China over Western Materialism. The recent history of China should not be dismissed so light-heartedly. It offers very valuable lessons for the Indians to learn. These lessons have not yet been properly learnt even by those who are anxious to learn them because of the confusion that reigns in the realm of facts. The lessons cannot be learnt unless the habit of reading facts to suit a predetermined theory is given up. Therefore in the following pages, my main purpose will be to set forth the salient facts in order to explain what really happened in China." Roy also wrote some articles for publication in newspapers. Some of them were published under different names in the Maratta of Poona and the Advocate of Bombay. The most significant amongst them was the article on the Joint Parliamentary Committee's report. The report was published in 1934. All political parties in the country were dissatisfied by it and advocated its rejection. But that was merely a negative approach. No plan of action was suggested for developing the rejection into a positive assertion of the people's will for independence. Roy had the imagination and boldness to suggest one. A few extracts will be useful as the line suggested by Roy was new, different from the usual Gandhian line and a line that he was to suggest again and again after his release. After pointing out the danger of the rejection being "an empty gesture," "a smoke-screen to hide the real policy of co-operation", the article suggests "a positive programme.... to give expression to the general discontent of the Indian people against the constitution, which would at the same time broaden the national movement and raise it to a higher level." The positive programme that is suggested is : "the most minimum demands of the Indian people may be formulated as amendments to the proposed constitution and a country-wide propaganda may be carried on in their support and for bringing out the real character of the J. P. C. scheme and for opposing its most obnoxious provisions." As the method of suggesting amendments was unusual, Roy explains its implications as under :

"The suggestion to propose amendments to the projected constitution may sound preposterous to orthodox Congressmen. It is not in conformity with the accepted tenets of Gandhism and the orthodox methods of struggle. But it is a method dictated by political realism, a method which under the given circumstances is best calculated to invigorate our national struggle for independence and to develop the political consciousness and education of the people. There is no illusion that British Imperialism can be persuaded to grant any of those demands or even to make any material alterations in its proposed schemes. Nor is there any suggestion that the proposed constitution should be accepted and worked for whatever it may be worth. The toiling masses of India will have nothing to accept, for nothing will be offered to them. They want Independence, and Independence cannot come as a gift of British Imperialism. The method of proposing amendments is suggested with the intention of forging the broadest possible united front against the constitution and with the intention of using it as a lever for, developing a mass movement which, if properly guided and conducted, will certainly rise to the higher level of actual assertion of the right of self-determination and intensify the struggle for the conquest of power." A broad-based united front is then suggested and the article concludes with the following "Word to Left Elements" : "A word requires to be said here for the edification of certain genuine radical elements who by force of habit may be disposed to consider this as a reformist or an opportunist move. They must remember the character of every move is to be judged by its aim and by its objective possibilities. The aim of this move is to mobilise the masses against the slave constitution. It holds the potentiality of developing into a mass struggle for the conquest of power. In any case, it will result in a political education for the masses and will rouse their consciousness. Under these circumstances, are they going to hold back from a method of struggle only because it does not conform to the orthodox Gandhian standards of the political movement?" This pseudo-revolutionary attitude of the Leftists posed several difficulties for Roy in later life. Brought up in the Gandhian tradition they would prefer mock heroics to concrete, rational actions suggested by Roy for raising the struggle from a lower to a higher level. They would condemn his suggestions as reformist, and waste their time and energy in empty gestures. He had that experience with the best amongst them such as Jawaharlal Nehru and Jayaprakash Narayan.

This will be seen later when Roy became free to engage in open political work. About this time, Roy also sent out his suggestion about changes in the constitution of the Congress, coupled with suggestions about a declaration of principles and a programme of national democratic revolution. Another article that was smuggled out was entitled "Whither Congress?" It was written a few days after Gandhiji called off the Civil Disobedience Movement early in 1934. It accused Gandhiji of throwing away the independence resolution of Lahore Congress and the fundamental rights resolution of Karachi Congress. It stated that the Congress stood at the crossing of ways and that the alternatives before it were, as indicated by an important Congress leader, relapse into liberalism or armed insurrection. It was clear, the article stated, that Congress leaders had chosen "the safe road of relapse into liberalism." It called upon the rank and file to convert 'the Congress into an organ of a new form of struggle "with a new programme under a new leadership inspired by a revolutionary outlook." If that were done, there was no harm in Congressmen entering legislatures under the strict supervision and control of the Congress. Speeches in legislatures would be more effective than those delivered outside and elections would provide an opportunity for popularising the Congress programme. This was rather an unorthodox line of thinking for a leftist. Roy gave further shocks to orthodox leftism when, after release, he advocated office acceptance. He was all along a non-conformist and he would not oblige leftists by merely following them in their beaten track. The article concluded with an appeal to develop a variety of mass activities with the slogan "land to the peasants and bread to the workers, manual as well as mental."

The most important and the most talked about of Roy's political writings of the period are his letters to the Congress Socialist Party. The C S P was formed in 1934 as a result of discussions in Nasik jail of some leftwing Congressmen. One Royist, Charles Mascarenhas, who was undergoing imprisonment for a speech in Bombay, was amongst those founders of the party. The party held its first conference in Patna in April 1935 at the time of a meeting of the All India

Congress Committee. The Civil Disobedience Movement was in doldrums at that time and the dominant opinion in the Congress was moving in the direction of a return to constitutional activities. Roy was getting information about all those developments in his prison cell. He was happy at the rise of a left-wing in the Congress, but was unhappy at its taking the form of a socialist party. He knew that the Congress, constituted as it was, could not adopt a socialist programme and that it was futile to seek to impose it. He knew further that the Congress would not tolerate the growth of a party within it and that, by forming one, radical elements within the Congress were rendering more difficult their primary task of radicalising and democratising the Congress. He further objected to the name socialist party, as it had acquired a bad connotation. The letters were written to convey these thoughts to the leaders of the party and make them concrete suggestions about the programme and policy that they should adopt. There were in all three letters, the first was written in May 1934, the second in May 1935 and the third in February 1936. As a good deal of controversy arose over them after Roy's release from jail, they were published in book form in 1937. Roy had stated earlier in the controversy in reply to the charge levelled against him by the General Secretary of the C S P : "Since the leaders of the C. S. P. have chosen to join issues publicly, I shall take up the challenge and, with the object of placing the discussion on a higher level, publish my letters written three years ago setting forth the reasons for my objection to the formation of the C. S. P. and suggesting the alternative method of radicalising the anti-imperialist struggle." They were published with an introduction by A. K. Pillai, a member of the All India Congress Committee of long standing, a prominent C S P leader and later an equally prominent Royist. He reveals in the introduction : "I do not think that these Letters were ever discussed at any meeting of the Party or its National Executive. The rank and file of the Party, at any rate, remained blissfully ignorant about these documents although they dealt with matters of supreme importance to the Party and even more to the movement." He came across them "just at a time when my mind was considerably exercised over the role and position of the Congress Socialist Party, of which I was then active member. To my pleasant surprise, I found that those very issues which were troubling me were specifically raised and, to my mind, most satisfactorily answered by Comrade M. N. Roy in the Letters which he had, more than two years before, written to the Executive of the Congress Socialist Party." The Letters constituted a booklet of over sixty pages. It is not possible to give its gist in a few paragraphs. An effort is, however, made to present a short statement of Roy's position in the controversy. In the first letter after defining socialism, drawing attention to the reformist role played by socialist parties, and pointing out how it was not possible to hoist a socialist programme on the Congress, Roy states : "The line adopted by the Congress Socialists, if consistently followed, will inevitably lead not to the capture of the Congress by the radical democratic, elements, but to the isolation of a small group of radicals, inside the Congress completely dominated by right wing. The struggle for the leadership of the Congress must take place not under the flag of Socialism, but of democratic national revolution.

The present political situation demands not the organisation of a Socialist Party inside the Congress, a party which by the logic of the relation of forces will inevitably be an impotent and isolated group, but the capture of the Congress as such by the radical national revolutionary elements." After pointing out that the struggle for the capture of the Congress, to be a matter of practical politics, must take place under the flag and programme of the National Revolution, the letter closes with such slogans as "Save the Congress as the Organ of Militant Mass Action." The second letter was written a year later after the Jabalpur meeting of the AICC. Among other things, it suggests a concrete plan of action. The plan suggested was as follows : "A mass agitation should be started without delay in support of the,demand for the Constituent Assembly. The most suitable method of starting an agitation will be a Conference of left-wing leaders to discuss the future of Congress politics. "The demand of the Constituent Assembly will be reaffirmed in a Manifesto issued by the Conference to the rank and file of the Congress. The Manifesto should be signed individually, the signatories appearing as Congressman and not as Socialists. It should remind the rank and file of the ideal of Independence and point out how the present policy represents a deviation from that ideal. The claim to the right of self-determination will be advanced and the Constituent Assembly demanded in accordance with that claim. The Manifesto will further set forth the fundamental principles of a revolutionary democratic constitution.

"The next step should be provincial left-wing conferences to consider the Manifesto and endorse it. Then the document will be submitted to the local Congress organisations throughout the country. Thus the question of the Constituent Assembly and a National Democratic programme (which will be formulated as the principle of the constitution advocated by the Congress) will become the issues at the next session of the Congress. And these issues will inevitably raise the associated issue of leadership.

"While preparing for the general attack with the purpose of raising the struggle against Imperialism to a higher level, demands should be made to alleviate the sufferings of the masses. These can take the form of forcing our parliamentarians to act under mass pressure. Partial and immediate, political as well as economic demands may be formulated by the local Congress organisations. When the demands got endorsed at mass meetings, the Congressmen in the Assembly should be called upon to press them on the Government. Repeal of repressive laws, release of political prisoners, implementing the recommendations of the Whitley Commission, relief-for the peasantry, measures to combat middle class unemployment, concrete measures for shifting the burden of taxation from the masses to the rich, specially the landed interests-these may be among the demands." 33 A real socialist party is essential, it is pointed out, but that "such a party cannot be inside the Congress. It must be independent of the Congress, although its members will individually remain in the Congress and constitute the driving force behind the leftwing." The letter closes with the following appeal :

"Comrades, you know that for years I have been trying to organise a political party of the Indian working class. Therefore none is more happy than myself to find the radical elements in the-nationalist movement embracing Socialism. But I fail to see why they should not join Parties already in the field.

"Concretely, and to put it frankly, I appeal to you, comrades,, to consider the proposition of amalgamating all those standing for the liberation of the toiling masses into a single political party, and from that base operate in the Congress with the object of freeing it from its present ideological, political and organisational deficiencies, and converting it into a mighty mass instrument in the struggle against Imperialism."

The last letter was written nine months later after the C S P conference in Meerut which decided to adopt a Marxian-Socialist programme and not to insist on the Congress accepting socialism. Roy welcomed these developments but pointed out again : "So, the immediate task of the party to capture the leadership of the Congress with the object of transforming it into-such a powerful organ of mass energy as will-hasten the triumph of the anti-imperialist struggle cannot be accomplished by the party as it proposes to function. This task will be accomplished by operating as the organised left-wing of the Congress." The letter further pointed out that a Marxian-Socialist party would not be allowed to function as an open legal party and stated : "The Socialist Party can exist as an open organisation if it will refrain from acting in the line dictated by its professed programme. It is riot I who is proposing liquidation. The form of organisation which you have chosen will bring about the virtual liquidation of the party. Therefore, I object to it, and advocate an organisational form and method of action suitable to the given conditions in which the party shall have to operate." The letter then makes some shrewd observations on the trends in the Congress. It states : "The Congress politics has run into a blind alley. So far only one way out has been indicated-that of office-acceptance. It is the logical consequence of the abandonment of the C.P. in favour of pure parliamentary action. Unless an alternative line of positive action is opened before the Congress, the drift towards neo-constitutionalism cannot be arrested. As the situation is at present, office, acceptance seems to be a foregone conclusion.

"If by any chance the ministerialists cannot have their way, there will be relapse into political passivity under the label of the orthodox creed of "no-change." Attainment of political freedom would be made conditional upon the accomplishment of economic impossibilities and removal of social cankers that can be carried out only after a social revolution. The cart will be placed before the horse, and consequently the progress will be in the reverse direction." Towards the end the letter asks for "a revolution inside the Congress itself-in its ideology, leadership, organisational structure, social basis, method of operation." The letter is written in a persuasive style and declared Roy's "readiness to join you ", in spite of his objection to the word "socialist" in the name of the party.

It is a pity that the letters were not considered seriously by the leaders of the C S P. They went on obstinately functioning in the name of the C S P. 'In the end, as Roy had predicted, they had to leave the Congress. While they were in the Congress, they never tried, again as Roy had suggested, to develop an alternative leadership. They hung on to the leadership of Gandhiji and just insisted on his moving a little faster. But that belongs to the next chapter as also the conflict that erupted between the Royists and the C S P.

As stated earlier, Roy used to write regularly on the foolscape size volumes that were given to him one at a time. A small part of that writing consists of comments on current political developments. It was not allowed to go out of jail and came out only when he was released. The comments were published as "Some Random Reflections" in 1941, in the book, The Ideal of Indian Womanhood. The "reflections" were written in 1936. They are important as Roy's reactions to contemporary events. They begin with the following significant autobiographical statement : "Lie-hunting is my profession. This is a thankless job. But someone must tell the truth, if it is not to remain an empty concept. I have been lie-hunting ever since I learned to think for myself, to distinguish facts from fictions. It has not won me popularity. The practice of suffering and 'sacrifice is not appreciated by the preachers of those virtues. I do not believe in them. Yet, not as a duty, but as a part of the game, I have made some sacrifice. Perhaps, that meant some suffering also. But having no martyr complex, I did not experience any feeling of suffering. It happened all as a matter of course, without any advertisement or ostentation." It continues : "I have not been hailed as a leader; nevertheless, none can deprive me of the satisfaction offered by the fact that several of the leaders of the nationalist India which has no use for me are tending today towards the direction I indicated years ago, when they believed in the Mahatma's miraculous power to win Swaraj in one year or to return from the Round Table Conference with the charter of Indian Independence dictated by him.

"The Congress has adopted the idea of the Constituent Assembly. As far back as 1927, 1 suggested that the agitation against the Simon Commission should be conducted with the demand for a Constituent Assembly. Then as now, the great leaders of "nationalist India" had no use for an insignificant person who dared disagree with them. It is foolish to shed tears over spilled milk; but one must learn from experience. It can be reasonably asserted that, had the demand for the Constituent Assembly been raised and persistently pressed from the time I suggested it, the political situation of the country might be entirely different today. Even in 1931, 1 found Congress leaders decidedly opposed to the idea of a Constituent Assembly. On the other hand, orthodox Communists denounced me as a bourgeois nationalist democrat for advocating the slogan. Today it has been taken up by both the sides. Those who came to scoff, have stayed to pray. Only, one still has no use for me, as Nehru informs, and others still call me a "renegade."

"I have been abandoned to my fate by the preachers of the virtue of suffering and sacrifice, although these patriotic heroes were living comfortable lives while, a quarter of a century ago, still a mere boy, I had undergone imprisonment for pioneering activities for the liberation for our country. But Imperialism seems to take particular notice of me-forsaken and friendless, as I am today. My imprisonment has not been a cheap price for applauded martyrdom. It has ruined my 'health, but my spirit remains uncrushed. As a matter of fact,

I am encouraged by this barbarous and vindictive treatment. It enhances my self-confidence, and affords me the feeling of satisfaction that, though not recognised publicly, my contributions to the cause of freedom have not been altogether negligible.

"I shall keep on hunting lies."

Roy then discusses the "social purpose" of nationalism and points out how the "dominant ideology of our nationalist movement is antagonistic" to it. After discussing Gandhiji's views and Nehru's reactions to them, he concludes : "the undoubted humanitarian sentiments of Gandhi are contradicted and rendered ineffective by his ethical principles and the religious approach to social problems."

In one of the "reflections", Roy objects to Nehru characterising Gandhi's critics its "arm-chair socialists" and writes In an aggrieved tone : "I, for example, plead guilty to the charge of having been a persistent critic of Gandhism ever since its ominous shadow was cast over the political life of our country. But I Would most emphatically refute the charge of being an arm-chair Socialist.

I do not say that Nehru had me particularly in mind when he castigated the critics of Gandhism. I know my place, and do not have the pretension of being remembered by the president-elect of the Congress, even to be castigated. I do not deserve such honour. Why should busy people think of a chap rotting in jail for the crime of having spent his entire life in modest efforts for promoting the cause of the freedom of India? Yet, it does seem rather strange to be so forgotten by those who talk so much about the virtues of suffering and sacrifice. I may not believe in the virtues. But I have had the perversity of practising them as much as anybody else, practising under no obligation, but voluntarily. Well, that is a different matter, and I could do a bit of experimenting with truth in that connection, if I wished. Perhaps, some day I would like-hunting has always been my favourite pastime. It is immensely amusing to play the gadfly." The "reflections" contain several other critical observations on Gandhiji's utterances and those of his defenders like Nehru and Kriplani and on a resolution of the Congress Working Committee. It is clear from them that years in jail had not brought about any change in Roy's views on the reactionary character of Gandhi, Gandhism and the leadership of the Congress. It will be interesting to observe how with such sharply expressed heretical views he would get along in the Congress which he looked forward to joining after his release. Roy was in prison, but jail walls did not stop his political work he was imprisoned and yet he was active. So, when his captors released him, he did not have to wait and watch and study; he walked into freedom to continue the work that he had already begun.

6

M.N. Roy : Theses on Chinese Problem

M.N. Roy on Chinese Problem visited to China with the thesis adopted at Moscow 1926. Roy had a large share in the drafting of the Theses. In an interview with Robert. C. North, Roy stated in October 1951 : "The Preliminary Theses prepared by Bubnov, Raskolnikov and Voitinsky were all but useless. So Stalin asked Bubnov, Bukharin and me to draw up another set of theses. These were divergent. On November 26, speaking of the Theses that were presented, Stalin stated : "Roy has written these Theses." In his book on the revolution and counter-revolution in China Roy writes the following : "The meeting of the Executive Committee of the Communist International in November 1926 adopted a new thesis on the Chinese question, the central point of which was that the Chinese Revolution must from that time be developed as an agrarian revolution. The leadership of the Chinese Communist Party as well as the representatives of the CI in China were of a different view. They still maintained that the nationalist bourgeoisie should be helped to lead the revolution and class struggle should not be accentuated for the sake of national unity. I was alone to advocate the different point of view that the Chinese Revolution had reached a critical moment in which it must strike out a new course and a fetish should not be made of the alliance with the Kuo Min Tang. The Executive of the CI adopted my point of view, which was opposed in the beginning by Stalin himself. But Stalin was brought around to my view and the Thesis adopted by the E.C.C.I. was drafted by me. Immediately afterwards, I left for China as the head of a new delegation of the CI." According to other sources, Bukharin and Bubnov had also a hand in preparing them. Whatever the fact, Roy was sent to China towards the end of 1926 as the Special Representative of the CI to oversee the implementation of the new Theses. The Comintern and the Russian Government had been taking keen interest in developments in China since long. The Russian Government was interested in weakening its opponents, the Imperialist Powers which by their military operations and through trade and aid to rival war lords had obtained a stranglehold over China. In contrast to them, it had in July 1919 renounced all privileges secured by the Tsarist Government. It welcomed and actively supported the nationalist movement which sought to unify the country and rid it of imperialist oppression and exploitation. In. January 1923 its Envoy, Joffee, issued a joint statement with Sun Yat-sen, the leader of the nationalist movement, assuring warm support of the Russian people and Government to the paramount task of achieving "national unification and attain full national independence." The statement made clear that "neither did the one seek to convert the other to Communism nor did the latter accept it." The common statement opened the way for close co-operation between the Russian Government and the Chinese nationalist movement. It continued for about five years. Comintern's interest in China started in 1920. Its first representative was Voitinski. He supported the establishment of the Communist

Party. A year later Sneevliet, known in China as Maring, was sent, he brought about an understanding between the CP and the Kuomintang, the central organisation of the nationalist movement. Later, the Kuomintang was reorganised and, on Moscow's advice, communists entered it. In the beginning communists were opposed to joining the Kuomintang which, they regarded, was the party of the bourgeoisie. In later years a bitter controversy arose in tile, CI, in the CP of Russia and also in the CP of China over the advisability or otherwise of communists joining the Kuomintang. In the starting, however, all Russian leaders, comprising Trotsky, supported the move. Roy also was of the same view. He has written : "It (Communist Party) had to be the vanguard of the struggle for national liberation. That task could be accomplished only when the Communists stood in close contact with all the forces of National Revolution. But these could not be all organised in the Communist Party. The Kuomintang was the common platform for all. Therefore, the entry of the Communists into the Kuomitang was a essential step. As long as the bourgeoisie were engaged in the struggle against foreign Imperialism, they must be supported with all means, because it was often evident that, left to themselves, they would not go very far. Only under the pressure of the masses could the nationalist bourgeoisie be driven to a struggle against Imperialism. For this purpose, it was essential that the masses must enter the Kuomintang. Should the masses do so, then the Communists as their leaders could not remain outside the Kuomintang. They must be there where the masses were. If the Communists called upon the masses to join the Kuomintang, but themselves remained out, then the masses would be revealed to the influence of the bourgeoisie. As the struggle against foreign domination was the burning issue of the day, the masses would certainly flock under the banner of the Kuomintang, as soon as it embraced a democratic programme of national liberation.

The Communists would be isolated from the masses if they stayed away from the Kuomintang!" Roy's old friend, Borodin was then the chief adviser to the CP. He was also an adviser to the nationalist Government which then had its headquarters in Canton. Borodin was in Canton from, October 1923 onwards. He had with him a number of Russian advisers comprising General Galen alias Blucher. Entry into the Kuomintang paid rich dividends to communists in the form of wide support amongst workers and peasants. On the ground of that support they were able to win several important positions in mass organisations and in the Government and the army. In 1925 opened a new chapter in the history of the Chinese revolution. It started on May 30 in Shanghai with firing by British police on demonstrators demanding the release of leaders of a strike which had taken place a few days earlier in a Japanese textile mill and had spread to Shanghai. The firing killed a number of workers. The news spread to all parts of China and there were angry demonstrations and strikes in several places. The people as a whole were angry and they pushed forward the Kuomintang to develop in right earnest its struggle against foreign imperialism and native reaction. With workers and peasants in revolt in several places against intolerable conditions of life, China was on the verge of a revolution. The leaders of the Comintern who wore watching the events in, China were happy at this revolutionary outburst of people's anger. They hoped that it would serve as a prelude to similar outbursts in other countries of Asia.

Expressing that hope, Zinoviev, the President of the Comintern, wrote as follows in the International Press Correspondence of July 9, 1925. : "The great events in China which are happening before our eyes, show the advanced guard of the European Proletariat very plainly what powerful reserves we have in the East. For a whole month now, a movement has been developing in China such as has never been seen before in that country, a movement which is spreading and intensifying with irresistible force despite of the predatory campaign of the united Imperialists of so many countries. The events in China will doubtless have a tremendous revolutionising significance for the other countries in the East and especially for the other colonies and the countries dependent on Imperialist England. Just as in its day the Russian revolution of 1905 had the greatest revolutionising influence on Turkey, Persia and China, the present great movement in China will without doubt have a great influence in Indo-China, India, etc. The many contingents of oppressed humanity who live in the East, numbering hundreds of millions, will greedily seize on every item of news from revolutionary China and will concentrate their thoughts on how they themselves can organise and revolt against their oppressors, the Imperialists. "The lessons of the events in China, however, must not be allowed to pass without bearing fruit, particularly for the advanced guard of the international Proletariat.... The Imperialist policy of kindling new wars at a time when mankind has hardly had time to draw breath since the universal slaughter of the years 1914-1919 facilitates this task of the vanguard of the International Proletariat. China has revolted today; tomorrow Indo-China and India will rise. Shanghai, Hong-Kong, Peking and Canton have revolted today tomorrow Calcutta and Madras will rise." A few weeks later another. Russian leader, A. Voznecienski expressed the same view. He wrote: "Lord Birkenhead and his colleagues have good cause to tremble with fear and to turn their glances to India even when mentioning those events in China. Such events constitute only the beginning of a slowly but uninterruptedly rising revolutionary wave, which in the next few years will sweep over the whole of Asia." This will explain why the Comintern leaders devoted so much attention to the happenings in China. Events moved rapidly in 1926.

Communists gained in strength in numbers and more in influence in all territories under the control of the national Government. The masses were on the move and there was constant pressure for more rapid strides in the direction of elimination of imperialism and liberation of the masses. Demands of the people for amelioration of their conditions of life received full support from communists but not from those who belonged to the Kuomintang.

There were several in the Kuomintang whose interests clashed with those of the broad masses. There were several industrialists, landlords and militarists who thrived on the oppression and exploitation of workers and peasants. Many of them did not like the alliance with the communists. Some of them, big landlords and capitalists, left the Kuomintang soon joined the opposition to it. Those who were left behind were equally unenthusiastic about the solution of the social problems of the revolution. There were constant conflicts with communists and several splits in the Kuomintang. On March. 20, 1926 Chiang Kai-shek, the Commander-in-Chief of the nationalist army, organised a coup against communists in Canton, the seat of the nationalist Government. Several communists were arrested and deprived of their position in the army and the Government. But that did not end communist co-operation with the Kuomintang. A few months later, when Chiang Kai-shek started the first Northern Expedition for the capture of Peking and the unification of the country, communists cooperated with him and helped his triumphant march to the Yangtse where he stopped and instead of proceeding North turned East towards Shanghai. That was a further step in the direction of betrayal of the revolution. But the Northern Expedition as such was an amazing success. In two months it swept the entire south of the country. In six months the nationalist army grew ten times larger. The Kuomintang, the CP and mass organisation such as trade unions and peasant unions increased their membership by lakhs. As Roy wrote later : "The most remarkable feature of the whole campaign was the enthusiastic support it received from the popular masses. The army had always been a dreaded and hated thing in China. But the Nationalist Army was hailed by the people everywhere as the liberator. The forces of the enemy were thus caught between two fires. Surrounded by the hostile people they flew in ail directions, even, before being attacked by nationalist troops. Many enemy commanders declared their adhesion to the nationalist cause, that being the only means by which they could hold their forces together. Not withstanding the motive with which the military expedition had been launched it became a means of developing the revolution." In the course of the campaign the three Han cities, Woochang, Han-yang and Hankow, collectively called as Wuhan, were captured and the seat of the national Government was shifted from Canton to Wuhan on January 1, 1927. Moscow, the headquarters of the Comintern and the Russian Government, was closely-watching all these developments and from time to time giving detailed instructions to the CP about the policies to be adopted. It had a number of trusted agents in China and was receiving from them reports which were sometimes contradictory and several a time confusing. Reports to Moscow and instructions from Moscow were always subject to long delays and on several occasions reached the destination long after the situation to which they related had undergone a complete change. That was the inevitable risk involved in directing a revolution from a distance of thousands of miles. It is always problematic for a far-away authority to understand and appreciate the subtle nuances of a fast changing revolutionary situation. The CP was the agency on the spot, but its members had become so habitual to rely for everything on Moscow that they had no independent view of their own. They slavishly accepted the instructions which they received from Moscow and tried their best to implement them. The Chinese revolution succeeded in later years only when this subservience was ended.

The CI had from time to time so many of competent representatives in China. But for the operation and implementation of the policies that it recommended it had to rely entirely on the CP and the Kuomintang, the only weapon in its hands in the case of the latter being the award or refusal of financial, military and other help from Moscow. The representatives of the CI were mere advisers on behalf of a distant authority. That was the fate of Borodin, of Voitinski and of Roy when he arrived on the scene. The Chinese problem was being constantly examined and reexamined by Comintern authorities. The Russian CP also had set up a special Politburo Committee to deal with it. The Committee used to meet from time to time, review the developments and issue instructions. There was a detailed consideration of the problem at the sixth enlarged plenum of the ECCI which met in Moscow in February-March 1926. It reaffirmed the importance of the Kuomintang and its Government in Canton. It warned against "two equally harmful deviations threatening the Chinese Communists : Right Wing liquidationism, which abandons the 'independent class tasks of the Chinese proletariat for a formless merging with the general democratic national movement" and extreme Left moods "which favor skipping over the revolutionary democratic stage of the movement straight to the proletarian dictatorship and soviet power, forgetting the most important and decisive factor of all, the peasantry. According to the plenum, the fundamental problem of the Chinese national liberation movement was the peasant situation. It stated : "Indeed, the victory of the movements' revolutionary democratic tendencies depended on how several of the 400 million Chinese peasants were drawn, "together with the Chinese workers and under their leadership" into the decisive revolutionary struggle. The main task of the

Chinese communists and of the Kuomintang was to explain to the Chinese peasants that "only by allying themselves with the working class to form an independent revolutionary democratic government" could they radically improve their national and political circumstances. Beyond this, the Chinese communists must develop a program "capable of rousing the whole peasantry to an armed struggle against the militarists and against the administrators, middlemen and gentry who support the semifeudal order in the villages." It was decided to continue cooperation with the Kuomintang and early in June 1926 Voitinsky, the Chief of the Far Eastern Division of the Comintern, was sent to China "to correct the separatist tendency." The seventh plenum met a few months later in November-December 1926. On the first day of the meeting Roy was elected to the Presidium and was also elected joint secretary of the Chinese Commission. The main business before the plenum was the consideration of the Chinese problem. The consideration started with a fervent declaration by Bukharin. He declared: "We address ourselves to the great Chinese people which carries on a gigantic revolutionary liberation struggle. We promise in the name of the entire Communist International in the name of the whole working class of the world, that we will support this world historic struggle with all means, with all forces, at any cost." Apart from Bukharin, other important speakers at the plenum were Roy, Stalin and Tan P'ing-shen, the Chinese delegate.

Roy spoke on November 30. The following is a gist of his speech as given by Robert C. North and Xenia J. Yudin on the basis of a report in the International Press Correspondence : "American imperialism, he argued, was trying to recover the moral prestige it had enjoyed in China when the Chinese nationalist movement had been oriented primarily toward the United States. "America tries to get stealthily into China under the label of a liberal, humane imperialism, "he said, "in the place of the old brutal and greedy imperialism. That is, America wants to kill China not with bombs and machine guns, but with kindness. We know that we have to be very careful with such a "friend". "In the meantime, since the revolutionary mass movement had broadened its base in China, imperialism by dialectical process must broaden its base proportionately by making alliances with some sections of the bourgeoisie which, up to now, had been marching with the revolution. These were the groups most likely to succumb to imperialist temptations. "These upper bourgeois groups, on the other hand, were a narrow segment of the population. In China the overwhelming majority of the people were peasants, and the revolutionary fight against imperialism depended upon their being drawn into the struggle under proletarian leadership. "The Chinese revolution in the immediate stages," Roy declared, "must primarily be an agrarian revolution". "In order to mobilize the peasantry and bring them into the anti-imperialist united front it was indispensable that both the Chinese Communist Party and the Kuomintang develop an agrarian programme.

But so far, in formulating this agrarian program, no one had touched upon the basic prerequisite, which was not merely a "program of action" or a program of daily demands but "the agrarian revolution-clearly put". There is the question of the nationalization of land, he reminded the plenum, "the expropriation of the big landowners' estates. This question cannot be avoided. It must be put clearly and answered in the negative or in the positive. The central point of the agrarian program of the Chinese revolution must be the nationalization of land. Stalin spoke on the same day. He emphasised the role of the army and called upon Chinese revolutionaries to study the art of war. There is nothing strikingly new in the Theses that were adopted. What can be said to be new is the emphasis on the agrarian revolution and the concrete tasks that were suggested in that connection. On that point the Theses stated : "The economic and political struggle of the peasantry, which constitutes the overwhelming majority of the population, must be developed as a part of the anti-imperialist struggle. The fear that the aggravation of the class struggle in the countryside will weaken the anti-imperialist front is baseless... Not to approach the agrarian question boldly by supporting all the economic demands of the peasant masses, is positively dangerous for the revolution. To refuse to assign to the agrarian revolution a prominent place in the national-liberation movement, for fear of alienating the dubious and disloyal co-operation of a section of the capitalist class is wrong. This is not the revolutionary policy of the proletariat. The Communist Party must be free of such mistakes." It was further declared "The national Government in Canton will not be able to retain power in the course of the revolution and will not gain complete victory over foreign imperialism and over the native reaction, unless national liberation is identified with agrarian revolution. The growing process of class differentiation in the rural districts intensifies the struggle between the peasants and the exploiting classes. This class differentiation and the struggle resultant from it, require the closest attention on the part of the Communist Party. The latter must assume the leadership in the peasant movement and develop it by adopting corresponding economic and political slogans". On the issue of the relations with the Kuomintang, the Theses advised communists and their revolutionary allies to "penetrate the new government so as to give practical expression to their agrarian programme by using the government machinery to confiscate land, reduce taxes and invest real power in the peasant committees, thus carrying on progressive reforms on the basis of a revolutionary pro-ram." It was further asserted : "For this reason and several other equally important reasons, the point of view that the Communist Party must leave the Kuomintang is incorrect. The whole process of development of the Chinese revolution, its character and its prospects, demand that the Communists must stay in the Kuomintang and intensify their work in it. In order to intensify their activities in the Kuomintang with the object of assisting further development of the revolutionary movement, the Communists should enter the Canton government. Since foundation the real power of the Canton government has been in the hands of the Right Wing Kuomintang (five out of the six commissars belong to the Right Wing). Even though the Canton government could not exist without the support of the working class, the workers' and peasants' movement has had to overcome numerous obstacles. Recent events have shown that the Communists must enter the Canton government in order to support the revolutionary Left Wing in its struggle against the weak and vacillating policy of the Right. The extension of the Canton governments authority to new areas makes the question of the participation of the Communists in it still more imperative... The Communist Party of China must strive to develop the Kuomintang into a real people's party—a solid revolutionary bloc of the proletariat, peasantry, the urban petty bourgeoisie, and the other oppressed and exploited strata of the population who wage a decisive struggle against imperialism and its agents. The Theses also drew attention to the "regrouping of class forces" that was taking place as a result of imperialism's efforts to win over the bourgeoisie through concessions and asserted that "the future development and the prospects of the Chinese revolution depend primarily on the role of the proletariat." It was to implement these Theses that Roy was sent to China.

The task that he had to perform was herculean. The Theses were contradictory in the sense that agrarian revolution was to be hastened along with preserving the alliance with the Kuomintang. Most leaders of the Kuomintang were small or big landlords and were opposed to the disruption of the status quo in villages. Agrarian revolution Could be effected, if at all, despite their opposition and not with their help. The CP, the sole agency with which he could work, did not, as Roy discovered in a few days, whole heartedly support the Theses. Even Borodin was opposed to them as, according to him, alliance with the Kuomintang was more important than Support of the peasantry. Besides, by the time Roy arrived in China the relation of forces had undergone large change. The counter-revolutionary forces had become much stronger than-the revolutionary forces. As he wrote later in 1931, "the game was nearly lost" by the time he reached China. Roy went to China along with an international workers' delegation. Apart from him, it consisted of Tom Mann from England, Jacques Doriot from France and Earl Browder from America. It was to attend the Pan-Pacific Labour Conference to be held in Canton on May 1, 1927. The Labour Conference was ail idea hatched in Moscow which attached a good deal of importance to it. It was to be attended by workers' delegates from India, Australia, New Zealand, the Philippines, Japan, Russia, U.S.A. and other countries bordering on the Pacific. The All China Labour Federation was to be the host. The conference was eventually held in Hankow towards the end of May. Roy was keen that some Indian delegates should attend the conference. He wrote to an Indian friend in December 1926: "In May 1927 the Pan-Pacific Conference will meet in Canton. We must send an Indian delegation there.... At least three or four people should leave not later than the middle of April.... There will be no difficulty as regards the financial aspect of the thing." Accordingly, four Indian labour leaders, K. N. Jogalekar, R. S. Nimbkar, S. S. Mirajkar and D.R. Thengdi applied for passports to go to China to attend the Conference. Their applications were, however, rejected. The delegation led by Roy arrived in Canton in February 1927. It had travelled from Russia via Vladivostok. The visit of the delegation was regarded as an event of much importance. The Canton Gazette described it as "a symbol of the militant alliance of the revolutionary workers of the East and West." An Intelligence report states : "The party received a great reception in Canton, where they made several violent speeches. They attended reviews of the Hong-Kong strike pickets and the Canton Workers' Defence Crops and were entertained on the 22nd February to a banquet, at the close of which Tom Mann is reported to have sung the Kuomintang song in Chinese." Roy was delayed in Canton for more than three weeks.

An air plane was to fly him to Hankow, the new seat of the nationalist Government. But there was an engine trouble and the group journeyed overland, "five weeks in chairs carried by coolies". According to North and Eudin, "On April 1, 1926, Roy and his party reached Changsha, where he was welcomed by the provincial government of Hunan province and by members of peasant, merchant, student, and labour organizations." A Kuomintang newspaper described the event : "Despite the rain, 100,000 people turned out to greet the (Comintern) delegate. Today the Government entertained Mr. Roy at a dinner. He will leave at midnight by special train and will arrive in Hankow tomorrow morning. Mr. Roy is accompanied by Mr. Tanp'ing-shan, Minister of Agriculture." "In Hankow Borodin received Roy warmly-though within a few weeks at most they were to find themselves in sharp disagreement." A few days after reaching Canton, Roy wrote an article on the significance of the Chinese revolution. It is Document 2 in the collection of documents translated and published by Robert C. North and Xenia J. Eudin in their notable work M. N. Roy's Mission to China. As stated by the authors, the documents were published in Moscow in Russian under the title Kitaiakaia Revoliutoua i Kommunisticheskii International.

Until his death Roy himself did not know of the existence of any copy of the book anywhere outside the communist archives in Moscow. Sometime later Richard Park, an eminent American academician and friend of I Roy, discovered a copy of the book in the University of California Library. A second copy was found later in the rare-book collection of the Hoover Library at Stanford University. "In view of the rarity of the book, the unique character of the documents, and the additional information they contain about the China situation in 1927 the two authors agreed to put the text into English and make it more widely accessible." The text is supplemented by six chapters of commentary setting out the historical context and explaining the significance of the differences of opinion that arose between Roy on the one hand and Borodin and leaders of the Chinese CP on the other hand. The article "Significance of the Chinese Revolution" pointed-out how it was taking place in an epoch of the decline of capitalism and how rival imperialisms were trying to "split the national ranks, to achieve reapproachment with the bourgeois elements, in the national movement, and to prevail upon them to betray and destroy the revolution." It was pointed out : "Times change—and essentially forms of imperialist domination in China must also change. Unequal agreements, extra-territoriality, concessions, were an essential under certain conditions, under certain forms of exploitation. At the present time, however, when conditions are different, capitalist domination in China can be maintained without these coercive privileges." The conclusion of the article was : "Consequently, the Chinese national-liberation movement will either continue to develop and emerge victorious either as a workers' and peasants' revolution or it will not win at all. Capitalism has become a reactionary force throughout the world. The bourgeoisie cannot lead the revolutionary struggle." Roy went to China with some certain views about the character and tasks of the Chinese revolution. What he saw in the few days that he was in Canton confirmed his views, as can be easily seen from the article that he wrote. By the time Roy reached

Canton, differences between the Right Wing of the Kuomintang and its Left Wing supported by communists had reached serious proportions. There were differences of opinion over the seat of the Government—whether it should be at Nanchang or at Wuhan, over the invitation to Wang Ching-wei to return-which Chiang Kai-shek had supported in the starting, and more particularly over the alliance with Communists. But there was a curious reluctance in Left Kuomintang and communist circles to talk about them. The Central Committee of the CP was aware that a great anti-communist tide had developed within the Kuomintang and that there was the danger of the Right Wing succeeding in winning over the moderate elements. The method that was suggested to counteract the danger was inter alia,-(1) allay the Kuomintang fear of the Chinese Communist Party, (2) convince the Kuomintang that the national revolution needs mass support to achieve an ultimate victory." In view of this, it is not surprising that in the "Warning" that was issued from Canton on February 27 on behalf of the Chinese Communist Party and a few unions Roy could not mention Chiang Kai-shek as the person who was trying to disrupt the unity of the Kuomintang. The "Warning "had therefore to content itself only with a vague appeal. : "We appeal to all popular organizations to rally around the Kuomintang with even greater solidarity and greater faith than ever before in order that the party's authority could become really supreme with respect to the organs of the revolution, that is, the national government and the national army." It further stated : "There still remain in the party persons who are seeking to undermine its Unity" and asked popular organisations to demand that the Kuomintang "categorically condemn the conduct of these enemies of the party." It supported the demand for the recall of Wang Ching-wei and stated in conclusion: "In order to make the national government the chief executive organ of the, revolution, the Kuomintang must rally the laboring masses around the government. This must be done by carrying out the workers' and peasants' programme of the national revolution through the proper organs of their revolutionary state. The progressive agrarian policy of the government will remove the danger of the disintegration of the revolutionary forces. The sympathy of the population in the rear will assure 50 per cent of the victory on the front. The peasant masses will give enthusiastic support to the revolutionary army if it brings to them the tidings of liberation from the more unbearable burdens-the exorbitant taxes, the fluctuating rentals, illegal requisitions, banditry, and so on." In a footnote added after his return to Moscow, Roy gives following information about the' circumstances in which the "Warning" was issued : "This is an appeal issued just at the time that Chiang Kai-shek was preparing to betray the national revolution. Within the Kuomintang, the struggle followed the lines of personal enmities. The Central Committee of the Communist Party which was still situated in Shanghai had taken no definite stand on this conflict. The first estimate of the political significance of the crisis in the Kuomintang was given in this appeal. This was the first attack against the feudal-bourgeois Right Wing of the Kuomintang. The appeal pointed out the imminent danger and advanced a political platform to counteract it. However, this was the first step, and it had to be made with great circumspection. Its formulation had to be very carefully done. However, the fact was that the majority of the working class in Canton had arisen under the Communist guidance to a struggle against the feudal-bourgeois reaction. Before it was published, the appeal was submitted through proper Communist factions for examination by all the organizations that were to sign it; it was discussed by them and accepted.

The Canton Committee of the Communist Party did not wish to take the initiative in the struggle and held up the appeal for one week after the decision to publish it had been taken." The last document issued from Canton was an article entitled "Watch the Leaders". It was written "for the organ of the Canton Committee of the Communist Party. The Committee refused to publish it under the pretext that it might provoke the Cantonese dictatòr, Chi-shen, into taking repressive steps against the Communist Party." The terrible massacre in Shanghai—when workers rose in revolt in anticipation of Chiang Kaishek's army's march on the city but the army failed to proceed further and allowed reactionary militarists to drown it in blood—had taken place before the article was written. It made pointed reference to that tragic incident and made I he following bold statement about what happened at Shanghai: "Were not these the "political heads" at whose counter-revolutionary advice the direct advance of the national armies on Shanghai was delayed at the very moment when the Shanghai proletariat declared a general strike in order to help the nationalists to occupy the town? The working class of the whole country has right to know why Marshal Chiang Kai-shek allowed the imperialist henchmen to stage a bloodbath of the leaders of the Shanghai proletariat while his army stood right by the city and could have dealt a direct blow and while Sun Ch'uan-fang's forces defending Shanghai were seriously debilitated, disorganized, and demoralized.

The Shanghai proletarians threw themselves into the front lines of the battle, they braved the imperialist cannon fire heroically in order to assure victory to the revolutionary armies. The proletariat took the stand at the most dangerous point of the battle and extended its mighty hand to the national army for a revolutionary alliance and brother-hood. But the national army, being evidently under some evil influence, did not accept this hand: it refused to take the road to victory and betrayed its valiant ally to the terror of the counter-revolution." It Stated further : "In the face of these formidable facts, our warning is not a false alarm. It is justified by the gravity of the Situation. A definite tendency toward compromise with domestic (otechestvennyi) militarism and foreign imperialism, toward a betrayal of the revolution exists in the national movement. This tendency is represented in the Kuomintang by a well-organized faction." It mentioned the secret negotiations with the Japanese Government that some Kuomintang leaders were carrying on and concluded by saying that the danger of a compromise and betrayal of the revolution was not a product of imagination. What Roy feared while in Canton came true a few days after he arrived in Hankow. Chiang Kai-shek on April 12 struck in Shanghai a great blow against the communists and the Left Kuomintang. "Just before dawn on April 12, squads of armed men left their hiding places and started systematically rounding up and disarming communist-organised labour pickets within the city. During the following days as Chiang pressed his attack, the Shanghai Communists and their forces of organised labour were all but decimated." The blow fell when the communists had least expected it. There were rumours in the preceding days about a rift between them and Chiang Kai-shek. But they were denied and dismissed as imperialist propaganda. Chen Tu-hsiu, the leader of the CP, had a few days earlier described Chiang Kai-shek as a nationalist revolutionary leader.

The same belief prevailed in Moscow and the suggestion that communists should withdraw from the Kuomintang was condemned as profoundly incorrect. Chiang Kai-shek's action also amounted to a revolt against the Kuomintang and the national Government. For that action he was removed from his position as the Commander-in-Chief and was expelled from the Kuomintang Chiang Kaishek replied by gathering around him a good number of older and more moderate leaders of Kuomintang and by establishing a rival national Government at Nanking. That completed and formalised the split between the Left Wing and the Right Wing of the Kuomintang. The split in the Kuomintang was not, as Roy pointed out in his book, a split on class lines. It was an artificial split between two factions neither of which was interested in developing the revolution. He stated : "The Kuomintang was split not as the result of the process of differentiation between the revolutionary and reactionary classes composing it. It broke into two factions both of which inherited everything from the mother organisation. In the place of one, there arose two nationalist combinations, Loth inevitably feudal-bourgeois in social composition, the superficial difference being a thin veneer of bankrupt petitbourgeois radicalism on the part of one. Swearing by the reactionary principles of Sun Yat-sen both were not only hostile to the revolutionary mass movement, but were opposed to the development of the bourgeois-democratic revolution.

For a Chiang Kai-shek in one camp, the other could boast of a Tang Shen chi, To drive the point home it was further pointed out : "Behind those two military leaders, there were to be found, in both the camps, representatives of the counter-revolutionary bourgeoisie, reactionary feudal lords and conservative patriarchal literati. C. C. Woo, in one camp, could vie with Sun Fo, in the other, for the distinction of a veteran rightwinger who had always opposed revolution. The youthful Wampoa cadet Pai Sung-chi, on the one side, could be well matched by a Ha Chien, on the other. Both eventually demonstrated their military ability by massacring the working class, one in Shanghai and the other in Wuhan. Later, Roy blamed the CP for not starting the campaign against Chiang Kaishek earlier, for not stressing class issues and for allying with feudal militarist elements. But faced with the concrete situation in April 1927, communists had no alternative but to go along with the left Kuomintang and try to push it further in the direction of revolution. It-is a different matter that at a later stage they made a fetish of that alliance, a policy that Roy, disapproved and resisted. Chiang Kai-shek had earlier expressed a desire that a-delegation of the CI should meet him to discuss the points in dispute between him and the CP. In a telegram sent to him on April 13, Roy explained why the delegation had not until then been able to meet him and then sought to dissuade him from convening a meeting of the Central Committee at Nanking as it was contrary to the agreement that he had arrived at with Wang Ching-wei.

Wang Ching-wei had returned to China in March and had assumed the leadership of the Kuoraintang and the national Government. The telegram warned Chiang Kei-shek that his convening a meeting of a few members would be "interpreted by the enemies of the revolution as a rupture in the ranks of the Kuomintang". It concluded with the following advice and assertion of the CI's desire to help the forces of revolution: "At this moment when international imperialism unites in an insolent attack upon the Chinese Nationalist Revolution the unity of the revolutionary forces is a supreme necessity. As a matter of fact it is the dissensions in the Nationalist ranks that have encouraged imperialism to assume such a highhanded attitude as to deliver identical notes of five powers. In view of the dangerous situation we advise you to abandon the projected Nanking conference which will practically split the party. And the grave responsibility of breaking the Nationalist front at this critical moment will rest on you. We advise you to stand on the agreement to place all contentions on inner party questions before a plenary session of the Central Committee. If you take this advice we shall be glad to visit Nanking in order to discuss with you personally all outstanding questions. "The Third International will lend all its services to help the formation of a united nationalist front of all revolutionary forces." The telegram was signed by Roy on behalf of the CI delegation. There was no response to the telegram and the two wings started a bitter war against each other until they united a few months later to suppress the widespread revolt of the peasants and the communists who were supporting it. Differences of opinion between Roy and Borodin and leaders of the CP became sharp after the split in the Kuomintang. The differences covered several points, but they centred mainly on three issues. The issues were: one, the second Northern Expedition; two, the peasant revolts and three, relations with Left Kuomintang.

The third issue became the crucial issue in June when, according to Roy, the Left Kuomintang was no longer an ally but an enemy, an instrument of the counter-revolution, as by that time it had begun its war against workers and peasants and was moving in the direction of an understanding with the Right Win-headed by Chiang Kai-shek. Earlier, Roy had accepted along with Borodin and others, the need of collaboration with the Left Kuomintang, but he had insisted all along that the collaboration was for a purpose and should end as soon as it ceased to serve that objective. All these differences were debated fully and frankly in party meetings and conferences. The positions that Roy adopted on various issues are now available in his speeches and writings of those days in M. N. Roy's Mission to China, thanks to the insight and industry of Robert North and Xenia Eudin. The issue of the second Northern Expedition came tip for consideration immediately after the split. According to Roy, "the father of the plan (second Northern Expedition) was Tang Shenchi" Tang Shen-chi, was a militarist who had attached himself to the Wuhan Government. Desiring to outshine Chiang Kai-shek who had captured Shanghai and Nanking, he wanted to hoist the national flag in Peking. He persuaded the Kuomintang and the Wuhan Government to accept the plan. Borodin and Chen Tu-hsiu also liked it, though there were some in the leadership of the CP who disliked it.

After studying the whole plan Roy became convinced that it was militarily impractical, politically dangerous and socially reactionary. He had to join issue on that point with Borodin and the leader of the CP, Chen Tu-hsiu. The debate started a few days after he reached Hankow: it continued for several days. Roy displayed in the debate a significant grasp of the military, political and social situation in the country. It centred around the concept of broadening the revolution as against deepening it. Borodin and Chen Tu-hsiu stood for the former while Roy advocated the latter. In a speech, to leaders of the CP made on April 13-15 Roy detailed his arguments against the Northern Expedition. To avoid misunderstanding he pointed out in the beginning that he was not against the Northern Expedition in general, but was against undertaking it immediately.

Dealing first with the military aspect of the Expedition, he pointed out: "If we really want to smash the Northern forces, we must set about this seriously. We will have to concentrate all our forces on the Peking-Hankow railroad. This would mean Wuhan will be left without defences. If we move toward the north, we will provide either Chaing Kai-shek or the Northern forces with an opportunity to attack us from the direction of Nanking...... Thus, on the right flank we are threatened by quite a substantial combination of armed forces. Our rear is not defended, we have no base, and yet we want to advance into a new region.. Under such condition the Northern Expedition represents nothing but a military adventure. The Expedition involved, he stated, alignments with militarists and, even if it succeeded in reaching Peking, the result would be equally disastrous for "right now we have to cope only with Chiang Kai-shek. But we are running from known to unknown territories where, in all probability, we will have to encounter several more like him."

Roy then criticised Borodin's suggestion of a "retreat somewhere to the bills, or to the Mongolian desert", pointing out that it amounted to leaving "the provinces where the revolution has a social base", and going into backward provinces "where the counter-revolution is stronger and better organised." The point of his criticism was: "Comrade Borodin thinks that the principal factor in the revolution is not the masses, but our ability to manouver not only with the petty bourgeoisie.... but also with various military elements." Turning to the political and social aspect of the problem ' Roy stated : "The fundamental task of the Chinese revolution at the present moment is the consolidation of the social and territorial base of the revolution. The bourgeoisie has turned against the revolution. The Left Wing bourgeoisie is disoriented and has no definite perspective. What is most essential now is the organization, concentration, and consolidation of the revolutionary democratic forces. Without this, there is no guarantee for the success of the revolution." Continuing he said : "The revolution is confronted with three tasks. These can be accomplished by consolidating our power in the central and southeastern provinces, but not by an immediate campaign against the North. These tasks are

1. Mobilization of the democratic forces through an agrarian revolution, and realization of the minimum demands of the proletariat;

2. Seizure of political power in the village by the peasantry;

3. Reorganization and centralization of the revolutionary army, in other words, the creation of a revolutionary army.

"The opportunity for this exists. Two of the most important ministries are in the hands of Communists and can be used for realizing these tasks. If we use our power in these two ministries properly and with sufficient energy, in a few months our position will not only become secure, but we will become almost invincible. Then we will be ready to go ahead to develop the revolution territorially." The fundamental question was, according to Roy, "whether to intensify or to expand the revolution." The way to intensify the revolution was to develop the peasant movement. The peasants were already on the move, demanding land and in some cases taking hold of it through confiscation of the lands of big landlords. An effort was being made to hold back the peasant movement on the ground that it would alienate feudal militarist, and bourgeois elements who would not then co-operate in expanding the revolution. The argument, therefore, was : expand the revolution before thinking of intensifying it; in other words, broaden it before deepening it. That was the argument of Borodin, Chen Tu-hsiu and others.

Roy countered the argument by pointing out that the bourgeoisie and feudal militarist elements had already betrayed the revolution, that workers and peasants and the petty bourgeoisie were the only reliable forces of the revolution and that they could be mobilised for its defence and advancement only by championing their interests. He was therefore all for intensifying the revolution which, being fundamentally an agrarian revolution, could succeed only with the support of the large masses of peasants. He could invoke in support of his stand the Theses of the seventh plenum which was the basis of his mission to China. Roy was not opposed to the military moves that were essential for the defence of Wuhan, but he was opposed to the offensive towards the north before, consolidating the base of the revolution in the south. In the end Roy succeeded in carrying his point. The resolution that the central committee of the CP adopted on April 16 was in accordance with the view that he had presented. It stated inter alia: "Under existing conditions, an immediate military advance to the north with the aim of capturing Peking, Tientsin, and so forth is not only undesirable, but will be harmful to the revolution. Military operations aimed at territorial expansion to the north must be preceded by a consolidation of the base of the revolution in those regions which are already under the control of Kuomintang or in which the revolution has already been partially accomplished." After detailing the defence measures it asserted : "The consolidation of the base will be carried out in accordance with the suggestions made in Comrade Roy's speech". If further assumed "that the opinion of the Communist Party will be taken into consideration before Kuomintang and the national government decide in favour of an advance to the north". However, Roy records that "two days later the Central Committee of the Communist Party retracted this resolution and supported the Kuomintang's decision on the immediate dispatch of troops to the north." On April 20 the central committee of the CP issued a declaration welcoming the Kuomintang decision to deprive Chiang Kai-shek of his command over the national army, to expel him from the party and to order his arrest. It is obviously written by Roy. Chiang Kai-shek represented, the declaration pointed out, feudal-bourgeois elements and they must be crushed if Chiang Kaishekism was to be crushed. It said: "Chiang Kaishek's expulsion from the Kuomintang does not remove the danger. He will effort, as before, to create a parallel "national government". In spite of the decision of the Kuomintang, a considerable number of military forces remain under his control. He wants to deceive the national democratic elements by a propaganda of lies about Wuhan, namely, that the Kuomintang has become an instrument of the Communist Party. By this cunning lie, he is efforting to cover up for the fact that he and the class he represents have become instrument of imperialism". The delegation of the CI made a similar declaration about Chiang Kai-shek on April 22. The new point that it made was about 11 open military intervention" of "international imperialism". It stated : "Not only is Shanghai virtually occupied by imperialist powers; other important points inside the country and', especially, Wuhan—the seat of the national government—are under the threat of an imposing line of warships. This is a grand-scale 'demonstration.' "Arguing with weapons, the imperialist bandits present the Chinese people with a demand for surrender. Identical notes from England, America, France, Italy and Japan Jay down impossible conditions to the national government." The point was made in order to display how Chinese revolution was a part of the world revolution against imperialism. The fifth congress of the CP opened in Hankow on April 27. It continued for two weeks and discussed all existing problems including the problems of the Northern Expedition, peasant revolts and relations with the Left Kuomintang. On all these issues Roy's views were in sharp contrast with those of Borodin and Chen Tu-hsiu. At the congress Roy delivered on those issues two speeches one on April 30 and the other on May 3. Both were closely reasoned arguments in support of his standpoint. Most arguments had been already urged in the speech that he made on April 13-15.

Only a few points need to be noted. Roy was blunt in pointing out the mistakes committed by the CP. They were: the failure, in the period of the united front, to develop the working class as an independent force; the neglect to consolidate the social forces of the revolution raised by the first Northern Expedition; underestimation of the role of the petty bourgeoisie and illusions about Chiang Kai-shek and militarists. While pointing out these mistakes, he did not fail to applaud the achievements of the party. He repudiated the suggestion that the revolution was on the decline asserting that "all objective conditions speak for the revolution being on the upswing."

Pointing out that militarism was an expression of all reactionary forces in the country he characterised as dangerous the theory that militarist forces could be won over to the side of the revolution. Criticising the party policy followed until then in its relations with the Kuomintang as a policy of acting "as an appendage and not as an independent force", Roy said: "We must have our own way in the matter of the development of the revolution." He recommended for the purpose factional work in the Kuomintang suggesting : "The Communist Party must create in various organs of the Kuomintang and the Government Communist factions under the political leadership of the Central Committee so that every decision of the national government would be embraced with the consent and under the influence of the proletariat and the peasantry." He concluded his speech by outlining a programme of action which was as follows First of all, and at the basis of all the agrarian revolution. Second, the arming of peasants for defending the gains of the revolution. Third, the organization of rural self-government for destroying the power of feudal lords in the village. Fourth, the creation of a state machinery through which the democratic dictatorship will be percepted. Fifth, the creation of a revolutionary army, not by converting militarists into revolutionaries, but by organizing a revolutionary army on a firm social basis." The second speech was delivered three days later to answer the questions that were raised. Roy pointed out that the line of action suggested by him was neither passive nor too left and that he stood for social as well as territorial expansion of the revolution. He repudiated as wrong the suggestion that work among peasants should be left to the Kuomintang as the CP was the party of workers.

On May 4 Roy spoke at the congress on the Theses of the seventh plenum. He showed how they were based on a deep study of the international Situation characterised by worldwide decline of capitalism. He referred in that connection to the

Colonial Theses adopted by the second congress in 1920 and how it had visualised that liberation movement in colonies would usher in "a period of non-capitalist development that leads directly to socialism" as the national bourgeoisie deserted and turned against the revolution, that was what had happened, he said, in China. He then analysed the structure of the Chinese society and showed how the bourgeoisie were incapable of leading an anti-feudal, anti-imperialist revolution and why, under the circumstances, it must be led by a coalition of workers, peasants and the petty bourgeoisie. He concluded by formulating the basic task of the CP at that stage which, he said "to organise the revolutionary bloc with the participation of the peasantry and the Wuhan petty bourgeoisie; to establish a democratic dictatorship: to lead the Chinese revolution on a non-capitalist path, and to transform the national revolution into a struggle for socialism." The Theses were adopted after a short discussion. Some Kuomintang leaders attended the congress. One of them was Hsu Chien who delivered a long speech describing CP as a party of workers and the Kuomintang as a party of peasants. This Kuomintang claim to be the sole leader of peasants was controverted by Roy and was not accepted by the congress. Another distinguished guest was Wang Ching-wei, the leader of the Kuomintang and the national Government.

He attended the session at which Roy spoke on the Theses of the seventh plenum. Speaking later, Wang Ching-wei declared that "the Kuomintang accepted fully the Comintern's interpretation of the non-capitalist development of the revolution. No one could reproach the Kuomintang for supporting the interests of the bourgeoisie. On the contrary, the Kuomintang was following a revolutionary path.

One question was not explicit, however the Kuomintang Left leader wanted the delegates to the Congress to tell him how they interpreted the position of the petty bourgeoisie.

Did they think that it could follow the non-capitalist development of the revolution?" Roy replied to the points raised by Wang Ching-wei. His reply "was censured by leading comrades as being a 'tactless attack on the Left (wing) Kuomintang." In the speech that is published in M. N. Roys Mission to China one does not see any attack on the Left Kuomintang. On the other hand Roy particularly said at the end of his speech: "The Kuomintang is a revolutionary organisation and shall remain a revolutionary organisation, because it is fighting against imperialism. And for this very reason, the proletariat will collaborate with the Kuomintang until final victory." Earlier he had made it clear that the CI had not asked the CP to work for "the immediate realisation of socialism", though the perspective was "of a development toward socialism." It was similarly made explicit that abolition of private property was not included in the immediate programme as the two classes, peasants and the petty bourgeoisie, the constituents of the three-class coalition, did not stand for it. But for the intervention of other things and forces these assurances might have satisfied the leaders of the Kuomintang. Roy spoke once again in the congress. The speech was devoted to the clarification. Of the concept of non-capitalist development and democratic dictatorship. The congress adopted in the end three documents : (1) Theses on the political situation, (2) Resolution on the agrarian question, and (3) Manifesto. They were on the lines suggested by Roy which meant that he succeeded in securing acceptance of his views in spite of the opposition of Borodin and Chen Tu-hsiu. The Manifesto drew attention to the desertion of the bourgeoisie and emphasised the necessity of drawing together the workers, the peasants and the petty bourgeoisie saying that the national revolution coincided with the agrarian revolution it called for confiscation of the lands of large landlords, struggle against the entry and organization of peasant militia. It expressed the conviction that the slogan "land to the peasants" would give, the revolution an army so enormous as to make it invincible. It assured the Kuomintang that the CP was participating in it and in the national government not as a rival striving to seize power but for consolidating the revolutionary elements.

Roy was happy at the result of the congress. In a speech to the newly elected central committee of the party he congratulated it on adopting a correct line and declared that it was "on the way to becoming a genuine Bolshevik party." He expressed the similar sentiments in an article written on May 10 and published in International Press Correspondence on July 14. With the withdrawal of "the large-scale bourgeoisie" the Kuomintang, he wrote, had turned into "a revolutionary bloc of the urban petty bourgeoisie, the peasantry and the proletariat" and that "mutual relations between the Communist Party and the Kuomintang had improved considerably." The happiness and the satisfaction were, however, short-lived. Soon after the congress differences between Roy on the one hand and Borodin and leaders of the CP on the other hand widened. Decisions of the congress were unanimous, but there were sharp-differences about the actual course of action. Borodin and Chen Tu-hsiu were in favour of making concessions in order to maintain relations with the Kuomintang even to the extent of exercising, restraint on the actions of workers and peasants; while Roy gave primary importance to the latter and a subordinate place to the former.

According to Tsai Ho-sen, a prominent member of the CP-who wrote later about the happenings the period, Borodin, being of the view that the congress had settled the problem of the petty bourgeoisie only in principle and had not provided any concrete practical formula, Suggested the following : "(1) To satisfy the trading and industrial petty bourgeoisie we should subside the demands of the shop assistants and others; (2) In regard to the village petty bourgeoisie, we should defend the small scale landlords; and (3) We should take measures against the practices of arrest and shooting of the counter-revolutionaries directly by the populace." Chen Tu-hsiu who followed him was reported to have suggested that "general leadership in the movement be handed over to the Kuomintang". Roy disagreed with both proposals. Tsai Ho-sen-notes Roy's disagreement but complains that be was not specific nor clear. The complaint does not appear to be justified if attention is paid to the proposals that Roy made to the party from time to time. Many a time his proposals were accepted but were not implemented. The decisive fact of the situation moreover was that Borodin held the purse strings and enjoyed the confidence of Chen Tu-hsiu and other leaders of the CP. Roy had during those days little effective power. Relations with the Kuomintang became strained as the influence of militarists and other reactionary elements became Tang Sheng chi had started the second Northern Expedition and in its name restraints had been placed on the agrarian movement and on workers' agitations. Roy wrote later : "As soon as the decision was made, the Nationalist Government called upon the masses to suspend all activities on the pretext that these would weaken the rear of the army fighting against northern militarism. Instead of fulfilling its previous promises, it asked the masses to make further sacrifices, so that new military victories could be won. While industrial workers were prohibited to strike for improving their economic condition, they were obliged to labour for longer hours to keep the army well supplied. Even the struggle against Imperialism was suspended on the pretext that the Nationalist Government should avoid international complications so long as it was engaged in the war against the northern militarists."

The Northern Expedition petered Out later owing to dissentions amongst militarists and paved the way for an understanding between Chiang Kai-shek and the Left

Kuomintang. While Tang Sheng-chi was busy in the north, one of his subordinates, Hsia Tao-yin rebelled in the middle of May and marched towards the seat of the national Government with the intention or overthrowing it. He had a small force at his command and could have been easily repulsed. But neither the Government nor its Commander-in-Chief, Tang Sheng-chi did anything against him which gave rise to the suspicion that he enjoyed the secret support of both. He was defeated when he approached Woochang by the combined action of communists and local members of the Kuomintang. Roy writes the following about the action: "The city was defended by a couple of hundred soldiers; but the garrison commander happened to be a Communist. The rebels appearing on the outskirts of the city, the Communist commander Could no longer wait for the instruction of the Nationalist Government, the headquarters of which were situated just on the other side of the river. As there was no chance of any reinforcement coming from Hankow, the garrison commander Yet-tin acted on his own initiative. He got together an irregular army of about 1500 men, including several hundred students from the local military school. They were mostly petit-bourgeois intellectuals, all members of the Kuomintang. After a weeks hard fight, the rebels were driven back." With reference to Hsia Tao-yin's revolt there are two documents in the collection of documents translated by North and Eudin. They seem to be written by Roy. One is an appeal addressed to the soldiers of the revolting common reminding them that they were peasants and that they should be loyal to the Kuomintang and the national Government as both were defending the interest's of soldiers, workers, peasants and small merchants. A foot-note by Roy states that the Kuomintang was to be persuaded to issue a same appeal, but that communists "working in the highest organs of the Kuomintang did not insist on this." The other document is a declaration of the CP. It was issued in order to reassure the petty bourgeoisie and to drive a wedge between them and the generals. The declaration said that the communists' bad pledged themselves to the protection of the interests of the petty bourgeoisie. It stated : "In the villages—the Communist Party is against confiscation of lands belonging to petty landlords and officers of the revolutionary army. In towns the Communist Party demands the reduction of heavy taxes which weigh on the petty merchants." It was explained that the "excesses" of the peasants were not caused by the CP and that "the lamentable incidents" were the outcome of the failure to implement the agrarian programme. The declaration made some concessions to the middle classes, but Roy thought that they were essential in order to intensify the conflict between them and the generals. Regarding the situation in the party he wrote in a foot-note to the declaration : "In those circumstances the "orientation toward Yang Shengchin" prevailed in the Central Committee of the Communist Party. The leading comrades considered him to be a-100 per cent revolutionary." The policy sought to create within the national government have been T'ang Sheng-chin. This policy was, of course, entirely erroneous. It aroused suspicions of the Left Wing Kuomintang, and particularly of Wang Ching-wei. The latter believed that the Communists were planning a militarist plot to destroy the, Left Wing. It was keeping in view of this strained situation, partly created in the Party by the erroneous policy of some Communists, that the declaration, presented above was issued, its aim was to win, the confidence of the petty bourgeoisie and to incite it against the, reactionary officers." Roy further stated that the central committee of the party decided to induce Wang Ching-wei to issue a resolution declaring Hsia. Toa-yin an insurgent, which might have brought about a break between the petty bourgeois Left Kuomintang and the militarists, but that the decision was not implemented. A fortnight later on May 20 a more serious incident took place at Changsha, the capital of the province of Hunan. General Hsu of the army staged a coup. It was an Ke-hsing and other officers open revolt against the Government and the Kuomintang.

The officers "overthrew the Provincial Government, put its members in prison, dissolved the local committee of the Kuomintang, closed the political school conducted by the Peasants Department of the Kuomintang, and adopted all the usual repressive measures against the mass organisations and the Communists. The insurgents were direct subordinates of the Commander-in-Chief of the Nationalist Army, Tang Sheng-chi. From the front, be remained in telegraphic communication with them." Under the pressure of Tang Sheng-chi the Government endorsed the action of the insurgents. The local CP and the Kuomintang did not, however, approve it and they planned an attack on the insurgents. Roy describes : "More than twenty thousand peasants marched upon Changsha from all sides. About at the gates of the city, they were ordered to go back and dissolve their military formations. The instruction came from the Communist headquarters at Wuhan. In the meantime, the Commander-in-Chief of the Wuhan Army, Tang Sheng-chi, had declared that he was personally going to Changsha, in order to establish order there. The counter-revolutionary insurgents there were his subordinates. The Communist leaders permitted themselves to be deceived by the unmistakably dishonest manoeuvre; they decided to call off' the armed uprising, since Tang Sheng-chi had taken the matter in his own hand. A sudden, unwarranted retreat is extremely demoralising even for a regular army; it is more so for an improvised force. The mobilised peasants retreated in a chaotic manner. The counter-revolutionary insurgents availed themselves of the opportunity. They attacked the retreating peasants and massacred them ruthlessly."

Several communist leaders believed at that time the stories of peasant excesses and thought it essential to check them in the interests of the revolution. It was decided to send for the purpose the communist Minister of Agriculture, Tan Ping-san to Hunan. Roy opposed the decision. A few years later he wrote the following on his position on that issue : "I vigorously objected to the Communists undertaking the task of checking the revolutionary action of the peasants, with a view to placate the reactionary army officers. I pointed out that the suicidal policy of restraining the development of the agrarian revolution on the plea of not disturbing the rear, when the army was fighting on the front, had already enabled the forces of reaction to go over to the offensive. Further restraint would demoralise the peasants' movement, and encourage counter-revolution to raise its bloody head in the villages. But my objection was disregarded.

"Thereupon, I suggested that Tan Ping-san might go with the instruction that, when on the spot, his mission should be not to check the 'excesses' of the peasants' movement, but to set up village self-government, investing the peasants' unions with the essential political power. That would be setting up Soviets if not in name. The peasants' unions were the rallying ground of the rural oppressed and exploited masses. In his capacity of the Minister of Interior, Tan Ping-san was in charge of local self-government and police. The action proposed, therefore, was within his official competence. Properly and courageously guided, the peasants' unions could easily become basic units of the revolutionary State, disarm the rowdies and ruffians in the pay of the landlords, and create a militia as the nucleus of a real revolutionary army.

"The rank and file Communists, working in the villages, were eager for such a line of action., but they were restrained by orders of the Central Committee of the party. Many of them lost patience, and acted independently under the pressure of the masses."*

In the meanwhile two communist leaders had joined the Government as Ministers, Tan Ping-shan as Minister of Agriculture and Su Chao-cheng as Minister of Labour. The proposal was brewing since March, but they were installed in office only on May 20. By that time the drift towards the right had progressed and the communist Ministers were not able to check it. After May it became rapid and ended in a complete break with the communists towards the end of July. Illusions about the Left Kuomintang persisted in the CP for a long time, practically until the time of the break. They persisted in the CI as well as can be seen from the writings and speeches of Stalin and Bukharin and the resolution of the eighth plenum which met in Moscow in May 1927. In a speech at the plenum Stalin described Wuhan as "the centre of the revolutionary movement" as against Nanking which, according to him, was "the centre of national counter-revolution". "The Wuhan Kuomintang must be supported", he said, "and the Communists must participate in this Kuomintang and in its revolutionary government." The resolution adopted by the plenum stated : "The task of the CCP, therefore, was to 'convert the Kuomintang into a genuine mass organization embracing the toiling population in town and countryside.' "The CCP was to see to it that the Kuomintang developed "into a genuinely broad, genuinely elective, genuinely mass, genuinely revolutionary democratic organization." While preserving its own independence, the CCP "must exercise to an increasing degree its influence over the work of the Kuomintang." Consequently, the CCP "must take a most energetic part in the work of the Wuhan Provisional Revolutionary Government." Trotsky was opposed to this line. He demanded the organisation of Soviets. He reminded Stalin of his policy of endorsement to Chiang Kai-shek and how disastrous it had proved. He foretold the same fate to the policy of collaboration with the Left Kuomintang, if the CP did rot build up soviets of workers and peasants. Roy was not also at that moment in favour of breaking off relations with Left Kuomintang though he had started making a distinction between the leadership and the rank and file. In his proposals to the polit bureau of the party of May 24 Roy made a sharp distinction between the leadership and the rank and file of the Kuomintang. Remaining in Kuomintang was essential, he stated, but that the task before the C.P. was of "freeing the Kuomintang from its leadership". He said : "We can no longer ignore the fact that the Central Committee of the Kuomintang is pursuing an anti-proletarian, anti-peasant, and anti-communist policy." he warned : "The continuing collaboration with the Kuomintang must parallel preparations of new forms of struggle and new organs of power, appropriate to the situation and essential for achieving the goal. Collaboration with the Kuomintang must continue, because it will give us an opportunity to make the essential preparations. If we collaborate with the Kuomintang for the sake of any other goals and nourish any illusions about the social character and the political aims of the Kuomintang leaders, we will lead our Party into liquidation and the revolution will be in jeopardy." The resolution that Roy suggested on the basis of his proposals was neither adopted nor rejected by the polit bureau. Later events proved that, even if it had been accepted, it would not have been easy to persuade the rank of the of the Kuomintang to revolt against its leadership. About this time there was a controversy in the CP on the issue of relations with the Left Kuomintang. Borodin and Roy were ranged on two different sides. A common idea of the respective positions held by them can be gathered from a report of Tsai Ho-sen. According to him Borodin's view was:

1. The present position of the Left Kuomintang is entirely acceptable. They do not display any devintionist tendencies or shortcomings. The

mistakes in the past were due to the extreme nature of the workers' and peasants' movement. Actually, the leadership in this movement Was not that of the peasants, but of the Society of Elder Brothers and bandits.

2. We must yield to the Kuomintang in order to be able to continue collaboration with it; if we break with the Kuomintang, the Chinese revolution Will suffer defeat.

3. Collaboration with the Kuomintang means collaboration with its CC, since the present composition of the CC is quite acceptable to us. The withdrawal from it, or its overthrow, would be equivalent to a break or a political coup. A tendency in favour of a break is evident among some of our party members.

4. Reduction of rent, elimination of usury and the introduction of local self-government in the countryside-these measures, the agrarian revolution.

5. The CC of the CCP must issue jointly with the workers' and peasants' organizations an appeal to the masses urging them to follow the orders of the CC of the Kuomintang and of the Nationalist government which require the discontinuation of the excesses in the workers' and peasants' movement, as well as the recently issued orders."

The view of Roy was :

(a) The CC of the Kuornintang and the Nationalist government no longer represent the Left Wing; rather, they support the interests of Tu-hao, the gentry, landlords, and imperialists. We must direct the people to overthrow them.

(b) The overthrow of the present CC of the Kuomintang does not mean as yet a political coup.

(c) At present we must aim at the democratic dictatorship of the workers and peasants.

(d) The CC of the CCP must issue immediately an appeal to the people and explain in it the reactionary nature of all orders which had been issued recently by the CC of the Kuomintang and its government. These orders aim at the suppression of the workers' and peasants' movement and the defence of the feudal system."

Early in June Tang Shen-chi, the principal advocate of the Northern Expedition, brought his forces back to Wuhan as his march to Peking was blocked by Feng Yuhsiang, the Christian General. Communists had for some time high expectation about the Christian General. He had been to Moscow and was making good use of Russian weapons and military advisers. Roy also had illusions about him as can be seen from the open letter of June 10 addressed to him as a representative of the CI. The letter congratulated him on his victories and talked to him about "the new enemy, the neo-militarism. Of Chiang Kai-shek, supported by imperialism and the counter-revolutionary national bourgeoisie." The same Christian General called the Wuhan leaders for a conference in Chengchow and after dictating his terms to them went from there to met Chiang Kai-shek at Hsu-Chow. According to him, unity in the nationalist camp was essential for the success of military operations against northern militarists.

According to Roy, "From Hsu-Chow, Feng sent an open telegram to the Wuhan Government urging the necessity of unifying all the nationalist forces in the struggle against northern militarism, while pointing out that Wuhan's insistence upon maintaining relation with the Communists was the only hindrance to that unity. In the telegram, he demanded that the Wuhan Government should soon dismiss its Russian advisors and suppress the Communist Party. The demand was supported by the thinly veiled threat that Feng would attack Wuhan from the north in case his advice was not accepted. The telegram strengthened the hands of those leaders of the Wuhan group who had been pressing for the break with the Communists and suppression of revolutionary mass movement." The Left Kuomintang and the national Government were thus compelled to make a choice between alliance with militarists and the bourgeoisie or alliance with communists and the big masses. The situation was grim, but not hopeless, according to Roy. On June 3 he addressed in the name of the CP an open letter to the central committee of the Kuomintang. On June 9 he made a long statement to the polit bureau of the CP in the course of which he surveyed the situation as it had developed in the country. The survey pointed out: "In political and social respects, the so-called Left-Wing group in Wuhan differs but little from Nanking. Today they both represent feudal-bourgeoise interests.... The Central Committee of the Wuhan Kuomintang is moving in the direction of counter-revolution". Referring to the Kuomintang demand for correction of peasants' excesses, it stated : "No, comrades, the Communist Party cannot do this. The Communist Party must give full support to the peasants who are seizing the land and expropriating the landlords, the users, and the gentry. The Party must head the peasantry and create a regime of terror with view to extirpate the reaction in the village." After defining the immediate tasks of the CP, the speech put forward the proposal of a one-day general strike of all workers including workers in the arsenal.

Referring to Chen Tuhsiu's criticism of the proposed general strike, Roy said : "Comrade Chen fears that a general strike, and especially a strike in the arsenal, would develop into an open fight and that workers are liable to be shot. But the attack on the working class has already begun. Masses of peasants are being shot. Workers are being disarmed. They are also being shot. If the working class does not put up a resistance to the attack of the counter-revolution and if it does not develop this resistance into a counter-attack, it will be crushed. I submit a proposal for a general strike and for a strike of workers in the arsenal not only as a demonstration of protest, strikes must become the beginning of an open struggle against the counter-revolution. Under the conditions that have arisen, the Communist Party must lead the proletariat to revolt.' There was disagreement in the CP over the general strike suggested by Roy. It was stated that in the critical situation then prevailing a general strike would mean a declaration of war on the Kuomintang and the national Government. It was not, therefore, organised. Mass meetings that were organised became meetings to welcome national leaders and not meetings of protest against Kuomintang policies as demanded by Roy. In order "to separate the goals from sheep" Roy proposed on June 15 a "platform of the national revolution" which, he suggested, should be put to the Kuomintang to test its revolutionary credentials. It was not a communist platform; it was only a revolutionary-democratic platform.

But Borodin and Chen Tu-hsiu had great differences with it. About those differences Roy said : "Both Comrade Borodin and Comrade Chen Tu-hsiu consider that this program lays down the maximum demands of the working class. In their view, this is what we want. They consider that our task is to ascertain what the Kuomintang wants and to find a way to reach an agreement with it. Borodin says that the future of our relations with the Kuomintang depends on our answer to the questions raised by the Kuomintang regarding : (1) diarchy (two parties); (2) control over the mass movement; and (3) industry and commerce. Borodin believes that if we do not make concessions on all these issues, a break at the present time is both undesirable and harmful. In his opinion, our break from the Kuomintang will throw it into the arms of the counter-revolution.' The rest of the speech is devoted to answering criticisms levelled by the two persons who controlled the party and its activities. This speech as well as the earlier speech lay bare the difficult conditions in which Roy had to operate in China. On several great issues Borodin and Chen Tu-hsiu differed from him, and they controlled-the machinery of the party. Roy could make suggestions; but he did not have the power or the agency to implement them. Keeping in view of all this, Ts-ai Ho-sen's later observation "if Comrade Roy had acted with more decisiveness and persistence, the Polit bureau would have given in and would have accepted his plan" lacks substance.

In the situation that had developed Roy was in favour of a determined offensive. His advice was rejected. A few years later he wrote the following about the effort that he made to save the situation: "In despair, I tried to act over the bead of the impossible Political Bureau of the Communist Party-I demanded a plenary meeting of the Central Committee to be attended by local leaders. The demand was opposed on the plea that important members of the party could not leave their respective posts in those critical days. The top leaders were against the plenary session, because local workers were impatient for decisive action and would have surely endorsed my plan. As the last resort, I sought to act with the co-operation of individual comrades, Chinese as well as Russian. Galen (the Chief Military Adviser to the National Government) was fully in agreement with me. Several other Russian comrades had also come around to my view by that time. But all power was centred in the hands of Borodin. Moscow had supported me politically as against his opportunism. Nevertheless, in other respects he was still left in the controlling position, and resultantly functioned as the dictator of the Communist Party. Being mostly his disciples and ideologically akin to his way, the top leaders of the C. P. Of China followed him, disregarding repeatedly the instructions of the International and in defiance of its representative on the spot. "It was possible to raise an irregular force, several thousand strong for temporary operations against Changsha, pending the formation of the revolutionary army with peasant volunteers. To secure the services of the improvised force, it was essential to pay the troops a month's wages in advance. Borodin controlled the pursestrings. In the beginning he promised to supply the required money. When all arrangements were made, in spite of the criminal non-cooperation of the leaders of the C. P. and the peasants' unions had been instructed to besiege Changsha, he failed to keep his promise. Consequently, the plan had to be abandoned. "At Wuhan, there was a demonstration, but not with the original purpose which was to give the signal for the planned insurrection. The plan was to declare a one-day general strike on the occasion of the return of the representatives of the Government to the Conference with Feng Yu-hsiang at the front. All the workers of the three cities were together at the meeting to be addressed by the nationalist leaders. From the platform, the representative of the Communist Party was to demand action according to the resolution of the party, and the rationalist leaders failing to sanction it, to take them prisoners as the signal for the planned insurrection. Ten thousand workers in the nearby Hanyang arsenal were ready to take possession of it on that signal. But the demonstration turned out to be a welcome to the commanders of the 'victorious' army." In the worsening situation in which the militarists were coming together and attacks on workers and peasants and communists were increasing, both Borodin and Roy turned to Wang Ching-wei, the leader of the left Kuomintang and of the national Government as the only person who could save the situation. Borodin still had faith in Tang Sheng-chi and suggested to Wang Ching-wei an Eastern Expedition in cooperation with him. Cooperation in Eastern Expedition would, Borodin hoped, convince Wang Chingwei that communists were behind him. According to Roy, "the foolish tactics of the Communists-Borodin's policy of a military combination under Tang Shen-chi's leadership-had driven Wang Chin-wei into the embrace of the reactionary clique." The effort that was made to reassure Wang Ching-wei of communist support is related by Roy as follows : "On his way back to China, he had passed through Moscow.

There he was promised full support of the Soviet Government as well as of the Communist International... I managed to send a radio message to Moscow demanding the reassurance. On the other hand, to him I proposed a concrete plan of action which should be undertaken to re-establish his effective leadership of the Wuhan Government. He agreed with the plan, provided that the essential help would be forthcoming. "A few days later, a telegram came from Moscow with the desired reassurance. Among other things, it suggested the following: 'Confiscate the land; destroy the present unreliable generals, arm twenty thousand Communists, and select fifty thousand workers and peasant elements to create a new army; put new worker and peasant elements in the Central Executive Committee of the Kuomintang to take the place of the old members; and organise a revolutionary Court with a well-known member of the Kuomintang as its Chair-,, man to try the reactionary officers.' "It was almost too late when the urgently required reassurance came. Meanwhile, believing that the Communists had betrayed him, Wang

Chingwei had entered into negotiations with the right wing which was clamouring for the blood of the Communists to propitiate Chiang Kai-shek.... I thought at that juncture, a final effort must be made to regain the confidence of Wang Ching-wei. I communicated to him the message from Moscow.... It was a repetition of the promise made to him personally in Moscow... Besides, the plan was already known to him. He had expressed his agreement with it. He was willing to stand by his agreement if I could produce definite proof that the essential help would be forth coming... It is reported that he showed the telegram to his associates who were already in communication with Nanking.... The counter-revolution was in open offensive in Wuhan itself several days before the arrival of the telegram. Associates of Wang Ching wei, known reactionaries like Sun Fo, Eugen Chen, Tan Yankee, trusted by Borodin and the leaders of the CP as left-wingers, had come to a secret understanding with Chiang Kai-shek and were only waiting to take Wang Ching-wei along into the camp of counter-revolution." Roy's showing Stalin's message to Wang Ching-wei and giving him its copy was not liked and resented by Borodin and the leaders of the CP. It was regarded as a serious dearth of tact and Borodin telegraphed to CI to recall Roy. Some irresponsible persons went to the extent of alleging that the Left Kuomintang turned against communists only after seeing the message and that, but for Roy showing it to Wang Ching-wei, it would have continued its co-operation with communists and that would have ensured the success of the Chinese revolution. They thus accused Roy of being liable for the defeat of the revolution. A whispering propaganda of this kind was carried on against him after his return to India in December 1930. In authoritative communist literature there is not a word to support this charge. According to Roy, several militarists who controlled the Left Kuomintang had already begun their war against communists and it was as a last desperate effort to prevent Wang Ching-wei from going along with them that the message which was meant for him was communicated to him. The author of The Inner History of the Chinese Revolution has given his own version of the incident. It is as follows : "Roy's idea was that the Left Kuomintang could only survive when in alliance with the communists, as otherwise they would be crushed by the Rightists. They should, therefore, be informed of Stalin's cable. Borodin, however, realized that the Left Kuomintang was much stronger than Roy thought it was, and knew that if they saw the resolution, they would at once sever their relations with the Communists. He had, therefore, suppressed the resolution, and was naturally annoyed when he learnt about Roy's recklessness in making it known to Wang. A majority of the Chinese communists sided with Borodin, being also of the opinion that the time for overt action had not come yet; and they drove Roy back to Russia." The version of another scholar is as follows : "In general the members of the Communist Central Committee, already confused and overwhelmed by the accumulated effects of their own previous policies, were dumbfounded and perplexed by these instructions. Ch'en Tu-hsiu somewhat inelegantly expressed their feelings when he said it was like "trying to take a bath in a urinal." Even Borodin, Stalin's deputy, he relates, "saw no possibility of carrying them out". After considering the communication from Stalin for some time, the Central Committee finally voted to wire its thanks to Moscow with the accompanying plea that the goals designated "could not be realized immediately." Roy, however, thought he had the solution. He promptly showed Stalin's telegram to Wang Ching-wei and asked him to support it. "I am quite surd," he is quoted as saying to Wang, "that you would approve of it." But Wang did not approve at all. He did not want to destroy the unreliable generals. He wanted to ally himself with them. Roy discovered, to his dismay, that the Left Kuomintang did not have to follow, Communist advice. It could go the other way.

This was the one small flaw in Stalin's whole programme; it required the approval of Wang Ching-wei and this it did not get." Even if these versions are believed Roy's action can be regarded only as indiscreet. And nothing turned on it. The militarists and other leaders of the Left Kuomintang had already determined their course of action. Roys' effort was too late and 'too feeble to have any effect on it. The Christian General's telegram asking for a union of all nationalist forces and expulsion of communists coupled with Chiang Kai-shek's ultimatum decided the fate of the Left Kuomintang and its national Government. They decided to reunite with Chiang Kai-shek and the Government that he had established in Nanking. A face saving formula was devised according to which Chiang Kai-shek went on leave for a short while.

But he returned soon and it was Wang Ching-wei who had to leave the country for a much longer sojourn abroad. Regarding the immediate developments Roy has recorded : "In the last days of June, events moved fast at Wuhan. Workers were completely disarmed; trade-unions were dissolved; meetings and demonstrations were forbidden; and the entire city was in a state of siege. On July 3, the Communist Party performed its last tragic act in an atmosphere of triumphant counter-revolution. An extraordinary meeting of the Central Committee adopted the so-called "programme of retreat" which practically nullified all the resolutions of the Fifth Congress of the party held only two moths ago. But the counter-revolution was implacable. It thirsted for blood. So long as the mass movement was not completely suppressed, the Communist Party was not fully crushed, the situation was not safe. The communists were driven out of all positions; hundreds were arrested, several executed.

Finally, there was an end to the relation with the Kuomintang, for the sake of maintaining which the communist leaders had committed mistake after mistake, one more fatal than the other. The communists were driven out of the Kuomintang." Later, the communists started an offensive the high point of which was the insurrection in Canton in December. It was a heroic but a futile attempt. A large number of workers and peasants, estimated at no less than a quarter of million, and more than twenty-five thousand communists were killed. Borodin left Hankow on July 27. Roy left in late July or early August. "The Comintern provided three large touring cars equipped with heavy duty springs and gasolin cans lashed to the running boards. The drivers were agents of the GPU. From Hankow the caravan headed to the North West, crossed the Mangolian deserts, and proceeded to the Soviet Union by way of Urga." After his return from China, Roy received his first jolt in Moscow when he could not get an interview with Stalin. He had hoped to win Stalin's approval for his work. He found, however, that he was being cold shouldered. He then went to Berlin and put together all documents connected with his work in China. They were published as a book in Moscow. Copious extracts from the book are given in this chapter on the ground of the translation of those documents by North and Eudin.

The documents are an invaluable source material of a contemporary character for the study of developments in China in 1927. Moscow published them with an introduction by Roy in which he examined the correctness or otherwise of the line recommended by the CI and the policies and actions of the CP of China. According to him, the CI line of collaboration with the Kuomintang was correct. He states : "By entering the Kuomintang the Communist Party was acquiring organic ties with the national revolutionary movement and was receiving an opportunity to exert influence on it. As a consequence of such a tactic, the national movement became a mass movement developing under the flag of the

Kuomintang. At the very same time, the Communist Party penetrated the proletarian and peasant masses and became their leader. The labouring masses could not have been mobilized so fastly into the anti-imperialist struggle had not the Communist Party participated in the national revolutionary movement as a component part of the Kuomintang." Continuing he states : "The Northern Expedition gave the Communist Party a brilliant opportunity to conduct revolutionary agitation among the masses of a number of provinces. Several millions of peasants and workers, not as yet touched by the revolution were not only drawn into the movement, but became organized under the exclusive leadership of the Communist Party. Collaboration was equally essential, he states in the Wuhan period : "Support of the Left-Wing Kuomintang as an organ of struggle against imperialism and national reaction, including the traitorous bourgeoisie, became all the more essential when the feudal-bourgeois elements turned against the revolution. The petty bourgeoisie, frequently constituting the majority of the population in Chinese towns, represents a highly important social factor in China. These petty-bourgeoisis masses were imbued with resolute anti-imperialist sentiments and they stood behind the Kuomintang. The peasant movement was spreading under the protection of the Kuomintang which commanded considerable authority among the peasantry. Even among the working-class masses, the Kuomintang still enjoyed a great popularity. Under such circumstances, the Communist Party had to remain in the ranks of the Kuomintang and use it as the center around which all revolutionary-democratic forces were grouping themselves."

For the defeat of the revolution he blames particularly the CP, the instrument through which the CI had to act. The CP, he states, did not understand the full meaning of the resolutions of the CI and was unable to act according to them. The leadership of the party was "weak, opportunistic and semi-Kuomintang." Roy states : "For collaboration they substituted capitulation. Their opportunism hampered the development of mass revolutionary action, and especially, the agrarian revolution which could crush the forces of reaction." In extenuation of these mistakes of the party he pointed to its youth and lack of experience. In conclusion he admits that the basic reason of the defeat was "the objective conditions, the unequal alignment of forces." One of the reasons for compiling the documents, writing the introduction and publishing the book was, it seems, to answer the criticism of the opposition in the Russian Communist Party and their adherents in other countries that the defeat of the revolution was caused by the erroneous and opportunistic policy of the CI. In a book written while in Kanpur jail in 1931, Roy is more just in apportioning blame. By that time he had ceased to be a CI functionary and could be, therefore, forthright in his assessment of the role played by the CI and the Russian CP. Pointing out that the defeat was because of the opportunist interpretation of a revolutionary policy, he states : "And it is a wilful misreading of history to shove the entire responsibility upon the leaders of the Communist Party of China." He states further: "Ever since 1923, the CP of China had been under Russian guidance. Its leading cadre was trained by Russian Communists. The opportunist deviations, which led to the disaster of 1927, took place not at the instance of the Chinese Communists but their Russian friends. Besides, when it is found that the leaders of a particular section of a centralised world party like the Communist International have systematically deviated from a correct line over a whole period of time, the liability for the same must be laid at the door of the International leadership." The guidance was exercised through, Roy points out, "inferior and indifferent" members of the Russian C.P, but to the Chinese communists their authority appeared to be "incontestable and infallible." One "evil result" of this arrangement was that the CP of China "grew as a spoon-fed child". The Russian representatives could not besides make a distinction between the revolutionary policy of the CI and the diplomatic manouvres of the Russian Government which in those days was extending liberal aid to nationalist bourgeoisie as well as left militarists. The latter fact coloured the outlook and thinking of several Russian representatives. According to Roy, the CI was as much responsible for the earlier opportunist deviations as for the adventurist live which brought about the disastrous Canton insurrection of December 1927. He writes :"Here again the responsibility lies with the International leadership. For the new policy of adventure was launched on mandatory instructions from Moscow." Harold R. Issacs, the scholar already mentioned, agrees with this assessment of Roy. He writes : "But the record shows that the Chinese Communist Party was with literal fidelity carrying out the directives it had received from Moscow." Roy wrote his major book on China, Revolution and Counter-revolution in China in 1929. The German edition of the book was published in 1930. The English edition was, however, published only in 1946 with the addition of two chapters to cover later developments. The book is more than a history of the revolutionary movement in contemporary China. It gives the "broad outlines of the social history of China from the earliest days. A number of social problems, which appear to be typically Chinese are theoretically treated." His third book on China is the already mentioned My Experiences in China, originally published as China in Revolt under the nom de plum S. K. Vidyarthi. In later life Roy wrote sketches of five great Chinese personalities, Madame Sun Yet-sen, Chiang Kai-shek, Yen Hsi-shan, Mao Tse-tung and Chou En-lai. They provide revealing insights into the thoughts and policies of the prominent figures of the period. They are collected, together in Men I met published in 1968. Much has been written about the extra-ordinary developments in China in the latter half of the Twenties, some of it by actual participants and by those who had the opportunity to watch events as they were taking place. A good part of the writing is vitiated by partisan spirit as the developments in China became the centre of a bitter controversy in the Russian Communist Party between Stalin and Trotsky.

The revolution having failed, Trotsky held Stalin liable for laying down wrong policies, forgetting in the heat of the controversy that he was also liable for those policies in the initial period. On the other hand, Stalin justified all policies and directives of the CI and placed all blame for the failure on the shoulders of the Chinese CP. Even the disastrous mistake of the Canton insurrection he utilised for bolstering up his case against Trotsky. He proclaimed the victory of the revolution in Moscow when it was being strangled and butchered in China. He did it for winning his factional fight against Trotsky; he could, however, do it with good conscience, for to him, Chinese revolution was more a battle in the world-wide struggle against capitalism and imperialism than a fight for the social liberation of the people of China. A temporary setback in a battle on one front is a victory if it damages imperialism and exposes its role as an oppressor. In that factional fight in the Russian CP several suffered. Roy was one of the sufferers, not because he agreed with Trotsky-because he did not-but because he did not bring Stalin the success that he required at that time. Roy's break with the CI did not take place then; it took place a year later and for different reasons, but the process could be said to have started at that time. In the writings on the period there are several references to Roy, adverse as well as favourable. They are of little importance at this distance of time. One oft-quoted observation of Mao Tse-tung may be, however, mentioned. Edger Snow reports it as follows : "M.N. Roy, the Indian delegate to the Comintern, 'stood a little to the left of both Ch'en and Borodin, but he only stood.' He 'could talk', according to Mao, 'and he talked too much, without offering any method of realisation.' Mao thought that, objectively, Roy had been a fool, Borodin a blunderer, and Ch'en an unconscious traitor. (Red Star Over China, 1973 Pelican reprint, p. 190) It is hardly fair to blame Roy for not "offering any method of realisation," as, though a representative of the CI, all effective power was in the hands of Borodin and Chen Tu-hsiu who disagreed with and vetoed in action the alternatives suggested by Roy. Mao was a minor leader at that time, but he is not known to have made any effort to place a different line before the party. His assessment of the situation in 1927 is of interest. Snow reports : "Mao did not think that the counter-revolution could have been defeated in 1927 even if the communist party had carried out a more aggressive policy of land confiscation and created Communist armies from among workers and peasants before the split with Kuomintang." If that was his reading of the situation, there is little justification for his condemnation of Roy, Borodin and Chen Tuhsiu. Roy's mission to China ended in failure. But it was a failure not of an individual, but of an institution. The Comintern had tried to foster and direct a revolution in a populous and complex country like-China from a centre thousands of miles away from the scene of operation. That in itself was an ill-conceived adventure.

None of the persons involved in it saw its quixotic character as all of them were operatives of the institution concerned which they regarded as the General Staff of world revolution and, as such, entitled to direct revolutionary activities all over the world. The institution was incapable of knowing and understanding the Chinese mind, which in that vast country was not one for a class or a region. It had hundreds of variations in each class and region. One remark of Mao Tse-tung, who was then the President of the Peasants' Federation, is full of meaning. According to Roy, he asked :

"How could foreigners have any idea of the Chinese reality" Comintern representatives were foreigners who stayed only for short periods and did not have much time and opportunity to dive deep into the mind of the Chinese people. The Comintern was getting contradictory and confusing reports from its representatives on the spot. Sometimes its representatives followed, as happened in the case of Roy and Borodin, contradictory policies. The CI directives were also often ambiguous and inconsistent and sometimes they were received after the situation on which they were based had undergone a complete change. A later biographer of Mao Tsetung stated the following as Mao's view on the position that existed : "No one can direct a revolution by telegraph, Stalin is reported to have said, yet this was now happening. The Comintern resolutions, Stalin's directives came thick and fast because the CCP leadership was incapable of making its own decisions... Envoys were sent who squabbled openly and contradicted each other. And there was the time element, the situation changed so rapidly that by the time the "advice" came from Moscow all was radically different. And in Moscow itself the Stalin-Trotsky struggle did not make things easier". The Chinese CP through which the CI had to operate was not of one mind. There were great differences of opinion amongst its, leaders. They had little freedom of action; they had to accept and implement the CI directives handed out to them by its representatives. Comintern representatives, however well-versed in Marxist theory and practice, did not have that intimate knowledge of the feelings and moods of the people which was inevitable for chalking out a correct course of action in a fast-changing situation. Roy suffered from that handicap as much as others. One is dazzled several a time by his theoretically correct analysis of the class forces comprised in the revolution. But how can one be sure that the oppressed masses, particularly the peasants, had at that moment the desire, the strength and the determination to wage a relentless struggle against their oppressors? How can one be sure that sporadic outbursts did not mislead him or that there was no overestimation of the rebellious mood of the masses? Whatever the answer, there can be no gainsaying the fact that Roy tried his best, resolutely and devotedly, to put into practice the directives of the CI which he had himself helped to formulate. His failure was because of mainly objective conditions) the overwhelming power of the feudal militarists and the bourgeoisie, backed as they were by foreign imperialisms, and the comparatively weak organisation of workers and peasants and the adverse conditions in which he had to operate. It is significant to note that, as stated by Roy, "there does not exist a single document of the Communist International in which I am accused of having done anything improper in China." Roy failed in China in his immediate objective of bringing about a revolution. However, the rich experience that he gained of revolutionary work in a predominantly agricultural country proved of great advantage. He put it to good use a few years later in India, the last field of his activity.

7

M.N. Roy : His Radical Humanism

M.N. Roy was sufficiently under the influence of Communism but as the time passed with that his faith in individual freedom increased. He developed his own philosophy called Radical Humanism. M.N. Roy was the exponent of Radical or New Humanism. He believed that science has proved to be an important factor for the development of creative faculties of man. For him renaissance opened a new era in modern civilisation. He stood for new humanism which was based on natural reason and in which conscience should be free. In it he laid stress on the sovereignty of individual and in his view society had no reason to impose itself on any one. For him a spiritually liberated individual is very essential for a better and happy society. He was believer of world federation in which none would be limited by the boundaries of national state as such ideologies as Communism, Socialism, Fascism etc. would gradually end. He said that ideas give birth to revolutions and as such ideas precede revolution.

Revolutions come when vast majority accepts new ideas. In dictatorship there can be no scope for human development. He believed that for establishment of free world it was most desirable that sources of production should not be used for personal ends but for the welfare of weaker sections of society, both in letter and spirit.

In his view freedom is biological heritage and closely linked with struggle for existence. Three pillars of his freedom are motivating power of social advancement, collective progress, individualism and rationalism. For him each one thinks in terms of cause and effect. Nationalism is not the final stage in his social philosophy but he feels it neglects social questions and as such it should be replaced by brotherhood. For him new humanism is cosmopolitan. He has made a distinction between cosmopolitanism and internationalism. According to M.N. Roy individual is an end itself and every other organization in the society simply means to an end. He was not ready to subordinate individual freedom even to religion or morality or to any other supernatural power. He believed that man had always been struggling for freedom and his joining the civil state and society was only on the condition that his freedom would be protected. In his opinion it was an evolutionary and continuing process. He said that those institutions and organizations which had been set up to safeguard individual freedom often have tried to master him and that was quite unhealthy. In his opinion state was primarily brought into being to check all impediments and hindrances which checked the growth of man individual today the state was trying to subordinate individuals and wanted to become an end in itself instead of being means to an end. Similarly religion had become the master of man's mind and tries to check individual freedom though gradually its grip is weakening. As already said Roy very much loved individual freedom and in his opinion freedom is above everything else.

He, however, feels that there are certain obstacles in the way of individual freedom. The greatest obstacle is the state which is trying to become an end in itself rather than retaining its essential character of remaining means to an end. The state is originally intended to be the custodian of human development and freedom but with the passage of time it becomes a hindrance on that very freedom. Similarly, he believes that religion is equally a hindrance in man's search for freedom. It is in religion that man is made to subordinate and put himself under the control of certain super-natural and heavenly revealed philosophies whether those are based on rationalism or not. Since most of the people have faith in religion and can not challenge the validity of religious principles, therefore, religion is becoming more and more an impediment in the path of individual freedom. Similarly he found that marriage and family life were also other hindrances on his path of freedom. He came to, the conclusion that these institutions try to establish harmony in their own Way with the result that people develop a very narrow outlook and in some cases even become irrational to protect their selfish narrow ends. In his philosophy both these institutions are even now great hindrances and man is gradually beginning to depend on others, thus sacrificing his wisdom and initiative. In his philosophy if these difficulties were to be crossed over for that it was imperative that the individual should depend on his inherited wisdom and rationality of thinking rather than depending on super-natural dogmas and institutions. He came to the conclusion that the curse of modem society was the notion of class rather than that of individual. He felt that Marx and many other thinkers just forgot that the individuals collectively constitute class which is an outcome of individual's willing association to come together and to perform certain functions. The present notion of giving priority to class over the individual is just reversing the course of history.

Roy, therefore, felt that the concept of class or society should be made relative and that it should be very clearly understood that society is means to an end not an end in itself. He, therefore, feels that the greatest hindrance to individual freedom, alongwith other factors, is society and class. In his Organized Democracy and in People's Plan he has suggested means by which individual can remain free by remaining a part of the class to which he belongs. M.N. Roy essentially believed in the basic doctrine of historical materialism as expounded by Marx, but he differed from him in details. In his opinion there was no difference between organic and un-organic matter. He was of the opinion that all living bodies were formed out of certain chemical matters and their combination resulted in the creation of other matters. In his opinion mind was a characteristic of matter at a high stage of development. Roy was also of the opinion that there was a constant inter-penetration and interdependence between man and matter. He thus tried to establish a close relationship between an individual's mind and matter. According to M.N Roy by nature man loves freedom and that he was born free and everywhere he was in chains. In his philosophy man was rational and as such above all the other living-beings. Rationalism was the most essential and basic standard of human development. In his own words, "It is the reason in man which harmonizes the people of human will with the law governess of physical universe."

Roy believed that rationalism was a part of human nature and in fact he inherited it from his very birth. There was no stage in human history when an individual was devoid of reason and thinking power. According to M.N. Roy in its present form democracy did not grant either economic or social or political freedom. It sacrificed individual freedom for the sake of collective freedom and required a fundamental change both in nature and character. He, therefore, pleaded for an organized democracy based on the concept of decentralization and which was to start from below rather than from above. In such a democracy every one will be a participant and that democracy alone can guarantee individual freedom. According to Roy, human history is nothing else but a record of struggle for freedom. The people have always struggled for their and that at no stage their struggle comes to an end. In his philosophy history normally develops according to the logic of thought and is an evolutionary process. In his opinion, evolution is the law of history and revolutions come but rarely. He believed that a revolution could not be a success unless it was required by the society for its collective development. In other words, in his opinion, Marxian interpretation of history of class struggle is rather defective. According to Marx, history is hitherto nothing else but that of class struggle, whereas for Roy history is not only an economic aspect of life but something broader and wider. It includes economic, social as well as political aspects of an individual's life. The life of Roy was a life of adventures, adventures in the field of action as well as in the held of ideas. The former dominated the first part of his life while the latter the later part. To a great extent the two went together.

His conversion from nationalism to communism would not have been possible without an adventure in the field of ideas. But that journey was not very difficult. There were several signposts on the way like the works of Marx, Engles, Kautsky and others and also several able guides like Borodin, Lenin, Trotsky, Stalin and Bukharin. The journey that he started in the last phase of his life, the journey from communism to humanism, was more hazardous. There were several pitfalls on the way and few signposts and fewer guides. He had to blaze a new trail. Many disillusioned and frustrated communists have turned from communism to religion and some others have reverted to liberalism or nationalism. That path was open to Roy but he rejected it and went beyond communism to humanism. By himself Roy could have completed the journey in a short time. But he was not alone. He had collected around him a large circle of co-workers, followers and admirers who looked up to him for guidance on all public affairs. A paraphernalia of a party and various other organisations had been built up and they all depended upon him to guide and direct their activities. Roy had a responsibility towards them, both persons and organisations. He had to make an attempt to carry them along with him. That needed a good deal of time and patience, and in some cases it did not succeed. It stands to his credit that he never ceased to make that effort, irrespective of the result that it produced. Developments that took place during the war and immediately thereafter in the political and the social field and in the field of science, technology and philosophy compelled Roy to re-examine all his ideas and to start a fresh quest for truth. He found that several of his hopes had not been fulfilled, that some of his forebodings had proved true, and that the world was moving not in the direction of peace and progress but in the direction of war and destruction Communism, which he had hoped would after its victorious fight against fascism assume the leadership of world forces of progress, had degenerated into nationalism and equated itself with the nationalist interests of Russia. That made Roy re-examine the basic concepts of Marxism and he discovered several faults not only in its political and economic programmes but also in its philosophical demands. Roy who was never an orthodox Marxist found it essential then to begin a search for a new philosophy. Roy's greatest disappointment was Russia and the policy that she adopted in international affairs. After the end of the war more information became available and, as she had weathered the storm and emerged strong and powerful, Roy did not think it essential to suppress or soft-peddle his criticism of her actions and policies. He revised some of his earlier views and wrote bluntly about her mistakes and miscalculations during the war and in the years that followed. In an article written some weeks after the end of the war, Roy pointed out various mistakes committed by Russia during the war. The first was the signing of the Nazi-Soviet Pact which was not altogether "an emergency measure", as he once imagined. After the Pact, Communist measure", as he Parties in several countries "actually operated as the fifth column of the Axis Powers," which happened he had reason to believe "on orders from Moscow". The next mistake was the policy of neutrality adopted when Hitler attacked France Roy wrote : "The Russians passively watching and perhaps indirectly helping the Germans overrun France cannot be justified by any political consideration."

These mistakes led to the moral isolation of Russia. Similar mistakes committed after the end of the war were depriving her of the great moral prestige that she had won during the war as a result of her heroic fight against Hitler's hordes. After reviewing the various moves made by Russia in the Peace Conference and other forums, Roy felt compelled to arrive at the following conclusion about her foreign policy: "The Post-war Soviet diplomacy of holding up the settlement of any major issue of international relations cannot be understood except on the assumption that the Russians want to precipitate another war, believing that in consequence, thereof the old world will be completely dissolved and, a thoroughly devastated and largely depopulated Europe will be a happy hunting ground for the intolerant architects of a communist new order. They seem also to believe that,, so long as Europe remains in unsettled conditions, they have the greatest chance of expanding their influence, working on the emotions of distressed, starved and desperate peoples by holding out the hope of a heaven on earth." During the next few years Roy examined from time to time diverse actions of Russia in the field of foreign politics, such as, setting up of communist dictatorships in East European countries, opposition to Marshall Plan, establishment of Cominform and general resistance to efforts to restore peace and stability, and became more and more convinced that Russia was not acting as a liberating or peace-loving force. Several of the articles that he wrote during the period are collected together in the later part of Russian Revolution. Some of the observations made by Roy in those thought provoking articles deserve mention. Drawing the balance sheet of the Russian revolution he wrote : "History declined to follow the course marked out by the Communist Manifesto. The failure of the proletariat to assume the leadership of society in developed European countries compelled the revolution in Russia to abandon the long-cherished ideals; instead of moving towards the Communist Utopia, it ended in establishing a National State—with a new type of economy; but that distinction, in its turn proved that planned economy was not necessarily liberating and equalitarian; that, on the contrary, it may continue the exploitation of labour on the plausible pretext of satisfying the abstract and imaginary collective ego. The transition from Communism to Nationalism was easy and imperceptible because the latter also makes a fetish of the deceptive concept of collectivity, which completely ignores its own constituent units." Pointing out how communism had discredited itself, he wrote at the end of the same article : "The experience of the anti-fascist war and its after-math has given birth to new ideas and new ideals to move civilised humanity towards a really new order. The leadership of that movement does not belong to any class, but to men and women who embody the totality of the heritage of human history and cherish the moral and cultural values created by human genius ever since the dawn of civilisation, the-very values which inspired the prophets of Socialism to issue the Communist Manifesto." After examining the developments in East European countries dominated by Russia, Roy stated : "National degeneration of Communism is the common feature of the political life of those parts of Europe which today fly the Red Flag of proletararian world revolution under the protection of the Russian Army. Evidently, the revolution is defeating its own end; opportunist means adopted as revolutionary tactics were bound to corrupt the end also. This inglorious fate has overtaken the Russian Revolution because, thanks to a fallacious theory and incompetent, short-sighted leadership, it failed to march abreast of time and seize the opportunities offered by epoch making events, which occurred very largely under, the impact of the Russian Revolution." In a later article he described Russia's regress from communism to nationalism and concluded : "The experience of the Russian Revolution has exposed the fallacies of Marxism as a theoretical system and the non-liberating implications of Communism in practice. In order to be a turning point in the history of civilisation, the revolution of our time, therefore, will triumph not where it has created a new status quo of terror and voluntary slavery, spiritual regimentation and moral degradation : it will succeed as a resurgent democracy, passionately holding on to the ideal of freedom, undertaking the task of building a new order under the banner of New Humanism." These developments in Russia saddened Roy and made him re-examine the basic principles of communism and Marxism which had guided him so long. If the product of a faithful practice of those principles was so undesirable and so ugly, there must be, he argued, something wrong with those principles. He was not prepared to place the blame for the distortion on any single individual like Stalin or Lenin. He applied himself to the task of discovering the defects in the principles. The quest which started in the closing years of the war ended in 1946 in the elaboration of a few basic principles of the new philosophy of Radical Humanism.

The quest continued throughout the remaining years of his life and resulted in the further elaboration and refinement of the new philosophy. In 1946 events in India were moving in the direction of transfer of power to the two dominant political parties in the country. Elections to the central and provincial legislatures which took place late in 1945 and early in 1946 provided conclusive proof of the hold that the two organisations had obtained on the mass mind. Congress disputed the representative character of Muslim League, though it had captured a large-majority of Muslim seats. That delayed the transfer of power by over a year and ultimately brought about partition of the country which was preceded and followed by an inhuman orgy of communal violence.

After the elections, it was difficult to contest the claim of the two organisations, whatever their social character, to represent the people of the country. RDP contested elections to provincial legislatures in so many provinces. It drew up an election manifesto presenting an attractive programme of popular welfare. But the people were not in a mood to read and think. They were carried away by high pitched nationalist propaganda. The franchise was narrow, but very likely a wider franchise would not have made much difference. There was a good deal of violence and intimidation. Nehru had to issue a statement deprecating their use. Reacting to it Roy stated in the course of a statement : "If Fascism triumphs in India, and it is as likely as not, given the active connivance of decaying Imperialism, Nehru may or may not be its leader; but the blood of the Indian people that it will shed in the name of patriotism will be on his head." The severity of the language expresses the depth of his feelings. In the election campaign several meetings were broken up and several Radicals were severely assaulted. At the end, Roy characterised the elections as "Typical Hitler elections." No Radical succeeded in the elections, but one Radical, Maniben Kara, IFL President, was nominated a member of the Central Legislative Assembly to represent labour.

Early in the year a British parliamentary delegation visited India. Roy's advice to it was to "discover India of the masses." A couple of months later the Cabinet Mission came. On that occasion Roy sent an open letter to the Mission which stated inter alia : "The idea of coming to give freedom to four hundred million human beings is so very intoxicating as to turn the wisest of heads. In such a state of emotional exuberance, amounting to self-hypnosis, one tends to lose sight of realities, preferring to live in a world of make-believe. Whatever might have been the reason, you and the British Government certainly over-simplified the problem of setting India free and suggested a solution which amounted to a negation of freedom for the vast bulk of the people, and therefore a betrayal of democracy. It is, indeed, a cruel irony that ambassadors of British democracy should undertake such a shameful mission."

He ended the letter with the following positive suggestion : "True to the commitment of transferring power to the Indian people, the British Labour Government is entitled to outline a constitution such as will establish democratic freedom in India. Having done that it should proceed to the next step of helping the formation of a Provisional Government which-will undertake the task of leading the Indian people through the successive stages of the process of framing the constitution and its promulgation by a Constituent Assembly elected by universal suffrage. For the interim period, all power will be transferred to the Provisional Government." This procedure, he pointed out, was impartial and fully democratic. While engaged in these day to day political activities, Roy had not stopped thinking about more fundamental ideological and philosophical problems. Why did communism degenerate into nationalism? Is it due to the collectivist approach of both? Is it possible to develop a liberating philosophy on the ground of the freedom and happiness of the individual" What is the relation between the individual and the society'? What is the relation between man and nature? Has scientific advance exploded materialism? Are wars inevitable? Has humanity reached a dead end? Is human civilization doomed to destruction? Is it possible to rationalise and spiritualise politics? Is pursuit of power through political parties the only goal of political activity? Is it possible to reorganise political and social structure and make it more compatible with individual freedom and social advance? These and several similar questions had tortured his mind for several years. He had discussed them with some of his close colleagues and also some others prominent in the field of thought.

By 1946 he had reached some tentative conclusions and was anxious to place them before a wider circle of his co-workers. The study camp held in Mehra Dun from May 8 to 18 according to a decision of the Central Secretariat of RDP gave him the opportunity. The camp was attended by over a hundred prominent members of the party drawn from various provinces. Some others interested in the ideas and programme of the party also attended it by special invitation. The discussions took place on the basis of an agenda previously drawn up and circulated through the party machinery. Roy inaugurated as well as concluded the camp. He also wound up discussions on some topics.

The speeches that he delivered are collected together in New Orientation, a book published by Renaissance Publishers towards the end of 1946. It carries a Preface by Roy and a Foreword by Philip Spratt. The camp played big role in the development ',of Radicalism as the first camp held in Dehra Dun in 1940. It had far-reaching consequences. It paved the way for the dissolution of RDP in December 1948. The ideas that Roy placed before the camp were forming in his mind "already for a long time." He stated : "I did not make a secret of them; they were hinted at, if not clearly stated in my writings. You could not help noticing the importance I have been attaching to the-need of a Renaissance movement to deal with cultural questions and philosophical problems. If I had absolutely no doubt about Marxism, why should I talk about a new philosophical movement'? I felt the necessity of further thought on certain philosophical problems which some may believe to have been solved once and for all by Marxism. I did not take that view." He felt the necessity of discussing those ideas because he found that several Radicals were suffering from, what he called "two psychoses", the major nationalist psychosis and the minor communist psychosis. Several Radicals felt that they were either revolutionary nationalists or camouflaged communists. He had in the first place to clear that confusion. Radicals, Roy pointed out, were neither nationalists nor communists. He said: "We have chosen anew name because we are not satisfied with the philosophies underlying the theory and practice of other political parties. A group of people inspired by certain philosophical principles, by a certain view of life, logically has a distinctive approach to all problems of life, including politics, trade unionism, propaganda, agitation and every thing else. Radicalism is not revolutionary Nationalism, nor is it slightly heretical communism. It is a distinctive philosophy," he then described as follows the features of the party and its philosophy : "Our party is not a political machine which holds that the end justifies any means. Its philosophy is not Jesuistic. Our political philosophy makes room for the individual, and moral value. Its basic principle is that man is the measure of all things. We judge the merit of any social order by the freedom it gives to its individual, members. That is our 'new philosophy', which has enabled us to discover the new way of revolution.

As a matter of fact, it is a very old philosophy. All prophets of human freedom, in all ages, were inspired by this philosophy, which places man in the centre of the world. 'Revolutionary' philosophies which hold that freedom is conditional upon individuals sacrificing themselves on the altar of a collective ego, be that the State or the Nation or a Class, have debased politics, and thrown the world in the present crisis. We want to revive the old philosophy of freedom to purify politics, so to say, and contribute to the solution of the crisis." Having cleared the ground in this manner, Roy proceeded to an examination of the national and international situation which led him to the conclusion that, having become a national State, Russia was indulging in power politics and that, therefore, "revolution can no longer take place under the banner of communism and that Marxism as vulgarised by its orthodox exponents can no longer give us a strong enough inspiration." Explaining further why communism had ceased to be an ideal and could not help the march towards freedom, Roy stated : "Both Communism and Fascism stand for collectivism. The Communist collective ego is the proletariat class; and the Fascist collective ego is the nation. Both sacrifice the individual on the altar of the collective egg, It makes no difference whether it is the class or the nation. That being the case, when Communists establish a National State and become the prophets of patriotism, their collective ego can hardly be distinguished from that of the Fascists. In either case, it is totalitarian.. So, the dividing line between Fascism and a decadent Communism is very thin." Another fatal defect of communism that Roy pointed out was its disregard of the individual. He said : "Communism does not recognise the individual; is very existence is ruled out as an abstraction. The theory is that the Individual exists only as a part of the collectivity. With this theory, Communism breaks away from its philosophical anchorage." Commenting on it, Roy said : It does not result from the fundamental philosophical principle of Marxism, namely, 'being determined consciousness.' Collective is conditional upon man's consciousness of the existence of others, and his consciousness is the result of his being. Social Organisation presupposes the existence of individuals. Collective attempt is the means to the end of man's self expression, which is another name for freedom. Man must be there before he can co-operate or collectivise with others. Marx was more explicit than the above philosophical formula; he actually declared : 'Man Is the root of things'. This liberating doctrine was formulated by Protagotas two and a half millenniums ago, and has been the basic impetus for all social and cultural progress over since." Roy asserted further that not socialism or communism but freedom should be the ideal of a civilized human being and that freedom could be experienced only by an individual. He attached supreme importance to the individual and asserted that a society which gave the greatest measure of freedom to the individual was the freest society, That became the basis of the philosophy of Radical Humanism as it evolved in the ensuing years. Pointing out its essential difference from the philosophy and practice of communism, Roy said : "We place man in the centre of our scheme of things; others would sacrifice him on the altar of the collective ego." Some significant statements Were made at the camp about the role of ideas and-the evolution of Marxism. Both topics became important in the further elaboration of Radical Humanism. On the role of ideas, Roy said : "Materialist philosophy does not exclude ideas, and the potentiality of ideas. As a matter of fact, ideas are the urge for all human activity, and all human progress. Materialism traces the origin of ideas to the physical being of man. They are not revealed; nor do they exist independently of our physical existence. But Materialism does not say that ideas have no more than a subsidiary place in the history of human progress. On the contrary, every great social or political movement was heralded by new ideas, which operated as the motive force of the movement. When these ideas exhaust all their possibilities and can no longer move men to great and heroic actions, the period of social and political development heralded by them comes to an end, and humanity begins to look out for newer ideas, new inspiration, new ideals, new faith, in order to begin a new surge ahead. The over-emphasis laid on the class character of ideas, the mechanical term 'super structure' compelled Marxists to overlook the very fundamental principle of philosophy. Consequently, Marxism ceased to be a philosophy and became only a mere political practice; and political practice or a theory of political action or social revolution without a philosophical basis is bound to degenerate into pragmatism." At one place Roy stated : "I do not regard Marxism as a methodology. You must have noticed that I have always insisted on the view that Marxism is a philosophy, something more than a system of economics, or apolitical theory, or again a technique of revolution, as it is called by some. Indeed, it is more than all that taken together. Primarily, it is a system of pure thought, a philosophy. The intolerant orthodox may condemn this view as idealism; it may be, and idealism may not be such a bad thing, after all. I do not stick to Marxian-methodology. I am concerned with its essential philosophical features, and these again ate to be seen in their historical setting. As a philosophy, Marxism is the outcome of the development of thought from the dawn of history; therefore, it is the heritage of humanity; it is the ideological equipment belonging to everybody fighting for a better world. Anything in Marxism that cannot be reconciled with that appreciation of it, I reject." At another place he said : "the discoveries of modern physics have rendered nineteenth century Materialism completely untenable; yet, the Marxist pandits even today fight philosophical criticism based, on twentieth century physics by quoting scriptures from Engles Anti-Duhring, written nearly a hundred years ago. Anyhow once you accept that it is permissible to adjust Marxian theory to human experience made since the days of Karl Marx, then you will come to realise that everything I have said can be fitted into the scheme of Marxism as a philosophy. If that cannot be done, then we shall have to place all the works of Marx in the dusty archives, attaching to them nothing more than historical value for today or for the future." In the course of discussions several other aspects were considered and doubts were expressed about Marxist theories of dictatorship of the proletariat and the withering away of the State. Roy's advice was not to accept Marxism as a dogma but to criticise and evaluate it in the light of new experiences and advances of knowledge. Criticism, he pointed out, did not mean rejection. Some political problems were also discussed. The most important amongst them was the new way of revolution. Roy called it revolution by consent or by persuasion. The old way of revolution through insurrection was closed, he asserted, owing to the tremendous military power of modern States. But a revolution was a necessity and it was, therefore, essential to think of a new way to bring it about. The revolution was required not only by the working class but by other classes as well, including the middle class. The revolution which is on the order of the day a philosophy which will not be a class philosophy but one which will appeal to all civilised human beings. Roy said : "We shall have to go ahead. But to go ahead, we must have a new ideological equipment, a new philosophical vision, a new faith, so to say. In my opinion, this camp will serve no purpose unless it will give not only to the Radical Democratic Party, not only to India, but to the tormented world, a new faith for civilized humanity. This is what humanity needs today." It must be recorded that the camp did serve a useful purpose in the sense that it laid the foundation for a new philosophical vision which in course of time blossomed into the philosophy of Radical Humanism. Initially, Roy was sceptical of the reactions of Radicals to the unorthodox views that he was going to place before them. He was especially sceptical about how they would receive his exposition of philosophical problems. One day he apologised to campers for discussing "questions which do not appear to have any direct bearing on politics" and suggested to them that they could regard his views on philosophical problems as "purely my personal views." Later, however. He showed the intimate connection that existed between practical politics and philosophical views. The same day he talked of his "desire to transfer power". Clarifying his meaning-he said : "It so happens that I had something to do with the foundation of the party, and did something for the development of its political theories. But of late, I have been losing taste for politics. I do not find enough satisfaction in political activities. But do not run away with the idea that it is frustration or defeatism. Nothing of the kind. I still believe that, if anything is going to happen in India, that will be the result or the political practice we advocate, and I further believe that, if there is going to be a new world as we all visualise, and it will be a new world of freedom, Radical politics will have an application even beyond the frontiers of India. Yet, I am not quite satisfied any longer with political activities. I can now do other work according to my inclination, because I am convinced that the Radical Democratic Party has come of age. It can stand on its own legs and go ahead." This desire to quit politics found expression in those days on many occasions. However, Roy was agreeably surprised at the end of the camp that, as a result of the discussions which took place in regular sessions as well as outside, and as a consequence of his psychoanalytical treatment of the two psychoses, a large majority of the campers accepted not only his political analysis but also his philosophical views. They also accepted the necessity of developing a new philosophy as the guiding light of their scientific, rational and moral politics. The camp displayed the Radicals a new way and gave them a new outlook. It also brought them much nearer to Roy as their friend, philosopher and guide. They felt so indebted to him and so enthusiastic about his mission that towards the end of the camp they decided to raise a fund to purchase 13 Mohini Road, the place where Roy and Ellen were staying.

Over Rs. 25,000 were collected in the next few months and given to the newly established Indian Renaissance Institute for purchasing the house for the permanent residence of its Founder-Director, Roy. Roy liked the place and stayed there until his death. A few days after the camp the Central Political Council of the party unanimously adopted a statement on the current situation based on Roy's formulations and philosophical outlook. It was greatly entitled : "A New Orientation". In the course of his speeches at the camp Roy made some autobiographical references which will be of interest as they throw a good deal of light on his thinking and his general approach. Chronologically, the first reference is to his days of militant nationalism and how even in those days he and his colleagues were inspired by the ideal of freedom. It deserves to be quoted in full. It says : "If the Russians could have their revolutionary way, I might not be here today. No, they did not want to kill me in a straight-forward manner by putting a bullet through my bead. They simply dropped me when I was seriously ill. That was the price Stalin paid to secure the control of the Communist International. And you might not believe me when I say that I thought he was right in doing so. The point is that gross injustice done to me personally did not influence my objective judgement.

On my return to this country, you know, I was sentenced to 12 years transportation. Shortly after my conviction, a high Police officer, who was in charge of the Meerut Communist case, visited me in Bareilly Jail. Beating about the bush for a while, he came to the object of the visit. He thought that I must be bitter against the Russians, and wanted to exploit my feeling. The central theme of the conversation, 'the Russians have treated you very shabbily.' After two hours' talk, he said in exasperation 'You are hopeless; you are a bit of a philosopher; how can you still stand by those people after the way they have treated you ?' I told him that I did not stand by anybody; I stood by my ideal, Before leaving, he said : 'Whatever happens, there is no future for Communism in this country.' I asked, why? he said : 'I have been dealing with your disciples for a long time; I know each of them inside out. If they had a fraction of your integrity, then Communism might have a chance in this country. I tell you there is none.' You can easily imagine the point of this story. If I allowed the sense of personal injury to get the better of my loyalty, I would have been rewarded like, Judas. But twelve years in prison could not terrify me to stoop so low. I could give several more instances to convince you that even the greatest personal injuries have never influenced me, and will never influence me." The last reference is to more recent times when the desire to leave politics was growing stronger in his mind and he was "something like a tormented soul." Referring to it, Roy said : "My whole political life, which is now nearly forty years old, has been nothing but a tormented soul's search for freedom. I am afraid I have not been able to impart that urge of mine to several with whom I came in contact. Because after all, when we are participating in politics, we shall have to deal with problems which cannot be always stated absolutely, and which cannot be always solved disregarding the context of the realities of our existence. As a matter of fact, I may tell you that I feel very uncomfortable in politics. I feel like a fish out of water. But having been drawn into this whirlpool since my early youth, I have not been able to get out of it. Perhaps the time is coming when I shall at last do so." The difficulty with Roy was that he hardly ever talked about himself. It was after a good deal of persuasion that he agreed to write his memoirs. The memoirs that he finally wrote cover a short period of his life and they tell only of political activities and the persons he met and the experiences he went through in connection with them. For most things his biographer has to rely on his books and speeches and try to catch glimpses of the man that on rare occasions emerged through them. The occasions were rare, indeed, as Roy was always putting forward or demolishing a thesis with facts and figures and logical arguments and examples from life and history. He had hardly any time to talk or write about himself, his personal life, its trials and tribulations or joys and sorrows. The camp, though it ended in a near-unanimous acceptance of Roy's point of view, was a disturbing experience for most Radicals who attended it. They had to purge themselves of several cherished notions; they had to accept a perspective which promised no glamour or early result, but a long, patient struggle for public enlightenment. Several of them had regarded themselves as Marxists; they were shaken by Roy's criticism of Marxism. It was apprehended that fragmentary reports of the discussions at the camp might confuse the rank and file of the party. It was therefore decided to organise provincial, regional and local study camps and membership meetings to give members a correct report and to publish in book form the proceedings of the camp. Senior members who were present at the camp were expected to attend the camps and meetings. To aid discussions at those gatherings, Roy addressed a letter to the study camps explaining the background and purport of the discussions. The letter is quoted in full in the Preface to New Orientation. It started by pointing out that "the ideas elaborated in the Dehra Dun camp constitute the philosophical background of our political theory and practice, and are indeed implied in the very organisation of our party." It stated further : "Our approach to the problems of political theory and practice is claimed to be free from any dogmatic presupposition. Otherwise, we could not pretend to be advocates of scientific politics. Freedom from dogma is the specific feature of scientific thought. We also proclaim that our thinking and action know no authority. Is that only rhetorics? Do we realise the seriousness of the declaration that our political theory and practice are determined by principles free from dogmas and not restricted by any appeal to authority? If we did, then we should not believe that we are unconditionally or irrevocably committed to any system of philosophical, social, political or economic thought. Any closed system of thought which, by its nature, precludes further development, including far-reaching revision in the light of new knowledge, is a bunch of dogmas. Those who regard Marxism as such a closed system of thought, cannot also pretend to subscribe to the iconoclastic principles of Radicalism, which knows no dogma and respects no authority "It will not be proper to judge my ideas by the standard of orthodox Marxism. You shall have to judge them on their own merit. If they have no intrinsic merit, you should reject them irrespective of their conformity with, or deviation from, Marxism. One could put absurd or highly harmful ideas on the strength of quotations from Marx, Lenin or Stalin. "It might be helpful for the discussion if I pointed out the fallacy of a fear which must be haunting some of you, and preventing you from judging dispassionately. The fear lurks behind the question : 'Are we not deviating from Marxism." This question is troubling the conscience of all the comrades who appear to be disturbed by my ideas. The implication of the fear is nothing short of Suggesting liquidation of our party. Adherents of orthodox Marxism must belong to the Communist Party.

The organisation of the Radical Democratic Party, therefore, represented a deviation from orthodox Marxism. It cannot be justified by quoting scriptures. Don't run away with the flattering notion that the Communist Party made mistakes, and we are better Communists. The fact is that Communist political practice in the Soviet Union as well as in other countries, logically follows from Marxism conceived as a dogma and an immutable scriptural authority." Continuing it asserted : "Radicalism is not a deviation from Marxism; much less a negation. But it does propose revision of Marxism. And precisely therefore it represents the scientific essence of Marxism, which is, that there is no absolute truth nor perfect knowledge. To insist that the deductions made from an analysis of the conditions of a century ago, hold good even today and will hold good for ever, is deviation from Marxism. Contrarily, Marxism is defended by those who realise that it should be revised the light of changed conditions, and have the competence to do so. Radicalism proposes to rescue Marxism from degeneration into orthodoxy." Roy made it clear, however, that those were his personal views and the party was free to accept or reject them. Rejection, he pointed out, would amount to the decision to liquidate the party. But the party was free to take that decision. In conclusion he stated : "Arid don't demand that I Should join you. The Radical Democratic Party is your party, if you are of the opinion that it has no fundamental reason to exist, and that opinion will follow logically from the rejection of the philosophical principles of Radicalism, you are entitled to liquidate it. But I am not your creation. You should not demand of me to think as you do. I shall continue my quest for freedom, wishing you luck in your new adventure." Getting away from Marxism and moving towards Radical Humanism Was not easy. It was difficult for Roy because he had grown with it and accepted it as the philosophy of his life for over, two decades. The brilliant intellect that he' possessed and his indomitable search for truth enabled him to effect that break. But it was much more difficult for his co-workers and followers. Several of them had accepted Marxism as a new faith, a faith that released them from bondage to Manu or Gandhi. It is always difficult to break- the bonds of a faith. Six months after the camp RDP held its third conference in Bombay in the last week of December 1946. In that period intensive discussions had taken place in the party and the large majority of members had expressed their adherence to the new outlook and the new philosophy. In the meanwhile basic principles of the philosophy were formulated as Twenty-two Theses. They were discussed in the conference and were adopted unanimously.

The party was thus firmly set on the road to Radical Humanism. The organisational structure of the party as well as the nomenclature RDP were not given up. It took two more years to realise the basic contradiction between the existence of the part), and the principles of the philosophy. The first step was, however, taken with the adoption of the Twenty-two Theses. Philip Spratt presided over the conference and Roy inaugurated it. The first English edition of Roy's book on China, Revolution and Counterrevolution in China was published in the middle of 1946. The book, written several years earlier, Roy added a few pages at the end to cover the developments after the end of the war. They seen in the book as Epilogue. The united national front had by that time broker down and a civil war had begun between communists and nationalists with Russia backing the former and America supporting the latter.

Roy was never happy with the united national front and was not impressed by press propaganda about Chiang Kai-shek. To him, to lionise Chiang Kai-shek as one of the top leaders of the international anti-fascist alliance was "the greatest absurdity of the contemporary history." He welcomed the change in the attitude of the press. He was happy that communists had dropped their "neo-nationalism" and begun their fight for democracy. "The civil war in China" Roy said, "has not been and will not be a struggle between Communism and Nationalism. It is a tussel between Nationalism and Democracy; between reaction and progress; between vested interests land the urge for social reconstruction required for promoting the welfare of the people as a whole." Communists, he said, were fighting for "democratic freedom" and that they were "Communists only in name." He went to the extent of writing : "It (CP of China) no longer pursues the object of setting up a proletarian dictatorship to establish Socialism. It strikes for democratic freedom, to be reared upon economic democracy. Consequently, for all practical purposes, in form as well as content, the Communist Party of China has become a party of the people Radical Democratic Party."

Roy made those statements on the basis of eye-witness reports published then by several Western correspondents. The reports were based on incomplete information or wishful thinking. As subsequent developments proved, Mao and his colleagues were not agrarian reformers as believed at that time, but were hundred per cent communists out to establish not democratic freedom but communist dictatorship. Roy's statements, based on those reports, did not, therefore prove true. Roy's book was welcomed by several scholars and critics. What the London Times Literary Supplement stated in its review of the book is noteworthy. It stated inter alia : "Much of what he has to say is therefore first hand evidence. But whether autobiographical or not his narrative maintains a high standard of factual impartiality. He' does not conceal his views, indeed, he argues them at some length. But the historian is never lost in the propagandist." That, indeed, is a big compliment from that august source. The process of the transfer of power from British to Indian-hands quickened in the latter half of 1946. An Interim Government was formed first with the participation of Congress and then with the joint participation of Congress and League. Joint work in the Government did not bring the two organisations nearer. As a matter of fact the breach between the two widened as the withdrawal of British power became imminent.

Communal tension developed in several parts and the League demand for Pakistan became irresistible. In the end

Congress accepted the demand and the British terminated their rule on August 15, 1947 after dividing the country into India and Pakistan. Roy did not like the division of the country, but he did not want to impose unity on the provinces which desired to separate. He was keen, however, that, whether united or separate, all provinces must have a uniformly democratic constitution. The Draft Constitution that he prepared provided for it. In March 1947 Nehru organised in New Delhi the Asian Relations Conference. He was then the leader of the Interim Government and was able in that capacity to mobilise for the conference wide official as well as non-official help. The conference attracted delegates from several Asian countries and became an impressive gathering of leaders of "resurgent Asia". Roy was not enthusiastic about it. In a manifesto addressed to the delegates he pointed Out that there was no cultural, racial or ethnic unity amongst Asian nations and to bring them together only on the basis of hatred of Europeans would not serve any progressive purpose. He invited their attention to the role played by Japan in the name of the Asiatic co-prosperity sphere and warned them of the feasibility of India trying to play a similar role.. He told them : "Modern civilization is the common human heritage. The Asiatic peoples belong to the great human family. They Must take their share of the common heritage as the asset for greater enterprise for conquering a brighter future and building up a higher civilization. It is an error of judgement to confound modernism with the aggression of Western Powers." He told them further : "Resurgent Asia need not imitate the political institutions and economic practices of the passing capitalist social order. Parliamentary Democracy is antiquated. No further economic progress is possible under the restrictions of capitalism, while technology renders that possibility unlimited. On the other hand, the call of Communism is losing its appeal. In the Asiatic countries, Communism has been corrupted by racial Nationalism. It is equated with the most extreme brand of Nationalism." He advised them to go beyond nationalism. "Humanism", he urged, "must replace Nationalism if Asiatic resurgence is ever to be a reality."

RDP also issued a similar manifesto. It is doubtful, however, if in the pomp and flourish that accompanied the conference any delegate paid attention to the two document. Roy had during the days of the conference long talks with an old acquaintance, Sultan Shariar, the leader of the Indonesian delegation, one amongst a few progressives who had risen to high position, in their respective countries. Shariar remained in that position only for a short while... The politics of the country shaped during the period as Roy had predicted. Years back he had propounded what came to be known as the decolonisation theory, that a time would come when Great Britain would have no capital to export and would be required to secure the help of Indian capital to develop the resources of the country in return for which she would have to give economic as well as political concessions to the owners of that capital. That process which started in the days of the first world war was now culminating in the grant of independence, which amounted to transfer of power to Indian upper classes. He reminded Radicals gathered together in the study camp in May 1946 of that prophecy made by him. He said : "Britain having ceased to export capital already more than twenty years ago, I came to the conclusion that the process could not be arrested. From that analysis, I came to the conclusion that the colonial economy of India, based on British capital would necessarily change its character, and a process of decolonisation would take place. And as a corollary to that, I wrote that decolonisation in the economic field must have a political repercussion; eventually British Imperialism would find itself faced with the necessity of transferring power to the Indian bourgeoisie... An eventual compromise between decayed Imperialism and bourgeois nationalism was a foregone conclusion. Is that not happening today?" Roy was at pains to point out to the people that the independence that was coming would not bring them freedom, but would establish a rule of the upper classes. That was then the constant theme of his speeches and writings. In a letter addressed to fighters for freedom he wrote : "The coveted goal of national independence is practically attained. The formality of transfer of power will be completed within another year." The British Prime Minister had then set June 1948 as the time for British withdrawal. It was later brought forward by about a year owing to the deteriorating conditions in the country.

Commenting on the plan evolved by the new Viceroy, Lord Mountbatten, Roy wrote : "Only power is being transferred not to the Indian people, but to a privileged minority. India is launched on the road not to democratic freedom, but fascist dictatorship. None in Britain may today be in the mood to see the dangerous implication of an apparently liberal policy determined by conventionalism, wrong reading of history and false expectations. But before long eyes will be opened and democratic Britain will have to hang her head in shame for having refused to do the right thing in India even when she was repeatedly advised to do so." Roy was not the only person to detect this trend towards fascism. Early in 1946, Sampurnanad, a socialist Congressman who later became the Chief Minister of Uttar Pradesh, wrote : "Fascism is an ugly word but it must clearly be recognised that, forces not dissimilar to fascism, are raising their head amongst us and gaining ground every day." Nehru also spoke about the danger from time to time. Early in 1947 some Congress Socialists, like Jayaprakash Narayan, thought of a new revolutionary mass struggle to halt the compromise with British imperialism and secure freedom for the people. Roy described the thought as romanticism. He advised Radicals to hold people's conventions to popularise the Draft

Constitution and the People's Plan. In a speech in Delhi in February 1947 he said : "The perspective for our politics was never better than today... India of 1947 is not the India of 1942. The National Government is in power. It is unable to solve people's problems. More and more people are getting disillusioned of nationalism. Imperialism is visibly disappearing.' The country is eager to listen to us." That reading of the situation did not prove correct. The people had not yet become disillusioned "of nationalism. They welcomed the advent of independence as the dawn of freedom.' They went delirious with joy when on the midnight of August 14 the Union Jack was hauled down and was replaced by the tri-coloured flag of Independent India. The joy was soured a couple of weeks later by the communal riots which followed the partition of the country. But they did not feel at that time that Independence was only a change of masters; nor did Roy's apprehension that the upper classes who had been entrusted with power would establish a fascist dictatorship come true. Roy's reaction to Independence was predictably different. It is expressed in editorial of August 10. It said inter alia "Independent India is in for a one-party government which is another name for dictatorship The goal of the Congress was attainment of national independence. The goal having been attained, the Congress should liquidate itself... The Congress was a totalitarian organisation, it claimed to represent the entire nation, which included all the children of Mother India-rich and poor, landlords and peasants, employers and employees, so on and so forth. If it continues to exist even after its goal is attained there will be no room for any other party in the National State The totalitarian claim advanced theoretically will be now enforced in practice.

With that objective, political power has been captured with the aid and connivance of obliging Imperialism. To place a totalitarian party of the upper classes in power was the policy of effete Imperialism. A wrong notion of democracy and conventional. Constitutionalism persuaded the British Labour Government to take over that undemocratic policy. Resultantly, India has become nationally independent with a totalitarian State, which spells the end of freedom... On August the vocal section of the Indian people, drugged and duped into a delirium, will ceremoniously enthrone the Leviathan. The exacting deity will demand more and more sacrifice. Ultimately, he will thirst for blood. The Leviathan is the God of War." A few days after Independence RDP issued a manifesto entitled "Forward to Freedom". It was addressed to the people of India as-well as of Pakistan. It was drafted by Roy. The main point of the manifesto was : "The 15th of August opens a new period of struggle. One obstacle on the way towards freedom is removed. Other obstacles remain and they will not disappear voluntarily.. They can be removed only through conscious purposeful activity." Attainment of Independence had solved one problem, the minor problem, of Indian revolution, which was to be both a national and a social revolution. The foreign power was removed which meant that the national revolution was completed. Its removal took place much more easily than visualised earlier owing to the conditions created by war.

The same conditions, Roy had accepted, would enable India to make significant efforts in the direction of social revolution. He made strenuous efforts towards that end during the years of the war. They did not succeed owing to the narrow nationalist outlook of Congress and other political parties. They were in a sense an effort to bring about a revolution from the top. As an outcome of their failure, India entered the new era with all her social and economic problems unresolved and with a system of government in which power became more and more concentrated. All the tasks of social revolution remained unaccomplished. Roy directed his attention to them. He looked at them now with the new insight that he had gained through the philosophy of Radical Humanism. In the year that elapsed since the camp in Dehra Dun he had elaborated the fundamental principles of the philosophy in the form of a manifesto. The manifesto was considered by Central Political Council of the Party at its meeting held in Dehra Dun in May 1947. It was adopted with a few modifications and it was decided to popularise it as Humanist Manifesto.

It was published a couple of months later tinder the title New Humanism. It reminds one of the Communist Manifesto propounded by Marx a little less than a century earlier. It makes a powerful appeal to reason as well as sentiment and displayed a new way to revolution appropriate to the conditions obtaining after the end of the second world war. It had a great effect on all Radicals and on the thinking of several others. A second edition was published in 1953. Last three paragraphs were amended as RDP had by then converted itself into a humanist movement. In his Preface to the second edition Roy pointed out that New Humanism, though presented in the manifesto "as a political philosophy", would be "a logical integration of knowledge about the various aspects of existence, showing how it is in the nature of man to be rational and moral, and therefore capable of building a free, harmonious and just social order." It is not feasible to give a summary of the manifesto. But a short description may be useful. It consists of seven chapters. The first three chapters deal with developments in the ideological field since the Communist Manifesto. They end with the statement : "We must look beyond the deceptive ideal of Communism, if the threatened catastrophe is to be avoided. We must have faith in human ingenuity and the creativeness of the human mind, Which are-far from being exhausted. Revolting against the fatalism of the prophetic theoretical system of Karl Marx, the heralds of a new order of social justice must concern themselves with social technology and social engineering, such as would reconcile freedom with planning, autonomy of the individual with the promotion of collective welfare and progress." The next chapter traces the liberal genealogy of Marxism. From the Marxian theory of revolution he arrives at the following conclusion : "The dogma of an uncompromising class struggle, and the false expectation of a polarisation of society into two classes, moved exclusively by economic incentives, led Marx and Lenin, particularly the latter, to visualise revolution taking place through an insurrection engineered by the so-called vanguard of the proletariat, to be followed by its dictatorship over the people. This theory not only defeats its objective, as proved by the Russian experience, by creating a new system of political domination, cultural regimentation and economic enslavement; but the uniform failure of Communists all over the world, after their accidental success in Russia, proves its utter inadequacy even as a technique for the capture of power. Scientific inventions since the days of Marx have vastly increased the military might and coercive strength of the existing States, and have rendered the idea of a minority-insurrection impracticable and but of date." There is the need for a new philosophy and the concluding chapter describes how Radical Democracy could be attained through "the collective efforts of spiritually free men and women united with the determination of creating a new order of freedom." Roy was engaged in developing those collective efforts of spiritually free men and women. Roy had by this time pursued vigorously his studies of natural sciences and philosophical developments. They enabled him to trace the growth of consciousness and reason in man to the laws of nature and to establish the relationship between man and society. These became in course of time the basic premises of Radical Humanism. Roy had pursued these studies since long, especially during the long years of his imprisonment. He wrote widely in the notebooks that were provided to him on philosophical results of modern science. Written in jail under very difficult conditions, when reference books were not available, the manuscript was defective and needed a good deal of editing and a certain amount of rewriting. Roy was not able to complete that work during his life-time. But some chapters were completed and they were published in the latter part of 1947 under the title Science and Philosophy. In his Preface to the publication Roy wrote : "The practical application of scientific knowledge has undoubtedly done a good deal of harm. Apart from the poison gas and atom bomb technology has not been an unmixed blessing, Therefore we hear so much lamentation about the Frankenstein create science. This regrettable situation has been brought about by an one-sided appreciation of scientific knowledge. Science not only enables man to conquer nature, but also helps him to understand nature his relation with it and with other human beings who arc integral parts of nature. In other words, scientific knowledge has a philosophical implication. As a matter of fact, science and philosophy have been interwoven from the very dawn of civilisation. Modern technological trends threaten to offer mankind at the altar of the Moloch, and create a Frankenstein lusting to devour its creator, because the practical, utilitarian value of scientific knowledge has been allowed to eclipse its ideal value, its contribution to pure thought, which alone enables man to behave rationally as well as morally, which also provides the standard for judging right and wrong, truth and error, good and evil. The following list of chapter headings will give an idea of the vast canvass that Roy covered : "Introduction; Reality and Appearance; Science and Philosophy; New Physics; Space and Time, Substance and Causality; The problem of Beginning and End; The Mystery of Life; Neo-vitalism, Materialism and A Scientific Theory of Knowledge." The ideas contained in the book became the foundation of the scientific part of the philosophy of Radical

Humanism. In 1947 and 1948 Roy's main task was to elaborate and expound the philosophy of Radical Humanism. He spoke on the subject at several places. Some of his more important speeches are comprised in a posthumous publication Politics, Power and Parties. Renaissance Publishers published it in 1960. Ellen Roy edited it. A few extracts from the speeches will be useful for understanding the basic principles of the philosophy that Roy had developed.

In a lecture delivered at the summer school of higher Studies held in Dehra Dun in 1948 he traced as follows the evolution of his ideas : "These are not abstract intellectual problems; I came to think about them as problems of my own active political life. I began, like so many, as a believing man, believing in something supernatural, superhuman, but at the same time felt that the old religious idea would not do, and that we must rationalise religion, conceive God scientifically. The experience of the nationalist movement made me doubtful about its possibilities, its methods as well as its "spiritual" ideology. Marxism appeared to indicate a more realistic and effective approach to the problems which had puzzled, the nationalist. The acceptance of Marxism as a philosophy of life implied breaking away from the old moorings of a rationalised religion. But I have never been an orthodox Marxist. My attitude to Marxism was critical from the very beginning. That experience again, the effort to solve the problems of life with the help of Marxism, brought me to the conclusion that Communism also was not a cure-all. I came to the conclusion that until the intellectual, cultural, spiritual atmosphere of the country was changed, it was not feasible to bring about a political and economic reconstruction of the country, such as would promote popular welfare, establish democratic freedom and social justice.' Roy accepted freedom as "the supreme value from which all human values are derived". He defined his concept of freedom as follows : "The function of life is to live.

The basic incentive of organic becoming is the struggle for survival. It goes on throughout the long process of biological evolution, until in man it becomes the conscious urge for freedom-the supreme human value. The beginning of man's endless struggle for freedom lies in the animal struggle for survival. Everything that man has done, everyone of his acts, cultural progress, scientific achievements, artistic creations-everything has been motivated by that one urge. Man is finite while the Universe is infinite, and his environment, in the last analysis, is the whole Universe. Consequently, his struggle for freedom is eternal; he can never conquer the Universe. Therefore, the urge for freedom is the only eternal thing in the human world. This urge enables man to acquire knowledge; he conquers his environment by knowing." A few months earlier, in a speech in Calcutta he had raised the following questions : What is the object of human existence? Raising the standard of living ? Reorganisation of Society? Replacement of Capitalism by a higher mode of production? Planned economy in the place of chaotic competitive free enterprise?" His answer was that they had "their merits," but they were not "our end," the real end of human endeavour being freedom, His contention was that "the social struggle for human progress, the entire process of social evolution is nothing but the continuation of the struggle for existence on a higher level, where that struggle is no longer guided by instinct and natural selection, but by intelligence, choice and reasoning." Radical Humanism, Roy stated, had taken over the tradition of the founders of modern civilisation, the tradition of "the revolt of man against the tyranny of God and his agents on this earth." Regarding Marxism, he stated : "Radical Humanism incorporates the positive contents of Marxism freed from the fallacies of its theory of revolution, from its postulation of dictatorship and from its greatest and basic fallacy of dismissing the freedom of the individual as a meaningless abstraction. Roy viewed Radical Humanism as a philosophy which covers the whole field of human existence from abstract thought to social and political reconstruction." The other two speeches included in the volume, one of January 1947 and the other of May 1947, are more political. The latter delivered at the study camp at Dehra Dun discussed organised democracy and politics without power. On the latter issue Roy said :" I say that politics, without the ambition of power is feasible. Otherwise, politics can never be rational and moral, will always remain a pursuit without scruple, without principle, without honesty, everyone trying to cut the other's throat. Having been active in politics all my life, I shall not play the dirty game. But I believe that an alternative practice is feasible.

The former was an appeal to young men of Calcutta to think for themselves and develop a standard to judge if any progress towards freedom was being made. In pursuance of the Humanist Manifesto, Radicals developed in 1948 several political and social activities. For example, early in the year they developed in Bengal an agitation against the Bengal Security Bill which put several restrictions on civil liberties. The Constituent Assembly was then drafting the Constitution. Radicals demanded that, when framed, it should be submitted to people's verdict. IFL unions were active in protecting workers' immediate interests as well as their general interests as citizens. IFL held its third conference in Bombay on December 31, 1947 and January 1, 1948. In the period Radicals established at several places Radical Students' Unions to acquaint students with their role in the society. Renaissance clubs and societies were established at various centres and prominent Radicals spoke under their auspices on important aspects of the Renaissance Movement.

Roy spoke at various places on Renaissance and wrote two articles, one on June 6 and the other on June 13, 1948. There was a summer school in Dehra Dun from May 24 to 31.

Earlier in February there was an Eastern regional camp at Uttarpara in Hoogly district which Roy attended. On that occasion Roy paid a visit to Dacca, which resulted in bringing together Radicals spread in different parts of East Bengal. Political issues-also claimed their attention. For example, they expressed clear, but unorthodox, views on Kashmir and Hyderabad. They also raised their voice against the growing danger of war. Roy issued a statement in April about Nehru's foreign policy welcoming neutrality, criticising arms build-up and declaring that there was absolutely no reason to take sides in the coming titanic struggle between U. S. A. and U. S. S. R. for world domination." Roy delivered several speeches in the period on topics like the international situation and the danger of war. There is, therefore, no substance in the criticism that, after the acceptance of Radical Humanism, Roy or Radicals became indifferent to current social or political problems and ceased working for their solution. A second edition of Scientific Politics, the report of the first camp held in Dehra Dun in 1940, was published in January 1948. That gave Roy an opportunity to explain the change in his thinking in the intervening seven years. In the Preface to the second edition he wrote : "I cannot unqualifiedly endorse everything said seven years ago... For me personally the intervening years have been a period not only of highly instructive experience but also of intellectual efforts stimulated by it... Seven years ago, I still spoke as an orthodox Marxist criticising deviations from or faulty understanding of the pure creed.

Nevertheless, the tendency to look beyond Communism was already there in a germinal form. While still speaking in terms of class struggle, I laid emphasis on the cohesive factor in social organisation. Already then I appreciated Marxism as something greater than the ideology of a class. I understood it as the positive outcome of earlier intellectual efforts to develop a philosophy which could harmonise the processes of physical nature, social evolution and will and emotions of individual man." Despite of what is stated in the preface, Roy was never an orthodox Marxist, even during the days of his association with C 1. Accepting it as a philosophy and method of study, he was all along trying to adjust it to new knowledge and new realities. Even in 1940, though he used Marxist terms he did not think or speak as an orthodox Marxist. He was all along a critical Marxist. A scholar writing several years later has expounded very well Roy's position on Marxism. The passage, though long deserves to be quoted. It states : "It is, however, worth mentioning her, that Roy was never, an orthodox and blind Marxist who considered the writings of Karl Marx as revelations of ultimate truth, as the last words of human wisdom. The acceptance of Marxism did not kill in him the spirit of iconoclasm. He retained fully the spirit of independent thinking even after the acceptance of Marxism and that enabled him to overcome its limitations and make some original contributions to the field of social philosophy. To Roy, Marxism was not a closed system of philosophy but a way of thinking. A study of the speeches which Roy delivered in the All-India Political Study Camp at Dehra Dun in May and June 1940 clearly displays that even when Roy was a Marxist his mind was free from Marxist dogmatism. In those speeches he too particular care to differentiate his Marxism from "a narrow mechanical conception of Marxism." He said : "Even Marxism, somehow or other, has been transformed into a sort of religion. It is conceived as a creed or held as a faith." Roy always tried to base his Marxism on reason and critical thinking. To Roy, the fundamental principle of Marxism as a philosophy was that being precedes consciousness. While explaining Marxism he always laid emphasis upon the principle that our being is not determined by consciousness, but our consciousness is determined by our being. He asked his comrades to base their thoughts upon their experience and not to talk of Marxism mechanically. Even in 1940, Roy was prepared to go beyond Marxism if experience so warranted. He said, "Our existence, our environment, our very being must determine our thought. From some books we have acquired a kind of understanding of Marxism. But we have our being in a peculiar set of circumstances. Our political consciousness and behaviour will be determined by these peculiar features of our social being. Necessarily, our thinking process, our ideology also must be very largely influenced thereby. And we shall be able to contribute to an amplification and enrichment or Marxism which is not a closed system of philosophy, not a bunch of dogmas. It is based on human experience, and therefore must adjust itself to new lessons acquired from experience... The result of our Marxist approach may be, and I am inclined to believe that it is bound to be, an amplification of Marxism. Don't be hidebound and believe that the whole truth has already been discovered, that the text should not be changed and that we can only interpret it. That is scholasticism. Marxism is something entirely different." He further said, "We must make our own experience. As the experience of a very large community of human beings, it is bound to be the basis of some contribution to human ideology, to the accumulated store of human knowledge. If that was not the real object of a revolution, personally, I would have no interest in it. It would not attract me, and I do not think that it would attract any civilized human being. If revolution is separated from that connotation, it becomes nothing bigger than rowdyism on a large scale.

We cannot go through all the dirt and squalor, suffering and sacrifice, unless there is something noble before us, unless our experience is going to make the light of human knowledge shine still brighter." These are certainly not the words of an orthodox Marxist but of a noble soul struggling for freedom and for truth. "Already in 1940, Roy found the necessity of revising or even discarding certain formulas which are considered by orthodox Marxists to be part and parcel, nay, the very essence, of Marxism, Even at the time Roy was against the dictatorship of the proletariat. Like the orthodox Marxist he did not think exclusively in terms of 'class.' "It is wrong and narrow conception of Marxism to regard it only as the philosophy of one particular class, as the ideology of one particular type of revolution... Marxism is the highest form human knowledge has attained so far. It is based on the accumulated store of human experience, gathered ever since the dawn of civilization. As such, it cannot be the property of any particular class. It is a human heritage." Again: "When that class creates a culture-art, literature, science, indeed anything of an abiding value, the creation naturally bears the stamp of the creator. But in so far as there is a relation of identity between that class and the entire society, the cultural values produced by it are the production of society as a whole. As such, it goes down in history as a heritage of humanity. Otherwise, there would be no culture, no philosophy, no knowledge." To the orthodox Marxists, the protagonists of the-theory of class struggle, there cannot be anything called 'human heritage', any culture with an abiding value' or any 'relation of identity' between a class and the entire society. Roy was also opposed to the concept of an inevitable process of social evolution preached by Marx. Thus, he was never a dogmatic Marxist; he always had an open mind which ultimately led him to formulate the philosophy of an open society." On January 30, 1948, a tragic event shook the country, the foul assassination. Of Mahatma Gandhi. It shook the world as well for no other Indian was as well-known and as highly respected. To India, the people as well as the Government, it was a shock which they found it extremely difficult to absorb. Roy, the constant critic of Gandhiji, was also shaken by it. He received the news in Calcutta when he was speaking at a meeting. After getting the news he could not continue his speech. He paid a hurried tribute and closed the meeting. The next issue of second could not be printed in Delhi because of disturbances. It published only one sheet carrying Roy's tribute. Thereafter it was lifted to Bombay.

The first issue from Bombay reprinted Roy's tribute under the title "The Message of the Martyr". It stated inter alia Leaders of aggrieved India have professed unswerving loyalty to the sacred memory of the martyred Mahatma and pledged themselves solemnly to be guided by his message. If the pledge is implemented, then death at the assassin's hand may still accomplish what a dedicated life could not. There is no doubt about the sincerity of sentiments felt in an atmosphere of poignant anguish and expressed spontaneously from the bottom of hearts moved by a dreadful experience. At the same time, it cannot be denied that, had nationalist India grasped the Mahatma's message and been guided by it without reservation, today she would not be mourning his death at the hands of an assassin. Therefore, having recovered from the initial impact of the stunning blow, the country should even now try to understand the meaning of the Mahatma's message, if his martyrdom is not to be in vain. "Even during his lifetime, the Mahatma was hailed as the Father of the Nation. Nationalist India's homage to his sacred memory will be to canonise him as such. He was the patron saint of nationalism, which triumphed during his lifetime. Yet he fell a victim to the very cult he preached. That is the implication of the terrible tragedy which stupefied the entire civilized world. But few seem to have learned the lesson. The patron saint of nationalism has been sacrificed at the ' altar of the geographical goddess of Akhand Hindustan, and all Indian nationalists, who today reaffirm undying loyalty to the Mahatma, also worship at the shrine of that goddess. Since that fanatical cult logically goes to the incredible extent of demanding the blood of its own patron saint, the Mahatma's message must have beep greater than a mere call for suffering and sacrifice for the country. Essentially, it is a moral, humanist, cosmopolitan appeal, although the Mahatma himself allowed it to be heavily coloured by the narrow cult of nationalism. The lesson of the martyrdom of the Mahatma is that the noblest core of his message could not be reconciled with the intolerant cult of nationalism, which he also preached. Unfortunately this contradiction in his ideas and ideals was not realised by the Mahatma himself until the last days of his life. During that period, he was a disillusioned soul, full of sorrow struggling bravely against the growing feeling of frustration with an apparently stout optimism based on the sand of an archaic faith." According to Roy, "the core of the Mahatma's message" was "that the end does not justify means", which he stated was not "compatible with power-politics." He regretted that "the Mahatma could not see the limitations of nationalism." In conclusion he stated : "He (the Mahatma) will be remembered for having vaguely visualised a humanist idea, while still groping in the twilight of medievalism. Mainly a religious man he set before his followers high ideals which could not feasibly be attained unless the human spirit broke out of the charmed circle of the religious mode of thought. Therefore, like all religious prophets of morality, peace and human brotherhood, die Mahatma was destined to fail in his mission." The tribute is symbolic of the change that had taken place in Roy's views about Gandhiji. He had started to appreciate and respect Gandhiji as a big moral force. The latter's one-man mission for communal harmony had touched Roy's heart as also his turning away from power, after the success of the nationalist movement that he led. This growing regard for Gandhiji is to be seen in the tributes that Roy paid to him in subsequent years.

Ten years earlier, that is, in 1938, Roy had written that he "appreciated Gandhiji's greatness better than any of his ardent admirers." But that was the appreciation of the role that Gandhiji had played in the national struggle. He regarded Gandhiji highly as the "political awakener" of the masses, as "the embodiment of the primitive, blind, spontaneous spirit of revolt of the Indian masses." It took him a few more years to appreciate the moral role that Gandhiji played in the country's public life. The appreciation developed with the development of the ideas of Radical Humanism. There was a close resemblance between some ideas of Gandhism and those of Radical Humanism. Both stressed morality and decentralisation. Both were opposed to the growing power of the State and desired to delimit its functions severely. Both attached supreme the individual and demanded the widest feasible scope for the development of his potentialities. Both abhorred power politics and stood for politics without power. There were, of course, some fundamental differences. Gandhiji did not elaborate a philosophy. His was a religious outlook based upon the dictates of his inner voice, while Radical Humanism is an integrated philosophy based upon science and reason. In later years there was co-operation on some issues between Radicals and Gandhists but the two could not move closer together owing to the basic difference in the outlook on the world. Developments that took place in 1948 in the national and in the international fields were distressing. In the national sphere, communal riots continued and there was growing tension between India and Pakistan, Nationalism was in the ascendant and there was a clamour for making the country strong militarily and industrially.

People's welfare was neglected and politicians quarrelled over loaves and fishes of power. In the international field the world became divided into two blocs and the danger of the third world war loomed large on the horizon. All these were, according to Roy, the signs of the spiritual crisis that had overtaken the 'world. Neither democracy not communism was in a position to show a way out nationally or internationally.

Roy continued his search for a new philosophy. By this time he had succeeded in laying down the philosophical foundation of Radical Humanism. He was able to explain, how growing out of law-governed universe man is engaged in quest-for-freedom and search For truth, how as a product of nature man is inherently rational, how morality develops out of rationality, how, in quest of freedom, man established society and State and various other institutions and how, if he is not to lose his significance, he must retain his supremacy over all his creations like society, State and all other institutions.

That brought Roy to a consideration of practical social, political and economic problems. He had already developed the idea of organised democracy. In the period following RDP conference of December 1946. It came to the conclusion that in organised democracy there was no place for a political party. The obvious inference was that RDP should be dissolved. Roy had reached that conclusion, but he did not put it brusquely before the party. Two summer camps were held, one in 1947 and the other in 1948, where the issue was quietly and dispassionately discussed. It was also discussed in numerous discussion meetings throughout the country. Those who had accepted the Twenty-two Theses and participated in the discussions that preceded them realised that the dissolution of the party was inherent in the Theses. Others also came round to the same view after some discussion. Steadily opinion in the party veered round to the view that there was no place for a political party in Radical Humanism. Opinion having thus crystalised, the fourth and the last conference of the party was held in Calcutta from December 26 to 29, 1948. The Sanskrit scholar, Laxmanshastri Jambi, presided over it. It was largely attended by delegates from different parts of the country. A thesis drafted by Roy entitled, "Practice of New Humanism" was placed before the conference opinion was already overwhelmingly in favour of the Ideas incorporated in the thesis. A few doubts which remained disappeared after the speeches of the President, Roy and others. The thesis was adopted and RDP decided to convert itself into Radical Humanist Movement. It died as a political party, but arose anew as a broad-based, socio-political, cultural movement. A chapter is appropriately entitled "From Party to Movement. "That was the essence of the decision that was taken by the conference. In the first part of the address Roy dealt with Humanism and explained how it developed out of "naturalist Humanism of the Renaissance, "Philosophical Radicalism and Liberalism of the nineteenth century and the thoughts of Feurbach and Marx. "It is", he said "the old doctrine of human sovereignty and dignity informed by modern sciences" In the latter part he dealt with the current political situation and showed why Radicals should get "out of the scramble for power." Congress cannot be kept out of power, he stated, "in the given atmosphere of blind faith,, religious morality and hero worship. "To displace Congress, opposition parties would have to do something worse "for deceiving the people to an even greater extent."

The situation could be changed, he stated, only by "changing the atmosphere, the outlook and mentality of the people." That could be done not by a political party but by a humanist movement devoted to the cause of the Renaissance which Radicals had decided to develop. Referring to that decision Roy said : "What we propose to do is the logical consequence of our thought developed over the last ten years, even when we were functioning as a political party. Even then we postulated a philosophical revolution as the precondition for any great social and political change. Having learned a lesson from the history of the world, we undertook to apply it to India. India has not yet undergone such a spiritual upsurge as was experienced in Europe at the dawn of the modern time. She is still clinging to old traditions. Unless she overthrows the ballast of a dead past hanging round her neck like a loadstone, India cannot march ahead towards democratic freedom, social progress and cultural reawakening. Unless we can alter the cultural outlook of the country, unless we can make people feel that they are human beings, that they are not puppets in the hands of a cruet Providence, that it is not their karma which made them what they are, today, but that they can alter their own fate-or no great change will ever be feasible." His concluding words at the conference were : "The Radical Humanist Movement will be based on individual initiative, individual endeavour and individual freedom. Such a movement cannot be tied by rules and regulations. Whoever agreed with us, we do not ask them to become members of any organisation; but we shall expect them to act according to their conviction. We are giving up a rigidly organised existence because we do not want to create a barrier around us, excluding anybody as outsiders. We do not want to monopolise the result of our efforts. Nor do we want any credit. But we are going to remain ourselves, travelling the path of knowledge and truth as we see it, as we have done in the past. If our ideas have any sense, if what we say is true, all lovers of truth and knowledge will join the caravan moving towards a future of freedom, harmony and happiness. Let us have faith in ourselves, if we want to remake the world. Let us behave like-free men-if we ever want to see a free world." It cannot be said that the decision was welcome to all. There were some dissentient voices. Several kept away from the conference. Some attended and expressed dissent, but did not press their view. Dissatisfaction with the decision continued for a long time amongst some sections of Radicals. But none of the dissentients came forward to run the old party or form a new party on their own. They wanted Roy to continue to lead the party which was not feasible for him in the light of the philosophy that he had developed. He was of the view moreover that even on practical grounds there was no scope in the country for a party pledged to follow rational politics. The preconditions for rational politics were, he asserted, yet to be created. He found it much more satisfying to engage himself in developing Radical Humanist thought and action. He was keen on liberating himself from party politics, and also others who had got involved in it at his instance or under his inspiration. The decision of the Calcutta conference liberated him as well as others. Having dissolved the political party, Roy now turned his attention to the development of the wider and more broad based humanist movement. The movement was to aim at not merely political and economic changes but at more fundamental social and cultural changes. Political and economic changes and agitation and propaganda for them were not excluded, but having percepted that they would not be feasible and abiding without social and cultural changes, more attention was paid to the latter than to the former. In a sense, that was not new to Roy. He had realised a long time back the necessity and urgency of the Renaissance Movement. He was the one political leader who in the midst or the national struggle had felt the need of a renaissance and had braved public criticism and opposition for championing it. Renaissance was to be now the major plank of his new movement.

Politics continued to demand his attention, but he looked at it now from the point of view of people's welfare and not from the point of view of advancing or counteracting the interests of this or that party. Similarly, in this new phase of his life which opened with the dissolution of RDP, he could not retire to Dehra Dun and lead a secluded life. He was in demand all over the country and had to undertake a good deal of travelling.

Moreover, 13 Mohini Road became more busy than ever with scholars, Indian and foreign, dropping in from time to time to discuss intricate questions of politics and philosophy or merely to meet him and learn from him. His desire for a quiet life of study and contemplation was never fulfilled. In January 1949, Roy delivered a speech in Bombay on "Humanist Politics". It gave in a systematic manner his views on the new politics on which he had embarked. It is significant for an understanding of humanist politics. It started by stating that the politics "which has of late become a veritable chaos can be cleared away only by introducing the human element into public affairs or rather by giving the human individual a prominent place in political practice." Society, it stated, was the creation of man and "originally politics was a concern, of human beings-with common interests and purposes." As societies became larger and larger and the state became more powerful, the problem that arose was : "how to regulate the relations between individual and State, how to carry an organised social existence without encroaching on the liberty of the individual".

Democracy was developed as the solution of the problem, but as nations became large it became representative government with the people delegating their sovereignty to their representatives. In this system "the individual citizen had no more right than to go to the polling booth and throw a slip of paper into it once in three, four or five years, in the period between elections, the sovereign people was completely helpless, and had absolutely no means or possibility to control their representatives who are virtually all-powerful." The representatives belonged to various political parties and struggle between parties, for capture of power became a standing feature of democracy. The party that made "the most glittering promises, had the greatest chance of obtaining the consent of the people." The result was that "democracy degenerated into demagogy" that "the most irresponsible demagogue came-to be the most successful democrat". In the meanwhile democracy had to face two challenges one of communists and the other of fascists. The fascist challenge was defeated in the war but the communist challenge still retained its appeal. The speech then proceeded : Confronted with this situation a growing number of thoughtful men have been thinking hard and searching for a new way of democratic practice. And curiously enough, it was discovered that living in varied parts of the world, often not known to each other, generally guided merely by the experience of their particular countries in which they were living, unaware of conditions elsewhere, several men throughout the world had been moving towards one and the same conclusion, and that conclusion is that, unless man, the individual, is restored to his proper place, that is, to his position of primacy and supremacy, there does not seem to be any way out of the present crisis." This was what Humanism proposed to do. Humanism arose in Europe in the Middle Ages. It receded to the background because it failed to explain man.

Man remained some mysterious elementary undefinable category." With greater knowledge it was now feasible to explain man. The humanist principle that "man is the centre of things, that man is the creator of everything in his world, can today be revived and Substantiated, and thereby a new inspiration given for that type of political practice which seems to offer the only way out of the modern crisis, namely, a really effective, humanist, radical democracy.." Recalling Plato's words that democracy is not Possible without education, the speech pointed out how modern democrats neglected education knowing through experience that "so long as the electors remained backward, it becomes all the easier for the political parties to deceive them by promises." As the large masses remained-ignorant and backward a class of elites arose and it became the ruler negating, in fact, democracy, the rule of the people, Humanism, however, asserts that "every single human being is potentially capable of, developing his creative powers, his intelligence, his discrimination as much as any other human being." The speech stated further : "Education for democracy does not consist in teaching just reading and writing, but in making the people conscious of their humanness, to make them conscious. Of their right to exist as human beings indecency and dignity. Education means to help them to think, to apply their reason. That is to say, the new humanist political practice must begin as a cultural movement. It must get out of the struggle for power of the political parties." Dealing with the argument that insurrection and dictatorship might provide a shorter cut, Roy stated : "Besides from the fallacious assumption that dictatorship could lead to a higher form of democracy, there is the factual and pragmatically established argument that this hypothetical shortcut to social change through insurrection is closed in our time, the days are gone when a determined minority party could capture power through air insurrection, as happened in the French and Russian Revolutions if you look at the history of revolution since the Russian Revolution, it is an unbroken history of defeats. Modern States are possessed of such formidable armed forces, and are so very highly mechanised and organised, that any effort of a minority to capture power by armed insurrection is bound to be crushed. "In a country like India, where the State may not have those advantages of other modern and highly militarised and organised States, the security of the established order is based on the blind faith and backwardness of the people. In the case of any effort to overthrow the present government by armed force, you will find the vast bulk of the population not on the side of the revolution meant for them, but rallying around the government which for all they are told is something almost divine, combining the qualities of father and mother, saint and worshippers of saints." His conclusion, therefore, was that the humanist way is the only way that leads "in the direction where we want to go." Roy then outlined as follows the political practice of Humanism : "Needless to say, a democracy cannot be educated from today to tomorrow. But a beginning can be made here and now. For example, if in the next elections there would be only two-hundred people throughout the country ready' to practise humanist politics, they could begin work in a dozen constituencies and there begin the task of awakening the urge for freedom in the individuals and raise the intellectual and cultural level of the people. These are after all not just high-sounding phrases; they express themselves concretely in a change of outlook and of their backward habits. When election time comes, we shall tell them; you may vote for any party you like, but before you vote, think; don't be carried away by election speeches; use your brains; examine the programmes and promises, and the record of the people who make them.

Anybody may come and say, for instance, that he will build Socialism when in power. Ask him what Socialism will mean to you, and then think if he can do what he promises. We don't say that he is telling a lie; but we shall also talk with the people about Socialism, and about the conditions in the country as they are, and what changes the people really want, and they will understand that no party with the best intentions can make of Indian society a socialist society, not in ten years time, assuming that Socialism is considered to be the highest ideal. "In that way, at least a few members in each community will be able to examine election promises in a critical spirit.. Half a dozen of them in a constituency will act as a powerful catalyst. They will infect others with their habit of thinking and critical discrimination, so that perhaps already in the next elections one or two per cent of the voters will cast their vote intelligently and with" a point of view of their own from which to judge the persons and programmes for whom their vote is canvassed.

A few independent men who are not professional politicians may not make themselves felt immediately in the legislatures. But the foundation will be laid for a really democratic practice. If this work will be continued in the five years until the next elections, the electorate of that constituency will have become a small democracy. "If we were to go on doing this in one constituency after another, it might take a hundred years. But it will not be so. Once the example is set and the spirit gets abroad, the momentum will grow and the movement will spread much faster than any-' body can imagine today. The humanist political approach is that by creating these small islands of democracy and freedom, the nucleus of a humanist democratic society will be created, the kind of society in which a Humanist would wish to live.

Example is better than precept, and by creating these small democratic islands, we are recreating society as a whole. Humanist democratic, education will not only create a discriminating electorate but also teach people to live a cooperative life, to transform their local democratic republic. As the example spreads, these will be the organised basis of the society we want." He asserted in conclusion : "We are not discouraged by the long way ahead of us. Every day of our life, by acting as Humanists, we approximate our ideal. This approach to political practice opens a new outlook and perspective before us, which can give us fresh hope and a strong conviction. When that spirit grows in a sufficiently large number of people, and they begin to function as a new catalytic element in society, that society is bound to be affected by their action and their spirit, and sooner or later by their whole philosophy. Because that philosophy does not just speculate and preach, but is practised by the people who are spreading it, and who are spreading it living it. It has become axiomatic that environment shapes men. But a Humanist will prove that men can also shape their environments." This was the essence of all that Roy wrote and spoke on politics in the period. He wrote regularly for II and for several other Journals. The name of II was changed to The Radical Humanist in April 1949. After Independence there was no point in calling the journal Independent India, The new name Radical Humanist was more in keeping with the ideology it was to propagate. Two years later, that is in May 1951, it was shifted from Bombay to Calcutta.

The journal was constantly its financial difficulties though everybody including the Editor worked for it without any remuneration. In spite of its wide circulation, it was not patronised by advertisers. That was the cause of its financial difficulties. The shift to Calcutta was made in order to reduce printing expenses. Roy spoke at several meetings and delivered several lectures. Not being associated with any political party made him acceptable to several institutions which had so long kept away from him. After RDP conference in Calcutta, Roy was in Bombay in the later half of January. In Bombay he gave two talks on philosophy and practice of New Humanism. One of the two talks was on "human nature and humanist practice". Roy pointed out in the talk, on the basis of sociology and anthropology, that primitive man was not a believer that human nature was inevitably rational, that every man was endowed with the capacity to know and that it was that capacity which Was responsible for man's progress as a rational and moral human being.

He asserted, "New Humanism says that the desire to be moral is inherent in man, and it is so because this desire results from man's innate rationality. New Humanism does not admit that certain men are inherently superior to other men, that some are gifted with the ability of acquiring knowledge and virtue, and others must always remain lowly and mean, in blissful ignorance, and forever be-guided by their, fortunate betters. Since Humanism starts from the fundamental principle that every human being is inevitably rational and therefore potentially moral, the corollary is that every man is capable of knowing, as well as of behaving, morally,' if he is-given the opportunity of developing his personality. Painting out that every Radical Humanist must begin from himself, Roy expressed the hope : "If the masses are regarded as what they are, namely, individual men and women, endowed with the same potentialities that I possess myself, then it should be feasible to make them think and feet just as I do, and react in the rational and moral manner that I endeavour to attain for myself. Increase the number of people who will not only dream of a better society, but immediately apply themselves to the task of living a better society, and you will be creating it in our own very midst, from where it will spread by virtue of being better and more reasonable." From Bombay Roy went to Poona where he delivered two lectures on the crisis of our times and its solution. Thereafter he visited Belgaum, Dharwar, Hubli and Solapur. In Dharwar there was a four day renaissance study camp. At the camp he made a characteristic observation which deserves to be recorded. He said : "I have worked in politics in different countries for the last forty years and have acquired a unique experience. And at the end of it all, I have realised the futility of what they call politics. I am old now, but I shall devote the remaining years of my life to this educative movement which I am convinced will be of lasting value."

It was inevitably a plea for a different kind of politics, politics pursued with a different objective, the objective not of capture of power but of educating the people. Politics did not leave him, but his approach to it was entirely different. A reference may be made here to Roy's article in RH of September 25, 1949 in which he wrote about RDP and its decision to convert itself into a movement. He wrote : "The decision of the Conference at Calcutta was a logical deduction from the philosophy of New Humanism formulated by !he Radical Democrats two years earlier. As a result, the Radical Democratic Party had already been engaged in developing a comprehensive social movement. Having abjured the aim of power, it had placed itself outside the scramble for it, the only sense in which politics seems to be understood in our times. The activities carried on by the Party could not lend themselves to be measured by the standards generally applied to a traditional political party. A certain, anomalous, position had thus arisen between those activities and the designation of a party, which on occasions created confusion even in the minds of those who otherwise sympathised with and supported the cause of Radical Democracy. The Calcutta decision ends that anomaly and thus removes what constituted, in a way, a limitation on those activities. "The Radical Democratic Party had the tradition of freedom and rationality in its own ranks. That enabled the Party to take such a decision. Throughout the period of its existence, it functioned as a school for the education of its members to develop into better human beings, and never as a collectivity with a transcendental significance, demanding the sacrifice of their individuality from its constituents." He then paid the following tribute to the party : "Built up in this manner, the Party never claimed a strong mechanical apparatus with huge mass membership which could be no more than a blind following in the prevailing atmosphere of cultural backwardness. But it did surpass any other group in the country in respect of its intellectual integrity and spiritual strength. These were often proved beyond doubt during the short period of its existence, when the Party had to struggle against overwhelming odds, and were recognised even by those who disagreed with it. In the successive waves of nationalist mass hysteria, Radical Democrats alone stood firm, reminding the people that so long as politics was based on emotion and prejudice, it could not bring them freedom. They went against the popular current because intellectual and moral integrity always counted for more than immediate and temporary success." Before returning to Dehra Dun, Roy passed through Delhi where he delivered two lectures, one of which was an extension lecture arranged by Delhi University. There was as usual a summer camp. It was organised by Indian Renaissance Institute and was held in Mussoorie for ten days front May 25. It was a camp for higher studies.

The following was the programme of studies at the camp : (1) Problems of Cosmology and Ontology, (2) Origin of Life, (3) Reason and Nature, (4) Foundation of Ethics : Sanction of Morality, (5) Historiology : Social Evolution and Dynamics of them, (6) Freedom and Organisation : Democracy and Political Parties, (7) Problems of Social Reconstruction : Economic Planning and Freedom. A glance at the subjects that were discussed will show how Radicals had changed the character of their movement. A political movement had converted itself into a wide humanist movement. The camp was attended by a number of prominent intellectuals who felt attracted by humanist Ideas propagated by Roy. Discussions at the camp helped Roy to give a more definite shape to the philosophy of Radical Humanism. During the year Roy wrote several articles on communism and the world situation a notable article was on Communism or Chaos in Asia. Another noteworthy, article was on Khudiram Bose in the course of which he paid a glowing tribute to that martyr and other heroes of militant nationalism. His winter tour started early in December. The first stop was Delhi where he delivered two lectures – one on Cultural Heritage and the other on Communism in China. The first was a Delhi University extension lecture while the other was tinder the auspices of Indian Council of World Affairs. In addition he gave a talk on India's New Constitution. The next halt was Bombay where he stayed for three weeks. From

Bombay he paid a two-day visit to Ahmedabad. At both places he delivered lectures and also held many meetings with local Radicals to explain the scope and purpose of humanist movement. Thereafter there was a two week visit to Karnataka and Andhra. The tour ended in Calcutta where he spent some weeks before returning to Dehra Dun. In Calcutta there was a Bengal study camp from February 10 to 13, 1950. Roy attended the camp and spoke on many topics. About this time there was serious communal trouble in the two Bengals. Hindus in East Bengal were attacked and in retaliation there were attacks on Muslims in West Bengal. Minorities realised unsafe in both areas. There was a flight of Hindus from East Bengal and of Muslims from West Bengal, Roy had not approved the partition of Bengal. He regarded it as a misfortune for both communities. It would not have been that bad, he was of the opinion, if the whole of Bengal had gone to Pakistan. A united Bengal, he was sure, would have broken away from the artificial connection with the distant centre and developed as an independent State." That came to Pass two decades later in the case of East Bengal, but even then the two Bengals did not come together. The communal situation in both areas was soon brought under control as a result of energetic action by both Governments. However, relations between India and Pakistan did not improve. Roy wrote on, the topic many times in those months. Another topic on which he wrote frequently was Russia, China and the Korean war. A cold war was tagging, between Russia and U. S. A. A communist regime had been established in China and the war in Korea was the biggest event on the international scene. There was ever), danger of the war spreading to other parts. In Europe, Eastern Europe had passed under Russian domination and an iron curtain had descended between that part including Russia and the rest of Europe and the world. Democracy was destroyed in Czechoslovakia and the German problem was deliberately kept hanging fire. Roy kept himself fully informed about all these developments and wrote penetratingly about them. What he wrote about China and India deserves to be remembered. He wrote : "There is not the least possibility of an alliance between Communist China and Nationalist India. For the leadership of Asia, Nehru has a rival in Mao, or whoever might replace him; the whole of East and South East Asia right to the land frontiers of India, has already made the choice. The Chinese Communist rival of Nehru has won this position because he represents the entire might of Russia.

Therefore, Nehru's expectations about the future behaviour of Red rulers of China and that of communism generally in Asia, are mere wishful thinking. Communists are Communists wherever they are. They are prepared to utilise everything and everybody; but finally it will be their victory; they must rule. No honest person can ally with them, nationally or internationally. One must be either with them or against them. They give no quarter, know no neutrality; nor do they allow any independence, either to themselves or to others. The tragedy of Masaryk and Belles is there to warn Nehru." About a year later he wrote the following about communist conquest of Tibet. "The target of attack, therefore, is India. It is the unkindest cut for quixotic Prime Minister, who dreamed of sharing with Mao Tse-tung the leadership of resurgent Asia; and perhaps with Stalin, that of a morally regenerated world.... The further militarisation of Communism heralds other conquests in Asia to make up for the setback in Korea. India's turn may not come soon; but she has reason to be nervous and doubt if Nehru's foreign policy can guard her against the menace." In the middle of December Roy was as usual in Bombay. For many years he had followed the practice of leaving Dehra Dun towards the end of November or early in December and spend the next three months visiting several places including Bombay and Calcutta. Dehra Dun gets very cold in winter and doctors had advised him to be away from the place during that period. That was also the time for meetings and conferences. In 1950 Roy was actually ill in November suffering from an attack of asthama. In that condition, climatically, Bombay was a better place to stay.

Illness did not, however, stop him from attending conferences and delivering lectures. The only difference was that the number of engagements-was smaller. During his about a fortnight's stay in Bombay he delivered two lectures and attended the Bombay State Radical Humanist conference held on December 24, 25 and 26. From Bombay Roy went to Hyderabad where he was invited to deliver the Khatri Memorial lecture at the All India Conference of Federation of Educational Associations. The lecture was delivered on December 29. Local Radicals took advantage of his visit for spreading the message of Radical Humanism. Roy met a number of public men and intellectuals and spoke to them about renaissance and other topics. After Hyderabad he visited Tenali, Vijayawada and Waltair where the Andhra Radicals had arranged a full programme of meetings and lectures and discussions. Thereafter he went to Calcutta. In Calcutta he attended the first All India Radical Humanist Convention held from February 2 to 5, 1951. He delivered at the convention an important speech on "the foundation of a new social philosophy." The speech is so important that it was included by Roy as Appendix D in the second edition of New Humanism published in May 1953. The speech begins with a discussion of the nature of man.

Two assumptions are mentioned : "Firstly, the general idea was that man is either selfish by nature and is instinctively concerned only with his own interest. Secondly, human nature is to believe in some benevolent supernatural power." On the basis of the two assumptions society became a prison-"penal or reformatory", in the one he had to surrender his freedom to the State, and in the other he had to accept the domination of some providential will, but in either case he was helpless and had "no freedom in social relations, and no initiative in political and economic practice." Roy then discussed the theory of economic man propounded by liberals, socialists and communists and pointed out : "The practice of any theory, conservative, liberal, revolutionary, which starts from the doctrine of the economic man, must lead to the loss of freedom and the degradation of man. If man is selfish and irrational by nature, society must be a coercive organisation, prison house to be guarded by earthly policemen backed up by heavenly colleagues. Economic determinism therefore cannot be the social philosophy which is required to lead civilised mankind out of the present crisis." Is Relying on history for the view that "neither is human nature incorrigibly selfish nor is it founded on the faith in the super-human", Roy stated : "The instinct of self-preservation and struggle for existence led to the foundation of civil society. Instinct is primitive reason. Man therefore is inevitably a rational being. Modern knowledge of biology also allows this deduction. Rudiments of reason, the ability to connect experiences, can be traced in lower animals. Rationality, therefore, is a biological function which can very highly develop in the highest biological form. Rationality can subordinate man's selfishness to enlightened self-interest, which is a social virtue." He then pleaded for discarding another idea, "the idea of conflict and competition" pointing out that "the desire to be helpful to fellow-men is a more fundamental human trait than competition and conflict." This more scientific view of human nature, said Roy, provides the basis for the philosophy of New Humanism. He stated : "To develop the human personality is the main purpose of life; political practice and social institutions, economic organisations, educational endeavours should all serve the basic purpose of life." Practical details of what should be done and, how were outlined in the two statements that were considered and adopted by the convention. One observation about communism in China made in the course of the speech also deserves to be noted. Communists had by that time established themselves in China and Chinese communism was attracting several young men.

Roy said : "It is argued that Russian Communism is bad, but in China Communism has taken the democratic path. There, Communism is supposed to have triumphed with the support of the people. This idea of Communism being purified by nationalism. In China also it means violence, suppression of all liberty and all the rest of the familiar story. Whether it be of the Russian or Chinese variety, Communism will bring in its wake a long period of terror, regimentation, suppression of liberty, most perhaps civil war and chaos. It is sheer madness to welcome that catastrophe with the hope that the golden utopia may be waiting on the other side of the uncharted sea of blood and tears. This was the period or the Korean war and the world seemed to be on the brink of the third world war. Deeply distressed by that grave threat of war, Roy wrote several articles criticisms the actions and policies of U. S. A. and U. S. S. R. He was convinced that USSR was behaving in an irresponsible and provocative manner, but strongly disapproved at the same time any move of a war against her. Roy was afraid that India might be dragged into an anti-Soviet war. He appealed to Indian political workers to "raise their voice against preparations for war." He wrote at the time a number of penetrating articles analysing the causes why communism was popular in Asia and pointing out how "in Asia Communism will be an unmixed, revival of oriental despotism with a thin veneer of modernism, marred by xenophobia, brutality and violence." He was alarmed by the rapid strides that communism was making in Asia, which, according to him, was nothing more than nationalism painted red. An impressive conference of prominent intellectuals from several countries was held in Bombay towards the end of

March. The conference was to be held in New Delhi, but owing to the last minute opposition of Government of India the venue was shifted to Bombay. The object of the conference was to mobilise intellectuals for the defence or cultural freedom and frustrate Russia's efforts to make them for her propaganda. It ended by establishing Indian Committee for Cultural Freedom as a branch of the worldwide Congress for Cultural Freedom with its headquarter in Paris. Roy was invited to attend the conference. He could not attend but he sent a message. He expressed his adherence of communism as it existed in Russia and communist countries, but warned at the same time against the danger of democratic countries losing their democracy in the name of fighting communism. The message stated inter alia : "The practice of Communism has exposed the fallacies of its utopian theory. All advocates of liberty and social justice must be repelled by the loathsome experience and recoil from the deceptive ideal." It stated further that return to liberalism would not help. It said : "The alternative to Communism is not a return to Liberalism, but to go beyond it with a reaffirmed loyalty to the humanist tradition of modern civilisation and a more steadfast adherence to the moral sanction of the ideal of social justice." The crying need of the time, Roy stated, was to develop "a new social philosophy which will enable the modern civilised man to devise patterns of economic relations and political institutions free, on the one hand, of the inequalities of capitalism, 'the inadequacies of parliamentary democracy and on the other hand, of the violence and tyranny of the communist practice." Roy did not develop closer relations with the international or national organisation for cultural freedom as he smelt in them more of anti-communism than positive pursuit of democratic values. By this time, the Constitution was adopted and the country was preparing for the first general election on the basis of adult franchise. It took place In February-March 1952. Roy was not oblivious of these political developments. In an article, he had written in September 1949 : "By resolving to dissolve their party, the Radical Democrats did not propose to retire into reclusories. The resolution simply was no longer to participate in a pattern of political practice which has done more harm than good, has soiled the fair name of democracy other forms of public activity."

Despite of his opposition to parliamentary democracy, he preferred it to dictatorship. He wrote in the same article : "In the transition period, parliamentary democracy, with all its manifest failure and inadequacies, will be obviously preferable to dictatorship. Civil liberties will have a greater chance of survival as long as several parties alternate in power or contend for power, than under one party rule." He did hot advise Radicals to keep away from elections. The article stated : "For these realistic considerations, Radical Democrats should have no objection to supporting parties which would challenge the system of one-party rule and the totalitarian claim of the Congress. This attitude will be consistent with the rejection of party politics and scramble for power, because of the difference between voting and soliciting votes. Radicals should support, and ask others also to support, the most promising opposition party, not with the illusion that the situation would materially change if it replaced the Congress in power, but only to shake the foundation of one-party rule, and provided that the opposition candidates are better even of proved integrity." Two years later, on the eve of the general election, Roy issued a statement pleading for a disinterested opposition and the return of at least a few candidates not associated with any party and not desiring to occupy any office. Roy was not optimistic about the future of democracy in the country. In a lecture in Guntur (Andhra) early in 1950 he said : "A Democratic Constitution can be worked in an atmosphere where the democratic way of life-is appreciated. A conscious will to freedom, the desire to take destiny in your own hands, a sense of responsibility and ability to judge what is good and what is wrong and to examine critically the promises and programmes put before the people by parties and politicians-these are the preconditions for a successful democracy. If we take a realistic view of the situation in our country, then we must regretfully come to the conclusion that, whatever be the letter and the spirit of our new Constitution, the prevailing atmosphere is not conducive to a democratic society." A few days later he said the same thing in Calcutta. He said : "The future of democracy in India is not-bright. Popular mentality is still authoritarian, and politicians and political parties glorify that reactionary cultural heritage as spiritual genius. People with an authoritarian mentality cannot establish democracy. If democracy fails in India that will not be due to the conspiracy of political parties and leaders; the failure will be predetermined by objective conditions, the mentality of the people which cannot conceive of human freedom and human creativity." Continuing he advised : "Therefore, whoever is concerned with the future of democracy in India, should give up the comfortable habit of blaming others. They should apply themselves to the task of creating conditions under which democracy is feasible. In the meantime, perhaps for another ten years, demagogy will vitiate political practice.

The scramble for power will continue, breeding corruption and inefficiency. That cannot be helped until the foundation of democracy is laid. And that means to promote in the people the feeling that they can be the masters of their destiny. Those who believe that democracy is the best form of government must apply themselves to the fundamental task of bringing about a revolution in the mentality of the people." Roy devoted himself to the fundamental task of awakening the critical faculty of the people. In the course of a speech in February 1949 Roy had drawn attention to the "prevailing psychological tendency of seeking security in the mass." He said on that occasion : "Helplessness creates in individuals the tendency of identifying themselves with others equally helpless, of merging themselves in some collectivity, be it called nation or class, in which the helpless individual constituents acquire an almost mystic power merely by losing themselves into a mass.

Collectivism offers security against the helplessness to which the individual is condemned under the system of formal parliamentary democracy." Psychologists and sociologists described that mass mentality, he said, as fear of freedom or flight from freedom. It could be counteracted, Roy asserted, by awakening man's faith in himself and by decentralising power. His scheme of organised democracy based on people's committees "endowed with specific constitutional rights':' was evolved with that twin object in view. He said, : "Instead of atomised, helpless individuals enjoying an illusory sovereignty, groups of individual citizens will be discussing and planning the affairs of their localities in the framework of similar neighbouring localities, together constituting the country for whose administration they will feel themselves liable. A growing network of such organised local democracies will be the instruments through which the electorate can assert its influence from day to day, and ultimately exercise a standing control over the State as a whole. The State will not then be able to become an all-powerful Leviathan, because State power will be decentralised, being largely vested in the local republics." With organised democracy, he stated, people can stand on their own legs and will not need political parties to represent them in the administration of the State. Later in the year Roy delivered several speeches on "politics without power." They were published in book form early next year. Early in 1952 the country went through the first general election under the new Constitution and also the first on the basis of adult franchise. Congress put up the largest number of candidates. There were several other parties in field and there was also a large number of independents. The emergence of independents was regarded as disintegration of Congress and lack of confidence in parties. Roy favoured the contesting of elections by independents. "As the first to suggest the idea of putting up independent candidates to challenge party rule," he suggested through an article in RH the following as the pledge to be taken by independent candidates elected I shall always remain directly accountable to my constituents. I shall not join any party which will stand between me and those who have elected me.

Ordinarily I shall act according to my honest and independent judgement. In the case of far-reaching issues, I shall seek the advice and direction of my constituents, and vote accordingly in the Parliament. I unreservedly acknowledge the sovereignty of my constituents to demand my resignation whenever a majority of them will think that I am not representing them faithfully. At the same time... I reserve the right to disagree with the desire of my constituents on any particular issue; but in that case, I pledge myself to resign so that the constituency may elect a substitute who would act according to its desire and direction." Though the number of persons contesting elections as independents was large-in the case of Lok Sabha the number was over five hundred and they polled over 15 per cent votes they were not of the type visualised by Roy, and several independent candidates joined Congress or other political parties after winning the election. Congress President, who was then also the Prime Minister, carried on whirlwind propaganda throughout the country for Congress candidates. About that propaganda Roy wrote : "The central theme of all his election speeches is "one country, one party." This theme has been preached by totalitarian movements of our time. They added a third term to the slogan, namely, "One leader." It logically follows from the other two. In India, it is already a fact. The sole leader of the country is calling upon the people to vote only for one party; and the implication of his emphasis on unity is that the country should not have more than on-, party." Roy characterised it as a "dangerous drift" towards a "totalitarian regime." Congress polled 45 per cent of votes but was able to win 74-4 per cent of seats. It scored similar successes in Assembly elections. Roy reviewed the results of the elections in a speech in Calcutta on February 9. He noted the emergence of CP as the most powerful opposition party as a disturbing factor. He noted also the fissures in Congress and the efforts to impose discipline. The perspective was, therefore, gloomy, he said, but advised democrats to build up "centres of resistance to the menace of dictatorship." Earlier on January, he spoke at the University Institute hall on "First Election in Free India." By this time, Roy had gained considerable reputation abroad as an independent thinker and shrewd observer of communist moves in India and Asia. From time to time he was approached by foreign journals to write on current developments as well as long-term trends. Whenever feasible, he wrote for them. Pacific Affairs, the journal of Institute of Pacific Relations, carried an article by Roy on "Communism in Asia" in a late 1951 issue. RH reprinted it in its 1952 January 12 and 19 issues. The article is a penetrating analysis of forces working for communism in Asian Countries. It pointed out : "The educated middle class constitutes the driving force as well as the social mainstay of Communism in Asia", In conclusion it stated : "The perspective is black indeed. Communism may not be able to conquer Europe in Asia. That is no longer the object of its global strategy. It wants to conquer Asia; it stands a good chance to succeed. And in Asia Communism will be an unmixed evil, revival of oriental despotism, with a thin veneer of modernism marred by xenophobia, brutality and violence. But neither war nor Nationalism is a preferable alternative to the ugly and frightful spectre of triumphant Communism... It would be wrong strategy to fight a numerically superior enemy all over the front stretched across a whole continent. Centres of resistance should be built up where the enemy is still weak. For more than one reason India is the most suited for the purpose. Pakistan also offers an opportunity. The whole of the Indian subcontinent could be fairly safe against any open Communist aggression from outside, provided that the internal security of both the States was not impaired by impatience... If India and Pakistan were allowed to find the realistic approach to their political and economic problems. Out of experience and independent thinking they might be the centre to generate and radiate the will to put up a moral resistance against the siren call of Communism... The will to moral resistance must be supplemented by political and economic reforms which need not conform with traditional Western or American pattern. A corresponding pattern of political institutions will have to be conceived... Democracy must regain its humanist,, soul and revert to the faith in the sovereignty of, the individual, and economic thought and practice must be radically-reoriented. Otherwise, the challenge of Communism cannot be met anywhere." Pacific Affairs published in its next issue a comment on Roy's article by Guy Wint, an English political commentator and author of The British in Asia. The comment was very appreciative of Roy's analysis but took exception to his contentions that communists succeeded in China only with Russia's help and that American intervention in Korea was unwise. Roy replied giving facts and arguments in support of both contentions. Wint's comments and Roy's rejoinder were published in R H of June 15. Manchester Guardian published in its issue of January IS Roy's article on "Indian Communists and the Elections." The same issue carried the following editorial comment on Roy : "Mr. M. N. Roy, whose article we publish on this page, has been one of the outstanding men of the age in Asia. He is a

Bengali Brahmin who in his earliest years dedicated himself to promoting revolution. He conspired against the British in India during the First World War, fought with Pancho Villa in Mexico, rose high in the Comintern, and played a dramatic part when the Kuomintang and Chiang Kai-shek were coming to power in China. Twenty years ago it might have been said that Roy was the Asian Revolution incarnate. Upon returning to India he was caught by the police and spent a fairly long time in prison. This gave him one of the first period of quiet in his stormy career. He examined the bases of his belief. Thereafter, from being a man of action expressing the ideas of others he became the expounder of original political ideas of his own. His following in India has remained small, and he has at present little influence on Indian affairs. But his ideas, which proceed from his penetrating vision of what are the real revolutionary forces in Asia, should be studied by everyone concerned with Eastern Affairs. Roy has now turned against communism, or at least against Stalinism. He has done so partly because of what he conceived to be Stalin's policies in the East. Recently he has explained his theme in a number of striking articles. "Mr. Roy was impressed by the fact that the force behind communism in the East is the educated middle class. Admiration for communism is found in wealthy professional men, among the army officers (for example in Pakistan), and among the extreme nationalists. Communism in Asia, says Mr. Roy, is not a revolt of the masses against unbearable economic conditions, though it uses, of course, whatever idealistic appeal lies in the idea. The ruling passion in most Asian countries is still fear of the West, despite of the British surrender of political control. This is so especially in countries which have been only superficially Westernised, for in them there is no appreciation of the values of Western civilisation to offset the dislike of Western influence, Another very strong passion is admiration for Russia, not because of the moral content of communism but because Russia is strong and a potential ally against the 'imperialists' of the West. The likelihood, says Mr. Roy, is of a so many extreme nationalist dictatorships which will call themselves Communist. 'Communism in Asia,' he writes, 'inevitably is nationalism painted red.' The triumph of Asiatic communism will thus mean a repudiation of the values of modern Western civilisation." Early in April Roy came across the comments of The Times Weekly Review on a constitutional issue arising out of A. Bevan's dispute with the leaders of British Labour Party. The issue was about the rigid party system which denied a member the freedom of expression. The journal commented that what Bevan was up against was not any particular decision but the whole party system. Roy appreciated that comment and in a note written for the journal explained his views on democracy and the party system. He wrote : "Commenting on Mr. Bevan's dispute with the leaders of the Parliamentary Labour Party (editorial : 'Caucus and Conscience,' The Times Weekly Review, March 2), you pointed out very correctly that his criticism is directed 'rather against the whole party system.. You were also right to characterise Mr. Bevan's remedy for the evil of government by caucus as 'impractical and undesirable'. It remains to be seen if he will himself act consistently with his critical opinion. In the mean time, the validity of his criticism of the party system cannot be ignored. You have endorsed it by indicating the stages of the development of the party system to the present position, where the member of Parliament no longer is a free agent'. If it is true, as you point out, that 'the pressure which party leaders can bring to bear on dissidents in their ranks has become formidable,' does not the experience lead to the conclusion that the party system destroys democracy? It is true. A crisis has overtaken parliamentary democracy, which challenges the ingenuity of all defenders of democratic freedom except the professional party politician. "Having pointed out that several constitutional writers have noted with regret 'the development of this rigid system, which undermines the authority of the individual member, and therefore the authority of the Parliament,' you seem to recommend their fatalistic attitude : the totalitarian degeneration of parliamentary democracy is inevitable ; therefore we must be reconciled to the regrettable process. 'It is the inevitable accompaniment of universal suffrage and of the comprehensive nature of modern government which leaves practically facet of the nation's activities outside the party programme.' Is it not an endorsement of the totalitarian doctrine which identifies the party (in power) with the State and the State with society?

The conception of a totalitarian State-the identification of the State with society may be formally reconciled with the broadest feasible democracy (universal franchise); but it is clearly inconsistent with the tradition of Liberalism. Nor is there any warrant for the assumption that universal suffrage must necessarily lead to totalitarianism. For, in that case, democracy must be given up as an impractical idea and an unattainable ideal. "The present regrettable position has been created by the party system which undermines the authority of Parliament. The parties stand between the people and their elected representatives. The latter are not responsible to their constituents; they are subject to the party whip, which can be defied only at the risk of expulsion from the party. It is obvious that loyalty to the constituents and loyalty to the party cannot always be reconciled. Party membership, therefore, is inconsistent with democratic responsibility. "If the party system is indispensable, then democracy is not feasible. It logically follows that survival of democracy is conditional upon the disappearance of political parties, which usurp the sovereignty of the people, between elections, at any rate. This condition can be created in Britain. The Mother of Parliaments is older than the party system. Traditionally, candidates offer themselves for election as individuals. Put life into that tradition, and democracy will survive the crisis. Make the British electorate aware of the crisis by showing that the party system transforms parliamentary government into a government by caucus, and the sound tradition of candidates seeking election as independent individuals will be revived. If the revolt of Mr. Bevan and his followers takes that, form, he may be not the next Labour Prime Minister; but they will greatly help, the survival of democracy." Pacific Affairs published in its June 1951 issue another article by Roy. It was on "Democracy and Nationalism." RH reproduced it in its issue of July 20. An international congress on humanist and ethical culture Was held In Amsterdam (Holland) from August 21 to 26. Roy was co-opted a member of the organisms committee. He was invited to attend the conference and also to contribute a paper. Roy could not attend but sent his paper. It was on humanist and ethical culture and was later published in RH.

The conference founded the International Humanist and Ethical Union. Roy was elected one of the Vice-Presidents of the organisation. In the later part of the year there was an interesting controversy in RH about Religion and Humanism. One John S. Conner, an American teacher and trade union counsellor attached to Xavier Labour Research Institute of Jamshedpur, started the controversy. Owing to pressure of work and other difficulties, Roy could not himself take much part in it. But he started it off with the following cogent and concise statement : "I am a working man; must drive my pen 8 to 10 hours a day to earn a living... I may tell you that I am fully at peace with myself without the Grace of any Divine Person. I have no quarrel with believers but expect a similar tolerant attitude from them. I am of the opinion that examination of the problems of life on this earth should not be influenced by the introduction of an Unknown Absolute factor in the equation of known variables. The believers of our time would be wise to take up the Nominalist position while discussing social problems. If some cannot be good and virtuous without the Grace of God, they are welcome to have their personal faith. But is it quite just and proper for them to question the moral integrity of others who may not share their faith though respect it ?" The first half of 1952 was a relatively quiet period for Roy returned to Dehra Dun early in the year after a heavy schedule of lectures in Calcutta. There was immediately no plan of going out. He settled down, therefore, to quiet literary work. He completed the Memoirs. He wrote during this period and the earlier couple of years pen portraits of some of the important people that he had met in the course of his travels around the world. They were later collected together and published as a book under the title Men I Met. He wrote some articles for foreign journals as well. The most important work that he did, however, was the completion of his monumental book, Reason, Romanticism and Revolution. 13 Mohini Road was in those years attracting so many visitors, several Radicals went there from time to time for short or long stays, But there were several personal friends, scholars from several lands, public men and eager young men and women anxious to meet the sage of Dehra Dun and get some of their problems solved. They were all received with courtesy and kindness. Some of them stayed on for meals which in the evenings were jointly cooked by Roy and Ellen. Amongst personal friends were Sudhindranath Dutta, the well-known poet of Bengal and S. K. Dey, an equally well-known administrator. They were family friends and on occasions stayed with their families at Mohini Road. Roy enjoyed discussing with them Bengali literature as well as Bengal politics. He also discussed with them his new philosophical and social ideas. Several American scholars and students also dropped in from time to time. Prominent amongst them were Robert North and Richard Park. Jayaprakash Narayan visited Roy once to discuss with him his ideas.of non-party politics and decentralisation. Jayaprakash stated several times later that his ideas on both issues were to sonic extent influenced by Roy's thinking. Prime Minister Nehru also dropped in once for a long talk. Retirement from party politics was thus making Roy more acceptable and his ideas were getting a better response. In June 1952 Roy went to Mussoorie, the hill station near Dehra Dun, for rest and recuperation. Ordinarily June is not a pleasant month in Dehra Dun; that year it was particularly humid and unpleasant. Having put in a good deal of literary and intellectual work, Roy and Ellen required a little rest and holiday. A friend secured for them a small cottage in Mussoorie. It was therefore decided to 'spend a month in that place.

The cottage, a little away front the town, gave a nice View of the mountains, Roy and Ellen liked the place and were happy at the little holiday that they were enjoying after a number of years. Every morning they used to go out after breakfast for a short walk. They preferred for their walks winding hill tracks on the slopes of the mountain to paved roads of the town. On June 11, Roy and Ellen were out as usual for their morning walk. After walking a couple of miles, they were on their way back to the cottage. Roy was in good spirits and was enjoying the cool morning air. He was a few paces ahead and Ellen was following him. And then he stumbled against something and fell down. He fell down and rolled down the hill some fifty feet. A rock stopped his rolling; otherwise he would have rolled into a steep valley.

Ellen was flabbergasted for a few moments; a moment ago Roy was there walking ahead and the next moment he was not there and was rolling down the slope. In a minute she realised what had happened and raised a cry for help. She rushed down the hill; Roy was in a heap and had sustained several injuries. In a few minutes a number of labourers from nearby cottages and a few others gathered in response to

Ellen's cries, They prepared a makeshift doli, put Roy on it and transported him to his hut. Ellen immediately summoned doctors. One of them was a heart specialist from Calcutta, Sunil Bose living in a nearby cottage. He and several others who were summoned from time to time gave Roy the best feasible medical treatment. The ever-alert Ellen was all along by his bedside and gave him the care and attention that he would have received in a well-equipped hospital. But it was months before Roy recovered and the recovery at its best was only partial. The accidental fall on June 11 proved to be the beginning of the end. The injuries sustained in the fall were mainly external, to ribs, head, face, hands and legs. They were treated by experts and in a few weeks Roy was moved back to Dehra Dun. There were ups and downs in his condition but it appeared at that time that he would be soon out of bed. On August 25, however, there was a serious set-back. Roy suffered on that day an attack of cerebral thrombosis resulting in a partial paralysis of his right side. On September 24, there was a further set-back when he went into a semi-comatose condition. It did not last long, but affected his speech for some days. Reporting in the first week of October, Ellen wrote : "There is not much difference in Com. Roy's condition except that while nights continue completely sleepless, he does sleep twice or thrice during the day for an hour or two. It has already had a good effect on his general strength. He did not have again those heart attacks after coughing; the pulse is better between 12-96 (respiration 22-25) and more regular; cough is less though the difficulty of expectoration remains. He looks clear out of his eyes and speaks a little more." In November there was a good deal of improvement. RH reported : "During the last fortnight Com. M. N. Roy's condition has been showing steady all-round improvement. He has now recovered voluntary movement of his right limbs and can not only lift his arms and legs but even move the fingers of his right hand. Although he still suffers from restlessness and inadequate sleep, he feels generally much better. He has also few coughing fits and attacks of asthama." These reports had to be published from time to time as all Radicals were deeply concerned about Roy's health since the news of the accident appeared in the press. There were several anxious telegrams and letters. Some Radicals rushed to Mussoorie and Dehra Dun on hearing the news and some of them stayed for many days to help Ellen. She required assistance particularly after the thrombosis attack in August. Prominent amongst those who stayed in Dehra Dun in this period were the two Radical doctors, Indumati Parikh and Indu Tarkunde, the famous Hindi writer, S. H. Vatsyayan and the American academician, Richard Park. Other Radicals from all parts of the country paid flying visits. One local Radical, R. M. Paul was in constant attendance.

The local physician, Durga Prasad, a close personal friend of Rays was in charge of medical arrangements. He consulted from time to time A. S. Erulkar of Bombay and some specialists in Calcutta. Erulkar visited Dehra Dun once to have a look at his distinguished patient. Radicals were generous as well in their financial contributions. Contributions towards medical expenses were received from several other friends and admirers, prominent amongst whom were President Rajendra Prasad and Prime Minister Nehru. As a result of the expert medical treatment that he received and the tender care showered on him by Ellen and others, Roy started to recover in the latter part of November. Steadily he recovered the movements of all his limbs and early in the next year he was able to move about in the house and the garden which surrounded it. Very soon he resumed his usual activities especially of reading and writing. Roy's first contribution to RH was a new year message. In the course of the message he stated : "Now the critical period is over, and I hope to resume my responsibility before long. I shall have much to say, the months of illness having given in.-plenty of time to think over the fundamental problems of human life. In the earlier days of my illness, few believed that I would survive. As a matter of fact, for weeks I lived in the dreamland bordering on life and death. That was a strange experience. Although I was half conscious much of the time, I retain a vivid memory of that bizarre dream. Of that memory could be produced a strange book. But I do not think that I would have the time for such purely literary venture. "However, I am back to this life, and shall be with you personally again before very long. Spiritually, I have always been. Death has no terror for me.

Indeed, in these days of despair, it might be a liberation for those who are feeling frustrated by difficulties. But the idea that I might not again be able to meet you all was painful. Although I am on the road to recovery, it will be yet some time before I shall be able to move about freely, and do sustained work." A few days later he dictated an article which appeared in RH under the title "Our Creed." It was a restatement of the fundamental principles of New Humanism. Thereafter he wrote frequently for RH, editorials as well as other articles. His first editorial after recovery appeared in RH of February 15. It was on "Indo-Pakistan Relations and Middle-East Defence Organisation." He wrote a few other editorials, but there was not the earlier regularity about them. Several a time they were written by others. Prominent amongst other articles that he wrote during the period were one on new democratic movement in China and two on Stalin. Stalin died on March 6, 1953. Paying his tribute to Stalin, Roy wrote in a long article : "During these years of cold war between the communist and the anti-communist worlds, Stalin personified the fearful spectre of Communism invoked by Karl Marx a century ago. He was the most hated, feared and maligned man of our time. As the leader of an admittedly dictatorial system, he was ruthless and at home committed and connived with several unnecessarily cruel acts, which shocked the civilised world. But at the same time, he led a numerous people inhabiting one-sixth of the globe out of mediaeval darkness and economic backwardness. Centuries before him, Peter the Great endeavoured to do the same thing. For that patriotic endeavour he has gone down in history as a great man. No great man has ever been an angel. Greatness is always purchased at the cost of goodness. Stalin did not do anything worse. He certainly deserves a place among the great men of history." Pleading that "some justice should be done to the most maligned man of our time," he wrote : "Stalin was a man of peace, although he disdained to have peace at any price. He would go far to avoid war because he believed that, under the present condition of the world peace would promote the cause of Communism. The future of the world will not be so very gloomy as it seems today if this truth will be recognised by the anticommunist world. If that happens, Stalin's death will mark the beginning of a new chapter in contemporary history – a chapter of mutual understanding and toleration. Stalin was undoubtedly the tallest personality of our time, and as such is bound to leave his mark on history" he stated, in support of his theory : "In the years immediately following-the second world war, there was no force in Western Europe to stop the Red Army if it was ordered to march ahead.

Even, if the Russians decide to overrun Western Europe, they can reach the Rhine and even the North Sea and the English Channel, in a matter of weeks. That is the opinion of several a strategist of the Western world. It is also admitted that not before another two years will the projected European Defence Community be in a position to resist a Russian attack. Why did the Russians wait all this time, if they really wanted to overrun Western Europe at the risk of plunging into the third world war? There are several Russians high up in the Soviet hierarchy who advocated that line of action. Zhadnov, who was for a time regarded as the heir apparent of Stalin, was the leader of that group. There is only one explanation why that catastrophic plunge was not taken. It was Stalin's caution and wisdom which restrained the ardent advocates of world revolution. Several will not agree with this assessment of the military situation and will be inclined to attribute Russia's decision not to venture further towards the West to the military might of the United States and not to the peaceful intentions of Stalin. A month later, Roy reiterated in his article "Stalinism Survives Stalin", the same views about Stalin while pointing out that "certain sensational steps taken by the new Soviet Government, peace offensive abroad and slackening of terror at home" were a continuation and not a repudiation of Stalinism. According to him, "Stalinism was not merely aggressiveness abroad and terrorism at home." He regarded Stalin as a "revisionist, indeed, heretical" interpreter of Marx, but he attributed Russia's survival and progress to the realistic policy adopted by Stalin in contrast to the orthodox Marxist policy advocated by Trotsky. Stalin followed the policy of peace not because he was a "Pacifist" but because "he knew that peace would be more advantageous for the consolidation of the Soviet Union than war." Stalin's successors, he asserted, were following the same policy for the same reason. He welcomed the "relaxation of terrorism" exemplified by "the release and exoneration of the condemned Kremlin doctors", but denied that it was due to "internal struggle for power." There was, however, an internal struggle for power. Beria was liquidated soon and a little later Khrushchev replaced Malenkov. Three years later, Khrushchev told the horrible story of the sordid crimes of Stalin. Roy did not live to hear the story. But he could not have been altogether ignorant of that dark part of Stalin's life. One wonders why he did not pay more attention to it. Was it because he was one of the victims? Or was it because he did not want to throw one more stone at "the most hated, feared and maligned man of our time"? During this period RH published serially several chapters of Roy's Memoirs. Tile publication continued in 1954. He wrote them in 1952 and they were published partly in Amrit Bazar Patrika and a couple of other papers. About this time there was a move to publish them in book form and Roy wrote for it a new chapter which was to go as the first chapter of the book. The chapter was entitled "Disintegration of a Priestly Family." It told of his visit to the village of his ancestors and to the temple of which his father and others before him were the high priests and of the decay and disintegration of the temple and the village. The article appeared in the M. N. Roy memorial number of RH published after his death in February 1954. He was to write a few more chapters, but fell ill before he could do that. The boo', was to be published under the title, "In Quest of Freedom". February 1953 saw the publication of the first volume of Roy's comprehensive work, Reason, Romanticism and Revolution. The second volume was published a year later after his death.

The Three Rs, as the book came to be known, is one of the books that Roy wrote as a book in his later life. The other books are generally collections of his articles or speeches. He took special pains to write the Three Rs. He was working over it for more than a year, It was to be the quintessence of his thought and to provide the theoretical basis for the philosophy of Radical Humanism. The book has fulfilled both objects. In his Preface to the first volume written in Dehra Dun on August 15, 1952 Roy described as follows the purpose of the book : "The cultural and moral crisis of modern civilization is compelling sensitive and thoughtful men throughout the world to turn towards its humanist tradition. The movement for a humanist revival grows stronger everyday. It is being increasingly realised that the baffling problems of our time call for a sober rationalist approach. The restoration of moral values in public' life is the crying demand....... "This, book is an effort to rescue rationalism and ethics from the devastating consequences of scepticism. In the light of modern scientific knowledge it is discovered that man's rationality is a biological property. Reason is not a metaphysical category. Moral values are placed on a firm foundation when they are referred back to the innate rationality of man. They need no other sanction than conscience, which is not the voice of God, but results from rationality. The discovery of the physical basis of reason and the rationalist secular sanction of morality frees Humanism from the mystic connotation traditionally associated with it... But comprehensive philosophy is indispensable to guide human life. A rationalist social philosophy must be deduced from a scientific interpretation of Humanism.

On the basis of a humanist interpretation of cultural history, this work endeavours to outline a comprehensive philosophy which links up social and political practice with a scientific metaphysics of rationality and ethics." The following from a long review of the book in The Plain View, London, will give a general idea of the book : "M. N. Roy tells an old, old story, the history of ideas and ideals in the West, the human tradition as it has been formed in Europe. We are shown again the famous scenes and acts, the successive constellations of great persons, and again and again we look at them once more with the proud and familiar eyes borrowed from our rationalist classics. But this is not a genuine performance. In every sentence, borrowed or his own, Mr. Roy relives the past, not with the exuberant make believe of the story-teller but with the passionate intensity of the philosopher at grips with the problems of his own time, for whom all history is contemporary history. Roy, himself an actor in the major events of our time, and their historian, makes us feel the future streaming up from the past and our own lives caught up in the exciting action of an unfinished piece.

The Renaissance, the Enlightenment, the Great Revolution, are not distant glories of an heroic age, they press into the present time with anticipations and presentiments of what is our very own, if we have the confidence and courage and creative energy of our grand inheritance and open future. And all this inspiration is communicated by one who is a thinker, a sufferer, a man of action and a man of his time, a mind and nature matured by experience and reflection, not a brain intoxicated by reading or dreaming or by science. "Roy's thesis is that reason and freedom are attributes of man's nature in virtue of his natural origin; they are not metaphysical categories, Nevertheless, although implanted as ineradicable impulses, they imply and impose disciplines, they are achievements. Reason, Romanticism and Revolution have manifested in history aberrations and extravagances, by which we should be warned and taught, but they are the standing clues to man's adventure in making his history.

The determinism of the physical universe from which he himself derives and his own self-determination are the two poles of man's being, and he is distorted by any idea or ideals which would deflect this axis. "One wants to stop and argue with Roy many, several times in the course of his book, on points of scholarship, historical judgements, or philosophical opinions, but that only means that he has written just the kind of book humanists need just now to stimulate their own reliving and rethinking of the past. On major points, we would all concur." The book was reviewed favourably in several Indian and foreign papers. The last three chapters entitled "The Crisis of the Twentieth Century," "The Way Out" and "New Humanism" are of particular interest as they deal with the contemporary crisis and the way out of it suggested by Roy. According to Roy, the crisis was "the greatest of all in history, being not only political or economic, but moral and spiritual—a total crisis affecting the whole of human existence."

As a result of the crisis, "the modern world," he wrote, "seems to be moving towards a position like that of the Roman Empire in decay and on the eve of its downfall". Roy attributed the crisis to "the eclipse of the humanist tradition as a result of which man was "subordinated to institutions."

The solution of the crisis, he wrote : "lies in the revival of man's faith in himself, in a humanist revival". The political aspect of the crisis was described by him as follows : "By making man into the masses, politicians and social engineers have created a monster which responds riotously only to appeals to passions-hatred, greed, lust for power. Man has been debased to the level of unthinking beasts, to serve the purposes of power politics. Political parties need votes to come to power. It is easier to sway the people by appeals to their emotions and prejudices than to their reason. The more backward a people, the more easily they are swayed by appeals to emotions and prejudices. Therefore, to keep the people in backwardness has become the result of modern democratic politics." Beginning with the proposition that "the civilised world needs a new hope, a new faith, a new ideal, a new philosophy of truly revolutionary theory and practice suitable for the conditions of our time", Roy elaborates a philosophy which will enable an individual to be free, "not only to enjoy economic sufficiency and security but in' a psychological atmosphere free from cultural regimentation and helpful to the development of his intellectual and other human potentialities." Tile inspiration for the new philosophy he found in "the traditions of Humanism and moral Radicalism". "The positive knowledge of nature-living as well as inanimate" should, Roy asserted, give us the conviction "that social relations can be rationally harmonised and that therefore appreciation of moral values can be reconciled with the efforts to replace the corrupt and disintegrating status quo by a new order of democratic freedom." "A moral order will result from a rationally organised society", Roy stated, because "man is inevitably rational and therefore moral". The philosophy of New Humanism will be activist and not passive but its action will be based on reason and not emotion. After tracing its roots in history and nature, Roy concluded : "New Humanism is a social philosophy, but as such, it is deduced from a general philosophy of nature, including the world of matter and the world of mind. Its metaphysics is physical-realist; and its cosmology is mechanistic. Conceptual thought and sense perceptions are harmonised in its epistemology. It merges psychology into physiology, and relates the latter to physics through chemistry. It bases ethics on rationalism, and traces the roots of reason in the orderliness of nature and harmony of the physical universe.

By tracing will and reason, emotion and intelligence to their common biological origin, New Humanism reconciles the romantic doctrine of revolution, that man makes history with the rationalist notion of orderly social progress." Emphasis is again laid on the fact that "man is the maker of his world" which he can be only as "a thinking being", that he can be a thinking being only as an individual, and that "brain is the instrument of thought" which again can be owned only by an individual and not by a collectivity. Stating that "New Humanism advocates a social reconstruction of the world as a commonwealth and fraternity of free men, by the co-operative endeavour of spiritually emancipated moral men," Roy expressed the hope that "boundaries of national States-capitalist, fascist, socialist., communist, or of any other kind-will gradually disappear under the impact of the twentieth century Renaissance of Man." By May there was such a remarkable improvement in Roy's condition that plans were made for his visit to the United States for medical treatment as well as for speaking engagements. Some American Universities and other organisations had invited him to deliver lectures on a variety of subjects. The original idea was that he and Ellen should leave by the end of May. But passport and visa formalities took a long time and it was finally decided that they would leave from Bombay on October 11. A reunion of Radicals was planned to take place in Bombay on October 2, 3, and 4. It was also resolved to collect a fund of Rs. 20,000 for the travelling and other expenses of Roy and Ellen. In May, Roy and Ellen went to Mussoorie for change of climate and a short holiday.

In Mussoorie, Roy felt so well that, as told later by R. L. Nigeria, a close associate, "He used to walk the whole length of Camel's Back Road-a distance of two miles. He climbed Montrose Cottage where he was staying. It was, a gentle climb but it took some endeavour even from us." After a couple of weeks in Mussoorie, Roy came back to Dehra Dun and resumed all his usual activities. He was in good health and was looking forward, eagerly to his trip to the United States. But the trip was not to take place. On August 15 when a few intimate friends from the city, Delhi and Bombay had gathered together to discuss about the visit and to celebrate Ellen's birth-day, all of a sudden, Roy got his second attack of cerebral thrombosis. Distressed and exasperated, Ellen called it "my birth-day gift." The left-side was paralysed on this occasion.

Durga Prasad was immediately summoned and he started his treatment. It continued throughout the period of the illness. There were several ups and downs. The first crisis came on August 24. But Roy survived it. Thereafter there was some improvement. It continued for some weeks and again there was a setback. In December he was again better. On December 12 Jawaharlal Nehru went to his place to meet him, R. L. Nigam has described the meeting as follows : "By the time Nehru arrived he (Roy) could talk a little freely. As Nehru stood by his side both holding each other's hands, Roy came out, "I am sorry to play the Mossadiq and receive you in bed."

Nehru said, while pulling the chair nearer, "I know it is not the habit with you". Nehru left saying with a warm handshake, "Get well soon. We shall have several things to say." A few days later Roy felt much better. He read some of the letters that came and wrote some. He dictated an article for RH. Nigam reports: "He started by saying that he would dictate a few sentences. But between Ellen's demonstrations and his own insistence a whole article grew. 'Just two sentences, just two sentences more', he would say. There was no stopping him." That was Roy's last article. It appeared in RH of January 24, 1954. It was about Radical Humanist Organisation, a topic under discussion amongst Radical Humanists for about a year. Roy suggested that the reunion planned to be held on the eve of his departure for America should discuss it in concrete terms after taking into consideration the aims and objects of the Radical Humanist Movement. Roy was at that time sure of his recovery of his visit to the States and of the reunion that was to take place. But none of the three events took place. In the new year there was a progressive deterioration in Roy's condition. The end came on January 25, ten minutes before midnight and the dawn of the Republic Day of January 26. Earlier in the day there was a heart attack which proved fatal. S. K. Das, a young Radical from Delhi who wag at the bedside wrote later : He didn't suffer much, I believe, in this last attack, the heart this time. Early on Monday morning he had complained of pain and was provided morphia. From then till the end the agony was ours; to him it must have been clear before consciousness went that he was on the last lap of what was once struggle for life-now only the routine of death. One is grateful that the last few hours were not spent in acute awareness of pain that had dogged his steps for nearly two years." The news went out by telephone, telegram and word of mouth. Newspapers flashed it the next morning. Some Radicals were already there; several more rushed next day as they got the news. Continuing

Dag wrote in his article : "Several of us from Delhi and Bombay were able to see him before the end.

Others started arriving soon afterwards, by car over long distances, by bus and rail. In the morning townspeople appeared and passed word round, for the papers come one day late. The callers were from several sections, from all political parties, and others who cared nothing for politics but knew him and loved him as a friend. One by one they came with flowers (for they knew he loved flowers) to have a last look. And they met him where he had been all these months, propped up on the bed in the long room, patiently suffering the physical disaster that had overtaken him. Now there was no trace of pain on his face, it was quiet and calm and serene, so usual indeed that one hardly felt he was not there. He wore his suit, ready it seemed for the journey." The funeral took place in the afternoon in the presence of a large gathering of friends and admirers and the people from the town. There was only one speech at the funeral, that by Dev Datta, a respected old, social and political worker and close friend of Roy. The news of Roy's death grieved people all over the country. Messages of sympathy poured into 13 Mohini Road. Prominent amongst those who sent messages were President Radhakrishnan, Prime Minister Nehru, Governor of Bengal, H. C. Mookherjee and public figures like N. M. Joshi, Jayaprakash Narayan, M. S. Aney, S. M. Ghosh, Vivekanand Mukherji, Ramanathan and several others. There were messages from Pakistan, from M. A. Khatib of Pakistan Federation of Labour, Hatim Alavi of Karachi and several others. Later they came from several other countries like England, U. S. A., Canada, France and Holland. Several condolence meetings were held throughout the country. To Radicals it was a stunning blow. It was not altogether unexpected, for they had kept themselves informed of his condition. But from time to time there were signs of recovery and they had hoped that with his indomitable will he would be able to beat back the second attack as he had done In the case of the first And, however, prepared one may be, the news of the actual end always comes as a big blow. To several amongst them, Roy was not only a political leader but a vital part of their lives.

They realised that a part of them had died. It took them some time to recover from the shock and to think of ways and means to continue the work that their Guru had begun. Several rich tributes were paid to Roy in the country and abroad. They were a recognition of his several qualities of head and heart and of the contribution that he had made to the political and social movement and to the world of thought, It is not essential to note them here. But one singular tribute deserves to be noted and quoted in full. It is by his wife Ellen Roy who-was his unfailing companion and close collaborator during the last seventeen years of his life. It deserves to be noted because it is not merely an eulogy but a candid description of the way that he lived during that period.

Ellen wrote it on March 4, 1954 four weeks after his death and on the seventeenth anniversary of her landing in Bombay to meet him after a separation of over six years. She wrote : "Today it is seventeen years since the day of my arrival in India to join him after his release from jail. Because we were always looking out for occasions to celebrate and have our friends with us for a good time, we gave this anniversary too the dignity of one of our 'Days.' There has never been in all these seventeen years a time when I did not think it an occasion well worth celebration, and I like to think that it was so for him too. "Usually about this time of year we had just returned from our winter tour, set the house in order, rediscovered the garden in full spring bloom, sorted out the papers accumulated here and in our luggage, and settled down to a good several months of new quiet work, to be interrupted only from time to time, by some 'Days' of celebration with friends and of course, the Summer Camps. "Life had become so perfect as I could not have dreamt even, in my most wishful imagination when I came Out to India. Not' that there were no worries and problems; there were plenty and they belong to a life not spent in passivity and isolation. But seventeen years ago, things looked very different. We lived in the midst of fierce controversies, and if there was much hero worship and even more loyalty of good friends and comrades, there were also meanness and misunderstanding and even more misrepresentation. And if he put up the face of a hard boiled hand at the game, which of course in a sense he really was, yet he never grew the thick skin required for it. I know that it hurt and disgusted him often, and me even more. "Then we had no place of our own and for long could not find one which was both suitable for us and within the means of our friends.

Because means too we had none of our own, and for several years I no chance to earn any. The little I had brought with me went straight into the 'Independent India.' One day he said : 'I have been a homeless rover all my life; I want a place attached to my name.' One of the first letters from abroad after he came out of jail was addressed (and delivered!) to M. N. Roy, India. Then we found a two room flat one for the 'Independent India' office and the other our home, of course flowing all over it. But we had hardly moved in when he had, to leave on his first Madras tour, on which he fell very ill. "Nobody knows how much he was ill ever since. Every one of our seventeen years together in this country was like a theft from fate or, if You will, a conquest of mind over matter. But of course, if his 'matter' had not been earlier so well organised in what he liked to call his 'iron constitution', It might not have produced a mind so powerful that it could make the body do its bidding even when it was so undermined as his was after those six years in jail. "On my arrival I had found him alarmingly run down, the heart dilated, the tummy all out of gear, but himself as if nothing had happened. And instead of getting slowly accustomed to life among people after long solitary confinement, he had plunged headlong into public life, while the sound of a cycle bell behind us on the road still made him literally jump and very annoyed with himself for doing so. "The doctors had told us that he required a prolonged period of rest if he ever wanted to live a normal life again. He simply did not heed or believe it. When he recovered from the fever in Andhra, the heart was in such a very bad condition that the doctors decided that there could be no question of touring any more, either now or later, and told me that, it I wanted him to live at all, I should see to that he never climbed a staircase again.' In those days, they would not allow him even to go down the two steps from the veranda of the house where we stayed, into the garden. "The next thing I knew, only a couple of weeks later, we were continuing the tour interrupted by the illness, into Foodless villages, in that humid heat which of all weathers affected him worst, and with such hot spiced food as was poison for him. I remember how in despair I asked once for nothing but boiled eggs, which were promptly supplied-neatly shelled and rolled in chilli powder. "As was to be, expected, in one of those villages he fell ill again, and I do not think there was even a doctor anywhere, nearby. I was all the while profoundly worried and upset and knew it was all wrong to go on like this. But I dreaded nothing more than the idea of making him feel a sick man, or that he could not now do for what he had gone to jail or generally to interfere with what he thought was right and essential. "Back in Bombay in the worst season of the year, at last he submitted for the first time, to systematic medical treatment for two months, and improved a lot. I set up household in our room, where heaps of papers had to be carefully removed every time he wanted to shave himself or when we had our meals, all on the one big table.

But the first time of settled normal life, with a strict routine, did him no end of good. Seeing that was what he required, I got the confidence that, if I only could strictly adhere to this, without making him feel that it was a 'regime' he might after all become alright and safe, and we would prove the doctors wrong and fool fate. "Well so we did for seventeen years. And good years they were. It was not always easy sailing, and my confidence was tried hard at times. Touring could not be avoided, and a strict discipline of work, sleep and diet, and some hours of rest during the day, not always, indeed seldom, be observed. Sometimes we toured for several months at a stretch. That was a great strain and almost every tour was interrupted and programmes upset due to illness. Often I was dismayed at the thought that time till the next tour would hardly be enough to make him recover from the previous one; and how long could he carry on like this? "He simply ignored his condition and worked even when ill. When he was too ill to work, he went quietly to bed and tried to sleep himself back to health; he had a wonderful sleep.

But he would not think of caution. Even if he knew that he could not stand some food offered, he would eat it, knowing that it meant a week's trouble, rather than hurt the feelings of the host. When people came and sat on late in the evenings, while he had some work to do, he would rather sit and do it until the early hours of the morning than ask them to go home, though lack of sleep would spoil his next day. "In the evenings, especially when on tour, after a day's strenuous work, friends usually invited us for meals and drinks, and the more they loved him, the more they plied him with drinks. Never a glass got a chance to be empty before it was filled to the brim again. Actually he had been medically advised to take some brandy, but much of it was bad for his heart. How often, when glass after glass was filled, I drank up the halves and more of his as well, hoping that none would notice. I saw no other choice.

Hospitality would have its way. And to express my worries would have spoiled the fun. He would have hated it. He would not like to need a nanny, nor to be one. So, what else to do? Luckily, I seldom, if ever, betrayed my ruse. "After the war, when we stayed at home for longer periods, he had started improving considerably in health, Then came the first severe asthama attack, and again I thought all hopes of a normal healthy life for him were dashed. For several years, these attacks recurred, sometimes lasting for several weeks and causing him intense suffering and almost complete suspension of work.

But by and by we found out what gave him relief and even how to prevent attacks, or at least breaking their severity. For the last three or four years they could be practically avoided and in the couple of years before the accident at Mussoorie, his health and general condition had been better and more vigorous in every way than ever since his release from jail. "We had created the form for the contents of his existence, and he was in his element here. At last my determined confidence lost the underlying fear for his life which had been haunting me ever since he left Europe for India, to face certain arrest. He too, I believe, was happy and content. With him, the question of confidence or otherwise did not arise, because he never thought of himself in that way. He made the most of every day, as if it was the last, though never thinking that it would be, much too intent on his work and ideas to have time for such thoughts, which he would have considered morbid; and anyhow there seemed to be no, cause for them. "During his illness after the first attack of cerebral thrombosis, he sometimes thought of it, as he described in his New Year's message in January 1953. In the last illness, ever since he was quite conscious, I do not think he ever seriously doubted that he was recovering again; and when he was depressed, I always reminded him how much worse he had been the year before and how perfectly well, after recovering from it. Indeed, during the last summer at Mussoorie, he was again in such good general health, and lived and worked so normally and happily, that there seemed to be no reason for worry, although I tried to take also no risks. "Once he started working, he never liked to stop. There was so much work; the more he did, the more it seemed to grow under his hands.

And he was so full of new plans in connection with the trip abroad. For a long time the idea of going out of the country again had not at all attracted him. Now he felt the time had come to renew old contacts and make new ones because he had something ready to say and to give. To prevent him overdoing and straining himself too much, I changed his habit of working on in the evening after dinner by persuading him to our games of chess. Life seemed to be more promising than ever, and happier too for having been practically reconquered from so near despair. Then came the second attack, and that too but conquered again. And then this. What an anniversary! " Thus came to an end on that night on January 25, 1954 a very eventful life which started in 1887 in an obscure village in Bengal. There are few people in India and may be in the whole world who had as eventful a life as that of Roy. As a boy in his teens he joined the ranks of militant nationalists and through his exploits and organisational ability rose to a position high enough to be sent as a representative to negotiate an arms deal with the authorities of the German military command. The search for arms proved futile, but it took him to the New World and to a new world of ideas and ideals.

A militant nationalist turned into a dedicated communist. He rose high in the communist hierarchy, but did not hesitate to leave those high positions when he disagreed with the policies that were laid down. He returned to India, sixteen years after his departure in search of arms, a lone fighter for freedom with a concrete programme of national revolution. He had to face the opposition of the British Government, Indian communists and orthodox nationalists. In spite of that opposition, he built up a sizeable political party, but dissolved it when in the course of his search for truth he came to the conclusion that political parties obstructed the growth of democracy. Roy was entirely a self-made man. With little education when he joined the political movement, he had to rely entirely on his wits, intelligence and courage to forge ahead in that dedicated group of revolutionaries. When he landed in the United States he was all alone in that wide land looking out for friends and for a new philosophy of life.

The same was the case in Mexico when he went there as a political fugitive. But when he left about two years later he had built up a communist party, the first outside Russia, and had risen to the position of an un-official adviser to the President of the country, all by his own unaided effort. He went to Moscow with the recommendation of Borodin but his subsequent rise in the communist hierarchy was entirely due to the brilliance of his mind and his mastery over the theory and practice of communism. He returned to India with a big reputation as a revolutionary but without any friends or patron to push him ahead. As a matter of fact the rightist as well as the leftist establishments were arrayed against him. Whatever he achieved in the country was his own creation aided by a few that he was able to gather around him. It will be pointless to say that he committed no mistakes. When he was in Europe he had an exaggerated idea of the revolutionary potentialities of the Indian national movement. He realised that mistake when he returned to India. His reading of the Indian mind was not always correct. The logic on which he relied failed to apply several a time to the Indian situation. His criticism of Gandhiji and other nationalist leaders, based on that logic, turned out to be misdirected. His faith in communism as a liberating force was misplaced as he discovered in the last decade of his life. But it must be said to his credit that disillusion with communitism did not turn him into an anti-communist, as happened with many. It made him go beyond communism and discover a new philosophy of life, Radical Humanism, his best legacy, to the world. His faith in Stalin was equally misplaced. It is because of that faith that he failed to take adequate notice of the inhuman terror that Stalin practised at home, though his actions and policies abroad were subjected to severe criticism in later years. These are, however, small blemishes in an intellectual giant constantly engaged in action to bring about social and political changes according to his ideas. One must resist the temptation of comparing or contrasting Roy with prominent people of his period. The circumstances in which he worked and the fields that he covered are so unique that no comparison or contrast is likely to be meaningful. None of the militant nationalists with whom he worked early in his life went through the transformations that Roy did and none of them rose to the heights of achievement that he did. Several of the communist leaders with whom he worked were already in positions of power or acquired them in Course of time by the grace of the Russian dictator, Stalin.

The only exceptions are Tito of Yugoslavia, Mao of China and Ho Chi Minh of Vietnam. But they were also in power for fairly long periods of their lives and a comparison will be pointless. Some have seen similarities between the thoughts of Roy and those of Mao. A search for them will be useful, but it cannot be efforted here. Nearer home Roy can be compared with Gandhiji. In the last phase of his life Roy moved nearer Gandhiji whom he had criticised throughout his life. Emphasis on morality in Roy's Radical Humanism approximated some Gandhian concepts. But there were several dissimilarities too, for example, Roy's rejection of transcendentalism and his insistence on a rational and scientific outlook. This and the general evaluation of Roy's place in the field of thought are exciting areas of investigation which must be left to others as this study is primarily concerned with the political life of Roy. Roy was constantly engaged in action, in agitation, propaganda and organisation. It was only in jail and during the last half a dozen years of his life that he had some free time to do serious reading and writing.

The fact highlights the massive character of his intellectual production which would do credit to any person who has devoted his whole life to nothing but reading and writing. A good part of that intellectual production is of permanent importance. It places Roy high amongst significant writers of the twentieth century. In the field of action, his capacity to attract people and weld them into a solid group of devoted co-workers was extraordinary. When he returned to India at the end of 1930 he had in the beginning a crowd of enemies around him and only half a dozen friends. But in seven months of underground work under constant threat of arrest he created strong groups at a number of places which not only survived six years of his imprisonment but increased during the period to be available to him for work after his release. Inspired by him the number multiplied in the subsequent period at a rapid rate in spite of several difficulties that Roy and Royists had to face. As a rule nobody who joined Roy ever went away from him. In a couple of cases that it happened, the persons leaving left with high regard and respect for Roy. The reason was Roy's high intellectual calibre, transparent sincerity and utter devotion to the cause, coupled with the personal interest that he took in each one of his colleagues and followers. He had nothing material to give, and yet those who were attracted by his ideas stayed with him through thick and thin. Few political leaders can claim such a record.

Roy's emphasis on reason and rational outlook and his insistence on a revolt against superstition, blind faith and all other forms of mental slavery made it difficult for him to secure a large following. In that respect he stood in sharp contrast with Gandhiji and most other leaders of the national movement.

All of them were advocates and defenders of the so-called spiritual civilisation of India and disliked doing anything that would weaken its hold on the Indian mind, free it from the shackles of that age-old civilisation. He attributed all the ills of the country, social, economic and political, to the spiritual slavery of the people. He was convinced that a mental revolution must precede asocial revolution. That is why alone amongst the political leaders of his generation he stood for Renaissance and devoted a good deal of his time and energy to the development of that movement. That had not make him popular. But he was uncompromising in his stand on that issue. Roy was uncompromising on all matters which he considered vital. With a little adjustment and diplomatic silence he could have avoided his break with CI and could have after a few years returned to India with its backing and then the history of CPI would have been different. With a little deferential attitude towards Gandhiji and some understanding with Nehru he might have found an important place in the national movement and then the transfer of power might have taken place earlier and the new State of independent India might have been more progressive.

But there is no point in indulging in these might have been. They did not happen because Roy was Roy. He was habitual to think for himself and arrive at his own conclusions. Once he came to conclusion, it was next to imfeasible to stop him front seeing it through. He was convinced that the ultra-left line adopted by the sixth congress of CI was ruinous and nothing could stop him from exposing its defects and working for its alteration. He was convinced that Gandhism was a philosophy of social reaction and nothing could stop him from exposing its reactionary character and struggling to liberate the national movement from its stranglehold. He held Gandhiji in high respect as a mobiliser of the masses; that respect increased when Gandhiji turned his back upon power and retired into the strife-torn Bengal of those days to pursue alone his mission of communal harmony. But Roy's opposition to the Gandhian programme, policy and outlook did not diminish a bit. His opinions were always well thoughtout, based on an objective consideration of all relevant facts and logically related to an overall view of the situation. Convinced of the correctness of his opinions, he stood by them in spite of the displeasure of those in power. Insistence on propagating the truth as he saw it was one of the dominant characteristics of Roy. It kept him away from popularity as well as power. Throughout his life he was indifferent to both. The intellectual eminence of Roy is beyond dispute. His intellect wandered over several subjects, social sciences as well as natural sciences, and whatever it touched it absorbed quickly. He had, moreover, the ability of reproducing whatever he grasped for the advantage of ordinary readers in a language that they could understand.

The books that he wrote on a variety of subjects bear evidence to it. Politics and social sciences were, however, his special subjects. Politics without parties and power, the basic constituent of Radical Humanism propounded by him, may yet show democracy a way out of the recurring crises which it faces all over the world. If that happens, Roy will have a permanent place in the galaxy of political scientists. He will also live as an eminent thinker. Few political activists have been thinkers. Day to day political work leaves them little time to devote to thinking. Roy combined thinking with political work from the beginning. It is thinking over the problems of national independence that converted him from a militant nationalist into a communist. Even after becoming a communist he did not give up his thinking. That explains his controversy with Lenin which ultimately led him to develop his theory of decolonisation. Whoever the father of the term, the theory in fact visualised disintegration of imperialism through the operation of economic forces and its efforts to enter into a partnership with the nationalist bourgeoisie. When the second world war broke out, Roy foresaw the acceleration of that process and could boldly declare that, after winning the war, England would not be able to continue her imperialist rule over India. Roy's prophecy came true, but he has received little credit so far for that rare insight into the future of Indian politics. Until the later part of the war his thinking was constricted by Marxism though he was never an orthodox Marxist. Developments during and after the war exposed to his eyes the limitations not only of communism but also of Marxism as a system of thought. He then moved beyond communism and Marxism and developed the philosophy of Radical Humanism. It came to him not as a revelation but as the ripe fruit of the Studies that he had carried on in jail and in the hours that he could snatch out of political work and as the response of a cultivated and sensitive mind to the seemingly insoluble problems of the world. Radical Humanism is Roy's abiding contribution to modern thought and to modern man's struggle for freedom. Freedom was the one aim of his life. He did not equate it with national independence though the early part of his life was devoted to work to secure it. He did Dot also equate it with the ending of the exploitation of the large masses to which his life as a communist was dedicated. These were incorporated in freedom; but to him freedom had a much wider connotation. It was "the progressive disappearance of all restrictions on the unfolding of the potentialities of individuals, as human beings, and not as cogs in the wheels of a mechanised social organism." That sets Roy apart from several other advocates of freedom. He was the prophet of individual freedom and it was his conviction that free individuals can alone build up a society of freedom and equality.

Throughout his life and, more particularly, in the last decade, he endeavoured to get together free individuals to work in cooperation in various fields for the development of a free society. He laid the foundation of a brotherhood of "spiritually free men united in the determination of creating a world of freedom" The ideas that he left behind are so vital that the brotherhood may grow even after his death. In the case of a man like Roy ordinary criteria of success or failure do not apply. According to those criteria, his was a life of political failure-for he did not attain any high political position nor did he leave behind any powerful political organisation to sing his praises. But the wealth of ideas that he has left behind will provide food for thought and inspiration for action to generations to come. Those ideas may in course of time find greater acceptance and help the growth of a society of freedom and equality. That will be his success and no success would have pleased him more.

8

M.N. Roy : An Overview

Manbendra Nath Roy was a great Marxist philosopher and Indian freedom fighter. He was one of the extremists in the struggle of Indian national freedom. For quite sometime he remained under the influence of Communism, but subsequently he changed his ideology and struggled even from the platform of Indian National Congress. His approach to the problem was absolutely different and quite untraditional. He had deep faith in individual freedom. He was a rationalist and wanted to test every philosophy by the yardstick of reason and rationality. He very strongly believed in the concept of freedom and placed that above everything else. For him state and society should come latter and the individual first in all social, economic and political arrangements. About human nature he said that it must be governed by the same principles as physical universe.

His significant contribution, however, is his concept of organized democracy which was quite different from indirect democracies in the East and the West In his philosophy organized democracy provided more freedom to the individual than indirect democracy. To a large extent he was indebted to Marx for his political ideas but with the passage of time he tried to interpret that in a way which was quite different from that of Marx. He even challenged his basic concepts of dialectical materialism and theory of surplus value. For the first time he gave it a very logical way, the concept of decolonisation. His ideas were also defective in many ways but all the more he is still studied seriously.

Early Life. M.N. Roy was a national revolutionary. His original name was Narendra Nath Bhattacharya. He was born in 1893 in 24-Parganas District of Bengal and got his education in Calcutta. From his very childhood he was influenced by the activities of India's revolutionaries and wanted to actively participate in country's national freedom struggle. He plunged himself in the national struggle which was then being fomented in Bengal due to the partition of that province. For the first time he was arrested in 1907 when he was hardly 14 in a political dacoity case in Calcutta. He was, however, acquitted because the trying judge could not reconcile himself to the idea of a boy of his age participating in a political dacoity. His activities, however, came to prominence during the First World War in 1914. The German revolutionaries, during the course of war came to the conclusion that one of the effective methods of checking British resistance was to create internal troubles in India and thus to divert the attention of Britishers to that side. They, therefore, decided to smuggle arms and money to India to aid Indian revolutionaries. The revolutionaries there also organized an Indian Independence Committee in Berlin which was to be mainly responsible to smuggle arms from Germany to India. Roy was given the responsible task of receiving arms in Java from a ship which was to reach there. With full determination Roy went there but he came back disappointed and frustrated because the ship did not reach there. A year later in 1915 he again went to Java in search of arms for Indian revolutionaries but again he failed in his mission. But this time lie adopted quite a different course. Instead of returning to India he proceeded to Japan from where subsequently he went to China, U.S.A., Mexico, Germany and U.S.S.R. He arrived in San Francisco in late 1915. It was here that he came in contact with many patriot Indian students and tried to organize them so as to provide a forum for Indian national struggle. It was at this stage that he changed his name from Bhattacharya to M.N. Roy.

Roy's Visit to U.S.A. His mission in America, however was not very successful because American Government, due to its policy of neutrality in war, virtually declined to provide its land to Indian nationals for their national propaganda. He therefore, decided to go to Mexico. In Mexico he moved with American socialists who had sympathies with India's freedom struggle and thus found a fertile ground for his activities.

Indulgence in Marxism

While in Mexico Roy contributed several articles depicting the poverty of India and the method by which the Britishers were exploiting Indians. His articles were so attractive that he was invited to attend a meeting of the Executive Committee of the Socialist Party. He was becoming gradually a moving force in the socialist camps and in Mexico he founded the first Communist Party outside Russia and became its Secretary General. It was at this stage that he came in contact with Borodin, a Russian favourite of Lenin, who was so much influenced by him that he recommended his case for an invitation to attend Second World Congress of the Communist International. On his recommendation he was invited and left Mexico for Russia. On his way he stopped in Germany and made friendship with leading German socialists. At the next Communist International Congress, Roy also played his part and even pointed out the defects of resolutions sponsored by official group headed by Lenin. He also attended the Congress of the Communist International. He was also elected a member of Central Asiatic Board constituted by the Communist Party to propagate the cause of Communism in India. In 1922 he went to Berlin to organize Indian National revolutionaries over there where he also started his journal the Vanguard of Indian Independence.' He was named a member of the Presidium of Comintern at its 4th Congress.

All along Roy believed that for the cause of Communism in India it was essential that there should be a separate Communist Party of India which should have an independent role and should not get guidance from outside organisations. He also proposed for the organization of People's Party with a revolutionary programme. He was sent to China to propagate the cause of Communism in that country. But he failed in his mission there and Communism could not develop in that country. Throughout this period Roy was developing his own political ideas and philosophy which was in many ways different from the traditional Communist philosophy. He gave his theory of decolonization which is being discussed in detail separately. On his return from China he left for Berlin and there he tried to contact the Indian Communists. He gradually became dissatisfied with Communist organization and 1928 he even did no, attend Sixth Congress of the Comintern and in his absence he was very vehemently criticised by his opponents and was expelled from the Comintern. It was during this phase that Roy-Lenin Debate took place which has been discussed separately.

Back to India. Thus having developed his differences with the Communist organization, Roy decided to come back to India and arrived at Bombay in December, 1930 with a forged passport and soon contacted Indian revolutionaries. For quite sometime he could not be detected by Indian police and thus Roy could consolidate his position. On the invitation of Jawaharlal Nehru he attended Karachi Session of Indian National Congress. In July, 1931, he was, however, arrested and ultimately sentenced to six years imprisonment. In 1936, after coming out of jail, he became a member of Indian National Congress which he wanted to organize on a revolutionary basis. It was with this end in view that in 1939, he formed a League of Radical Congressmen which, of course, remained a part of the Indian National Congress. His programme of action envisaged decentralization of authority and snatching of independence from British Imperialism. Soon, however, Roy developed differences with the Indian National Congress on the outbreak of Second World War. Whereas the officially dominant group in the Congress wished to boycott war efforts by Indians and not to favour British Government, Roy was of the opinion that England was fighting the war against Fascism and Nazism and as such it must be won. He even condemned Quit India Movement launched by Gandhiji.

The result of all this was that he became unpopular and lost his prestige and honour. In 1940, Roy founded a separate party known as Radical Democratic Party which ultimately led to his breaking away from Indian National Congress. In 1944 he founded Indian Federation of Labour. Roy was of the opinion that Congress had no inherited right to get rights of ruling over India after the Britishers had withdrawn from India. In 1948 he dissolved his Radical Democratic Party and in its place he founded Indian Renaissance Movement. In 1952 Roy was elected as one of the Vice-Presidents of the International Humanist and Ethical Union founded at Amsterdam. He died in 1954, comparatively unknown.

Influences of Marxian Philosophy. On him was the most significant influence of Marxian philosophy which he studied very thoroughly and which remained virtually the basis of his subsequent ideology though he differed from it in detail. In addition to this he was inspired by social and political leaders of Indian life. He was educated in the national school, and as such the movements started by Swami Ram Tirth and Swami Vivekananda reminding Indians of their supremacy and past cultural glory very much influenced him. Similarly, Roy was inspired by those national leaders who worked through the forum of Indian National Congress and devoted themselves to this national struggle.

On him, was the influence of Bankim Chandra Chatterji who wrote his famous Ananda Math. Roy was absolutely dissatisfied with the methods through which the Britishers tried to exploit the Indians and denied individual rights and liberties. From his very early age the growing poverty of India was an eye-sore for him and freedom, both national and individual, was the only solution to the problem. He was very much influenced by the revolutionaries who devoted themselves thoroughly in undoing the evils of partition of Bengal and were determined to revoke the action. He found that Swadeshi and boycott programmes were active and a realistic approach to Indian political problems. On the international field the victory of Japan over mighty Russia in 1905 was a great moulding and motivating factor on him. He gained confidence that colonial subjects in Asia, including India, could also win their freedom if they had determination and proper organization.

Significant Works of Roy

Some of his significant works are: 1. India in Transition: India's Problems and Its Solution; 2. Revolution and Counter-Revolution in China; 3. Our Differences, 4. Materialism; 5. Science and Philosophy; 6. On the Congress Constitution; 7. People's Plan; 8. National Government. 9. The People's Government; 10. Rise, Romaniticism and Revolution. In addition to this Roy contributed very many articles in several papers and also started his own journals through which he tried to propagate his ideas and philosophy.

Debate with Lenin. In order to have strong set-up of Communist organisation Congress of International Communists was set-up. Second such Congress paid attention to developing strategy for bringing about world revolution. Lenin believed that international capitalist system structurally was basically linked with metropolitan country and for its survival such linking was unavoidable. He therefore believed that conflict in colonies was an integral part of bringing crisis in imperialist world system. It was the pivotal point of Roy-Lenin debate.

The Communists believed that the decision about what in politics depended on the kind of society, its class structure and its likely behaviour political life. Lenin believed that whereas European societies had seen capitalist transformation, colonial societies had not and as such there could be several ways of applying Communism to the latter particularly with regard to the analysis of classes in colonial societies and following of political strategy. From analysis the Communists under Lenin understood not simple class analysis but also the application of methods. Thus it was not merely a set of conclusions but a set of resources from which conclusions could be drawn. What kind of conclusion would be appropriate to a particular case depended on what particular set of resources were considered appropriate for use. Lenin in his preliminary draft thesis to the Congress expressed the view that the task of Communists in colonies was to assist the bourgeois in their democratic liberation movements. They should support nationalist movements not as a finished product but as ongoing process. They should try to bring radicalism in these. If necessary they should have temporary alliance with bourgeoisie democracy in colonial countries but should not merge in it.

Preparation of Draft Thesis. On the eve of Second Congress of Comintern Roy was invited by Lenin to prepare a draft thesis on colonial question and also on his own about colonies. Unlike Lenin, Roy believed that a crisis in world capitalist structure should be expected from the colonies and not from metropolitan centres. He therefore, stressed the need of arriving at a correct evaluation of these societies. Whereas Lenin saw between countries like Russia and the colonies a difference in kind, for Roy it was only a difference in degree. Lenin believed that compromise was a temporary procedural truce with the enemy before hostilities could be begun again on more favourable terms, but for Roy it meant fundamental reversal of position and a decisive one for all acceptance of a subordinate position to imperialist bourgeoisie and selling out to imperialism. According to Roy there was likely to be a continuous process of radicalisation in the national movement. He believed that every change in leadership was likely to bring with it a new polarisation in the movement and that only the Communists could lead the movement to final victory. Then for Lenin dualism meant contradictory patterned behaviour which indicated a deliberate strategy between politics of confrontation and compromise. But for Roy dualism was existence of two stages in political set up of bourgeoisie class.

The first stage being progressive phase which will be disturbed by compromises whereas second was that of final political crisis in which bourgeoisie would betray the national movement. Roy also made a distinction between national movements led by the bourgeoisie trying to have political compromise and reformism on the one hand and social revolutionary trend on the other, in which efforts ill be made for national independence and end of exploitation. According to Lenin during finance capitalist and imperialist phase of economy it was necessary to achieve an integration between bourgeoisie nationalistic struggle of colonial world and the rising proletarian movements in the advanced Western countries. But Roy tried to expose anti-proletariat 'attitude of Asian leaders. He did not support Russian Revolution which was fought under Lenin, as according to him Revolution was not in mechanical conformity to a previously laid down law of History. He called it fluke of history, which occurred because of combination of several circumstances. He considered Russian Communism as State-Capitalism. Though Lenin-Roy debate came to an end in 1920 yet the issues raised continued to concern of Comintern, which admitted Roy's intellectual worth and entrusted him the leadership of the communist movement in India. Roy's long term analysis of Indian society which he has given in India in Transition is considered one of his major contributions to Communist world. He has given the views on the changes which Indian society is to see in the long run and fluctuations which may come in it in the short term, because of changes in political and economic set up.

Study of the Existing Condition of India. According to Roy British colonialism brought Indian economy into contact both European capitalism and capitalist economic structure. Thus Indian economy was brought under the controlling influence of international capitalist structure. British colonialism, according to him, implanted capitalist economy in India. In this connection Roy paid attention to four classes namely labour bourgeoisie, the petty bourgeoisie, the peasantry and the proletariat.

Roy believed that India was not under feudalistic system, which has been destroyed because of gradual domination of entire economy by British capital. Indian economy was landed aristocracy, the bourgeoisie intellectuals and petty peasantry and working classes, including landless peasants. The bourgeoisie was the product of colonialism and dependent on colonial domination. Industrial capital in India has come under British domination. Roy has said that bourgeoisie are gradually moving towards lower forms of industrial enterprise. According to him colonial administration in India after some resistance would acceed to political pressures and he saw a narrow relation between economy and politics. According to him secret of poverty and misery of rural India can be traced the fact that capitalist economy had brought under its control almost the whole of agricultural production.

Indian peasantry was thus subjected to both Indian and foreign capital. He also said that existence of huge amount of capital invested in land was forcing rapid concentration of capital in the possession of non-agrarian sections. He has said that on development of large scale industry would depend the future of India. In M.N. Roy's views as industrial base of India will increase with that rank of labour will not only increase but will become strong. There will then be a situation of compromise between bourgeoisie of India and imperial bourgeoisie. He said that the task of winning liberation of India would be shouldered by the workers and the peasants on the basis of class struggle. He has also discussed Indian situation under three broad headings namely (a) the rise of Indian bourgeoisie, (b) the pauperisation of peasantry, and (c) poverty of urban proletariat. According to him the future Indian nation was going to be shaped by progressive forces latent in Indian society.

Suggestions to Solve Problems of India. In his book 'India's Problems and Its Solution' brought out in 1922, Roy has criticised Gandhian philosophy and also constructive programme of Congress adopted at Bardoli in that year. He was in favour of creation of revolutionary mass party which could create discontentment among the people and also organise strikes. He put forth his programme of militant action of masses. It was with this end in view that at the end of 1922 his Vanguard Party sent a programme for the consideration of Gaya Congress. In it Roy suggested abolition of landlordism, eight hour work day, creation of a national militia to replace standing army and fixation of minimum wages for workers by legislation. His programme also included reduction of land rent, free and compulsory education, development of modern industries with state aid and separation of state and religion. In his programme Roy also included creation of workers councils in big industries, state aid for modernising agriculture, profit sharing system in big industries, abolition of indirect taxes, legislation of labour organisations and nationalisation of all public utilities. He also favoured progressive income tax. His programme however, did not receive much attention at that time because it was felt that it aimed at introducing Communism in India.

Concept of Radical Humanism. M.N. Roy was sufficiently under the influence of Communism but as the time passed with that his faith in individual freedom increased. He developed his own philosophy called Radical Humanism. M.N. Roy was the exponent of Radical or New Humanism. He believed that science has proved to be an important factor for the development of creative faculties of man. For him renaissance opened a new era in modern civilisation. He stood for new humanism which was based on natural reason and in which conscience should be free. In it he laid stress on the sovereignty of individual and in his view society had no reason to impose itself on any one. For him a spiritually liberated individual is very essential for a better and happy society. He was believer of world federation in which none would be limited by the boundaries of national state as such ideologies as Communism, Socialism, Fascism etc. would gradually end. He said that ideas give birth to revolutions and as such ideas precede revolution. Revolutions come when vast majority accepts new ideas. In dictatorship there can be no scope for human development. He believed that for establishment of free world it was most desirable that sources of production should not be used for personal ends but for the welfare of weaker sections of society, both in letter and spirit. In his view freedom is biological heritage and closely linked with struggle for existence. Three pillars of his freedom are motivating power of social advancement, collective progress, individualism and rationalism. For him each one thinks in terms of cause and effect. Nationalism is not the final stage in his social philosophy but he feels it neglects social questions and as such it should be replaced by brotherhood. For him new humanism is cosmopolitan. He has made a distinction between cosmopolitanism and internationalism.

Freedom of the People. According to M.N. Roy individual is an end itself and every other organization in the society simply means to an end. He was not ready to subordinate individual freedom even to religion or morality or to any other supernatural power. He believed that man had always been struggling for freedom and his joining the civil state and society was only on the condition that his freedom would be protected. In his opinion it was an evolutionary and continuing process. He said that those institutions and organizations which had been set up to safeguard individual freedom often have tried to master him and that was quite unhealthy. In his opinion state was primarily brought into being to check all impediments and hindrances which checked the growth of man individual today the state was trying to subordinate individuals and wanted to become an end in itself instead of being means to an end. Similarly religion had become the master of man's mind and tries to check individual freedom though gradually its grip is weakening.

His Approach About Obstacles on Individual Freedom. As already said Roy very much loved individual freedom and in his opinion freedom is above everything else. He, however, feels that there are certain obstacles in the way of individual freedom. The greatest obstacle is the state which is trying to become an end in itself rather than retaining its essential character of remaining means to an end. The state is originally intended to be the custodian of human development and freedom but with the passage of time it becomes a hindrance on that very freedom.

Similarly, he believes that religion is equally a hindrance in man's search for freedom. It is in religion that man is made to subordinate and put himself under the control of certain super-natural and heavenly revealed philosophies whether those are based on rationalism or not. Since most of the people have faith in religion and can not challenge the validity of religious principles, therefore, religion is becoming more and more an impediment in the path of individual freedom. Similarly he found that marriage and family life were also other hindrances on his path of freedom. He came to, the conclusion that these institutions try to establish harmony in their own Way with the result that people develop a very narrow outlook and in some cases even become irrational to protect their selfish narrow ends.

In his philosophy both these institutions are even now great hindrances and man is gradually beginning to depend on others, thus sacrificing his wisdom and initiative. In his philosophy if these difficulties were to be crossed over for that it was imperative that the individual should depend on his inherited wisdom and rationality of thinking rather than depending on super-natural dogmas and institutions. He came to the conclusion that the curse of modem society was the notion of class rather than that of individual. He felt that Marx and many other thinkers just forgot that the individuals collectively constitute class which is an outcome of individual's willing association to come together and to perform certain functions. The present notion of giving priority to class over the individual is just reversing the course of history. Roy, therefore, felt that the concept of class or society should be made relative and that it should be very clearly understood that society is means to an end not an end in itself. He, therefore, feels that the greatest hindrance to individual freedom, alongwith other factors, is society and class. In his Organized Democracy and in People's Plan he has suggested means by which individual can remain free by remaining a part of the class to which he belongs.

His Approach About Materialism. M.N. Roy essentially believed in the basic doctrine of historical materialism as expounded by Marx, but he differed from him in details. In his opinion there was no difference between organic and un-organic matter. He was of the opinion that all living bodies were formed out of certain chemical matters and their combination resulted in the creation of other matters. In his opinion mind was a characteristic of matter at a high stage of development. Roy was also of the opinion that there was a constant inter-penetration and interdependence between man and matter. He 'thus tried to establish a close relationship between an individual's mind and matter.

His Approach About Nature of Man. According to M.N Roy by nature man loves freedom and that he was born free and everywhere he was in chains. In his philosophy man was rational and as such above all the other living-beings. Rationalism was the most essential and basic standard of human development. In his own words, "It is the reason in man which harmonizes the people of human will with the law governess of physical universe." Roy believed that rationalism was a part of human nature and in fact he inherited it from his very birth. There was no stage in human history when an individual was devoid of reason and thinking power.

His Approach About Democracy. According to M.N. Roy in its present form democracy did not grant either economic or social or political freedom. It sacrificed individual freedom for the sake of collective freedom and required a fundamental change both in nature and character. He, therefore, pleaded for an organized democracy based on the concept of decentralization and which was to start from below rather than from above. In such a democracy every one will be a participant and that democracy alone can guarantee individual freedom.

His Approach About History. According to Roy, human history is nothing else but a record of struggle for freedom. The people have always struggled for their and that at no stage their struggle comes to an end. In his philosophy history normally develops according to the logic of thought and is an evolutionary process. In his opinion, evolution is the law of history and revolutions come but rarely. He believed that a revolution could not be a success unless it was required by the society for its collective development. In other words, in his opinion, Marxian interpretation of history of class struggle is rather defective. According to Marx, history is hitherto nothing else but that of class struggle, whereas for Roy history is not only an economic aspect of life but something broader and wider. It includes economic, social as well as political aspects of an individual's life.

Radical Humanism : Criticism. Roy has been criticised for his concept of radical humanism. It has perhaps rightly been said that though Roy condemned Lenin and Marx and called himself a radical humanist yet he could not shed away the influence of Marxism. He also failed to give logical and adequate reasons as to how the matter was capable of producing life, and as such without giving any satisfactory alternative concept of materialism he denounced Marxian theory of dialectical materialism. It has been said that Roy based his whole theory on a very important and essential basis namely rationalism. The pivot of his philosophy is that everything should be decided by reason before that is accepted but unfortunately he has failed to clearly and precisely define the term 'reason'. He has also failed to give any standard and acceptable definition of judging rationality and irrationality. Similarly, he has denounced religion on the plea that it is a hindrance in the development of freedom.

But who can deny that religion has all along been responsible for cultural and intellectual development and as such it is essential for development of human life. To deny and to criticise an institution which deserves a rightful place in the society is obviously undesirable. Similarly, Roy has failed to satisfy his thinkers how human urge for freedom will not result in clashes. It is but natural that while struggling for individual freedom collective freedom is bound to suffer and clashes between the individuals are bound to come to the fore. Then another defect of his philosophy is that if all are capable of satisfying their reasonable urges then there is no need for the state or similar other institutions but again we find that is not historically correct.

Another serious defect in his philosophy is that he has tried to establish that physical and social beings are governed by the same principles but such an analogy does not appear to be very correct, as he himself subsequently establishes, that social beings are rational whereas physical beings are bound to obey certain pre-determined and decided laws without testing them on tests of rationality and reasonability. M.N.

Roy's radical humanism was not Something new. Long before him, both in the East and West, many political thinkers and philosophers had championed the cause of individual freedom. Roy only tried to give a new outlook by freeing human beings from all other social obligations which is not a practical proposition. Each one is a member of State. He has faith in some religion or the other. Similarly he is a member of society and family. He is bound to lead a married life and all these are most essential requirements of his life. Therefore to think of an individual beyond these pressures is only utopian and not real to life. He wants to create a free man above class and society which is rather not practical. In his love for individual freedom he went to extremes and became an idealist rather than a realist. Both, in Europe and in India, he joined very important organizations, namely the Communist Party and All India Congress but nowhere he could permanently adjust himself with the result that his philosophy could not get much prominence, importance and popularity.

Roy's Approach About Organized Democracy. Roy, like Jayaprakash Narayan, very severely criticised parliamentary democracy based on party system. In his opinion introduction of party system in a democracy is not only unhealthy but frustrates the very meaning and purpose of this institution. Roy was so much opposed to the system that he gave the concept of organized democracy which he based on decentralization. In his organized democracy there was no political party system and the power was to be vested in the hands of the masses who were to remain sovereign in the real sense of the word. He, however, himself laid down certain prerequisites or conditions for the success of his organized democracy. One such condition was that the people should be educated and made to realise their sense of responsibility. They also should have high moral character and the power should be vested only in the hands of those who have established their integrity and high standard of intelligence. Roy stood for perfect elective democracy but in his opinion it was not possible to immediately introduce that because the people have as yet not attained high intellectual and moral standards. He, therefore, suggested that in the initial stages there should be elective as well as selective democracy. It was on this basic presumption that Roy also gave a draft constitution for India which was to be a model of organized democracy.

Roy's Approach on Modern Democracy. Roy was an individualist and believed in individual freedom. According to him, individual is above everything else and all institutions and organizations in the society should work with this end in view. He even left Communist party as that did not provide any opportunity for individual freedom. He tried to establish that the individuals always struggle for achieving freedom which is eternal and the most natural urge. He felt that democracy essentially accepted, though in theory, the ideal of individual liberty, yet in practice it acted to the contrary. Roy was very much critical of political party system which had become a part of parliamentary democracy. He was surprised to see that with the passage of time party system was gaining more and more strength, and leadership in the party expected all its members to work like dead machines simply obeying the commands of their leadership. He also felt that politics was becoming a scramble for power and there was now no regard for morality. He tries to establish that with the introduction of party system democracy has not remained a form of government of the people and by the people. He, therefore, came to the conclusion that for preserving individual freedom it was essential that whole concept of democracy should be radically changed and replaced by another system known as the system of organized democracy.

India's Draft Constitution. In his organized democracy ultimate sovereignty was to be vested with the people. In each village and city there were to be local people's committees to be elected for a period of one year on the basis of adult franchise. In his arrangement the system of proportional representation was to be adopted with a view to giving adequate representation to the minorities. Instead of joint electorates lie favoured the system of separate electorates in-so-far as India was concerned. These Committees were to be responsible for electing members to the higher legislative bodies namely provincial and federal legislatures. These were also empowered to express their opinion on matters pending before the legislatures and giving guidance and instructions to the representatives elected by the Committees. Like Switzerland, Roy also wanted to introduce the institutions of referendum and initiative so as to make the democracy useful, purposeful and effective. At the centre there was to be a Supreme People's Council which was to consist of an elected Governor-General, a Council of States and a Federal Assembly. The Council of States was the Upper House of the legislature and had an advisory role. It was supposed that its members shall not actively participate in politics. Each professional group was to recommend a number of representatives to be elected to the Council of States who were to be elected only by the Head of the State.

The Council of States was to have no control over the executive authority. The Federal Assembly was the Lower House and consisted of persons elected by indirect election. It was a supreme body responsible to Supreme People's Council. The Governor-General was to preside over the joint sittings of both the Councils. More or less the same pattern was to be adopted in the provinces. Part I of his proposed Constitution relates to the declaration of rights and fundamental principles. It says that the supreme sovereignty belongs to the entire people who have absolute right to modify or change any political organization or society. He also has a right to rise and revolt against oppression and all provinces shall be formed on the basis of linguistic and cultural homogeneity.

There will be a democratic constitution and the land as well as the underground riches shall be collective property of the community. Modem means will be introduced for increasing production and basic industries shall be under state control. There will be collective ownership of large-scale industries under state management and the cultivators shall be entitled to hold land. There win also be encouragement to cooperative agriculture and adequate employment and relief shall be given to the citizens. There shall be an 8-hour day and social security for old and sick people. Children upto the age of 14 shall be free and there will be freedom of the press. People shall be given freedom to safeguard their economic interests by forming associations and no person shall be placed under arrest without legal validity. Private correspondence shall be protected and people shall have freedom of worship. Men and women will have equal rights and responsibilities and legitimate rights of the minorities shall be protected. Discussing the sources of authority he said that people will be the final source of authority and shall exercise that through People's Committees which shall be annually elected on the basis of adult franchise by citizens of 18 years of age. The number of members of people's committees will be 1/5 of total number of voters in the locality. The committee shall help the citizens to exercise their sovereign right and make democratic power effective. They shall nominate candidates to seek election to higher legislative bodies and guide their representatives there. They shall also be competent to recall their initiative in legislative measures.

Federation of Provinces. The Federal Union will cover both the British India and Indian states and the provinces shall be formed on linguistic basis and cultural homogeneity. The Provincial People's Council shall have the right to entertain a proposal that the province concerned may be kept out of the proposed federal Union. There shall be the system of referendum also, provided the proposal is supported by a majority of voters in the province. The provinces can also remain out of the Union and constitute another federation. The Federation of India shall be a member of British Commonwealth to be renamed as Indo-British Commonwealth of Free Peoples. India shall be a democratic State and the provinces shall have a right to break away from the Union. The supreme power shall be in the Supreme People's Council.

Composition of Federal Assembly. The Federal Assembly shall consist of elected representatives each representing 5 lakh people. They shall be elected on the basis of adult franchise through a system specially devised for the election. Its life shall be 4 years and shall have paid members. It will meet atleast quarterly and can be dissolved earlier by the Governor-General on the recommendation of Prime Minister. Supreme People's Committee will be the final authority to take decisions about the dissolution.

Appointment of Council of States. The Council Of States will be appointed by the provincial Government of the federating provinces and its numbers shall be equal for all provinces. Each provincial group will nominate a panel of 10 names out of which provincial Government will appoint two as members of the Council of States. The Provincial Government shall also have a right to appoint two more persons of repute and 3 civil servants as members of Council of States. The Provincial Government shall have no power to cancel the appointment once made. Each member will remain in office for a period of 6 years and shall also be eligible for reappointment. Both the Council of States and Federal Assembly shall have simultaneous sessions. The Council will guide and advise the Assembly. Both these will meet in joint sessions with the Governor-General and the Supreme People's Council, and shall be final authority in the State.

Elected Governor-General. There shall be an elected Governor-General for a period of 5 years to be elected by the entire electorate. He will preside over the joint sessions of the Council and Assembly and shall be competent to give final approval to every legislative measure. He shall also be empowered to dissolve the Assembly.

The Federal Assembly shall be the legislative body with the power to legislate on all matters. Its decisions shall be ratified by the Supreme People's Council and for their application to the provinces these will be sent to the Provincial Legislatures. On certain matters there shall be no need for ratification of the decisions. The provinces shall also have a right to challenge the laws passed by the Assembly with regard to the subjects requiring ratification by the provinces. There shall also be provision for referendum. The Council of States shall also be consulted but its disapproval in no way shall adversely affect Assembly's decisions. Each law must he approved by the Supreme People's Council, which will have a right to Veto. The provincial Government could also appeal to the supreme federal court against such Veto. In cases of conflict between a federal and a provincial law the former was to prevail. There were also provisions about the exercise of executive power and economic organization of the society. He also dealt with the organization of judiciary which was to have original jurisdictions and was required to deal with cases brought before it both by the individual and the provinces. There was also a section dealing with local self-government

fullest advantage of scientific and technological advancement. There will also be a planning body which shall be responsible for allocating priorities in the use of national resources and improve our social utility services. In the arrangement tile superstructure of the large scale production of basic needs of the society will he on co-operative basis. Such an arrangement is bound to end exploitation.

Roy's Planned Economy. In his opinion if individual freedom is to be preserved then there should be perfect economic democracy and purchasing power of the people should be increased. That could alone be possible in a planned economy by two ways. First, the goods should be produced at very cheap cost and secondly, government should subsidise the goods to be exported; but in both the cases the burden should be put on the tax-payer who could in turn expect to get back the profits after sometime. In-so-far as India was concerned, Roy was of the opinion that purchasing power of Indian masses could only go up if there was an extensive programme of setting up new industries. In his opinion burden should shift from land to industry as land is already over-burdened. He, however, does not fail to realize that in India there is uneven distribution of land which is responsible for the mal-production and mal-distribution of agricultural produce. He, has therefore, suggested a proper scientific re-distribution and adjustment of land so that there is rational and reasonable distribution and production of agricultural commodities. He also felt that if large-scale construction programme including that of roads and bridges etc., was taken up that might help in the distribution of wealth and thereby living standard of the labourers might go up.

Roy on Indian Economy. Roy was conscious of the fact that his economic arrangement should be such which suits Indian conditions and environments. He, in fact, differentiated between tile economies of industrially advanced and underdeveloped countries. In his arrangement, India rightly fell tinder the category of a country with all under developed economy. According to him, in India advancement can only be possible when there is large scale industrialization. He however, realizes that introduction of agricultural machinery was bound to result in unemployment of thousands of peasants and workers working oil our fields. He, therefore, hesitated to suggest introduction of agricultural machinery for our peasants. He, has suggested that instead of manure we should use cattle dung. Similarly, he has also suggested the use of tubewells as an alternative to wells for watering our fields. In his constitution of India he has devoted a section to economic organization of our society.

Under his arrangement economically India will be a cooperative commonwealth where goods shall be produced Primarily for satisfying the requirements of the people. There will be proper planning and regulation for production and distribution which shall ultimately be the entire responsibility of the state. He has also suggested a national planning authority consisting of experts with proper representation of State Bank. Such a body shall be subordinate to the Council of States. In his arrangement industrial and agricultural enterprises financed by the state shall be the collective Property of the people and State Bank will control the entire credit system Of the state. The ownership of land, underground riches and railways will be transferred to the people. The freedom of enterprise, individual as well as corporate, will be guaranteed subject to the condition that the Production will satisfy the requirements of the people.

Critical Appraisal. Like his political arrangement his economic theory has also been severely criticised. The basic principle of his theory is co-operative arrangement. In his arrangement co-operatives will work as independent bodies looking after mutual interests. He has, however, forgotten one very essential fact namely that of co-ordination. For a successful system there must be proper co-ordination of various institutions and organizations devoted to the cause of production and distribution. Under Roy's arrangement there is no authority to coordinate these functions. If his intention is to leave that job to the State then that must intervene in the functioning of co-operatives which is not acceptable to Roy. Similarly, Roy has also not created an organization to settle disputes which are bound to arise among various functional groups. Similarly, if his arrangement of co-operative is taken to its logical conclusions then that shall mean in agriculture, putting of land under a joint management. But who can deny that such a system will kill initiative and incentive resulting in low production and negligence of land which is a national loss. Even if co-operative is accepted as the logical end of his philosophy one thing is very essential namely a cooperative spirit for running cooperative enterprises. As things stand at present no nation in the world has successfully implemented cooperative system at national level. To think of implementing such a scheme under Indian conditions, where the people are poverty stricken and keenly look after their personal interests, it shall be only an ideal arrangement, not suited to India. Roy's arrangement appears to be sound in theory but is utopian for a country Re ours. Our Planning Commission and Five-Year Plans are however, very close to the arrangements suggested by him in his proposed economic system of planning. Roy was a born revolutionary and like many other revolutionaries, in the very initial stages of development he was receptive to Marxian philosophy. In fact his love for Marxism was so deep rooted that under his arrangement the only solution to existing Indian problems lay in Marxism. His enthusiasm in Marxian philosophy is evident from the fact that he was the first Indian who founded a Communist Party outside Russia and that too for the first time.

Gradually, however, his interest in Marxism slackened and tried to seek a solution of Indian problems under the flag of Indian National Congress. No doubt he could not adjust himself there also and continued to remain a revolutionary but certainly not a Marxist. Some of the points of criticism put forth by him against Marxism areas under:

Nationalism of Roy. As already said in the beginning Roy was a Communist and believed that the workers and peasants had no fatherland. It was under this influence that Roy gave the idea that nationalism was undesirable because it was based on hatred and created many unnecessary and unwanted problems. In his opinion nationalism has degenerated itself into racialism and colonialism. He also thought that if national borders were removed, many of our social, economic and political problems would automatically be solved. In Roy's opinion the greatest problem of the modem time was this narrow outlook which nationalism brought with it. In actual practice Roy did not very much adhere to this principle and he struggled to achieve freedom for India on national basis.

Marxism of Roy. Roy criticised Marx for its denial of individual liberty. In-so-far as Marxism was concerned Roy was of the opinion that there was complete regimentation in that and party bosses expected the masses to act according to their instructions. In Communism he felt, there was at all no place for individual freedom. Similarly Roy did not agree with Marxian theory of dialectical materialism as well as that of historical interpretation given by Karl Marx. He was not convinced that history of hitherto existing struggle was only that of class struggle. In his opinion there were many other factors, responsible for proper interpretation of this struggle.

He, similarly criticised the Communists for their dogmatic outlook. He, criticised Marxists for their narrow outlook. In the same way Roy criticised Marx for his prophecy about the disappearance of middle classes. Though Marx had made a prophecy that gradually middle classes would disappear yet history was a witness that middle classes were emerging as a powerful and forceful factor and influence in moulding national policies and programmes. As such Marxism was not coming true with the changing conditions and required radical change. Roy also did not agree with Marx in his rejection of their liberal concept of individualism and as such felt that by such a concept Marx virtually betrayed his ideas about Humanism. Not only this but he felt that ,ethical foundations of Marxism were weak because of its overstressing the role of working classes in the future set-up of our society. Thus, whereas Roy continued to adhere to the idea of increasing association of people in their administration which was the basic principle of Marxian philosophy, he was pained to see that the Marxists denied this increasing, share, and in fact, in practice, kept the masses aloof from their administrative machinery.

Twentieth Century Jacobism of Roy. During Second World War (1939-1945) M.N. Roy was strong supporter of twentieth century, Jacobism, which he believed was historically fore-runner of Bolshevism, in spite of the fact that it is the creed of a bourgeoisie revolt. For him it was in between the bourgeoisies revolution and proletariat revolution and had two implications, firstly the Indian revolution was to be led by a multi class party and not by proletariats who were in minority and secondly that immediate problem before India was not Communism or socialism but a democratic revolution.

Gandhism of Roy. Roy, fully well appreciated the role of Mahatma Gandhi in India's national freedom struggle. In his opinion Gandhiji consolidated Indian National struggle for freedom and united the masses. He was also responsible for providing a forum to the masses where they could fearlessly and frankly express their opinion. Not only this, he also appreciated his love for the down-trodden and the poor and raising them to higher standard of living. He praised Gandhiji for his technique of civil disobedience and non-cooperation especially in the field of non-payment of taxes to the Government. By and large he also supported him in his ideas about nonviolence. But at the same time he was not all praise for Gandhism. In his opinion it was not a co-ordinated system of thought and that its social basis was cultural backwardness and its intellectual mainstay, superstition. He felt that Gandhism was not very logical in its economic programme. He could not reconcile himself to the idea that by spinning on the wheel or by the use of khaddar India could be economically advanced. Similarly he felt that Gandhism tried to reconcile the interests of the peasants and the landowners which was rather impracticable and impossible. In his philosophy both could not go side by side and suggested that some effective steps should have been proposed by Gandhiji to solve this economic problem of India.

Revolution of Roy. M.N. Roy very thoroughly studied Marxian theory of revolution, which in practice implied forceful over-throw of social set-up. In other words Marx believed in radical changes and the use of force for achieving ends. Roy was, however, not very much convinced of the Marxian theory of revolution. According to Roy, Marx was wrong about the role of middle classes in forging revolution in capitalists societies. He, however, did not under-estimate the necessity of introducing a revolution or in other words radical reconstruction of society as a necessary step for improving our present set-up. In his opinion middle class was the most backward section of the society and careful attention should be given to this class. In his opinion, it was wrong to ignore one class and to bring the other to prominence, as was the case with Marxian theory. He came to the conclusion that revolutionary forces must include people of all shades and opinions except those which had vested interests and were not prepared to accept changed social set-up. According to Roy, a revolution could be successfully brought about by appealing to the good sense of the rulers. It is a human urge to remain in power and those who somehow manage to get power will like to continue and shall also listen to public opinion with care and attention. In his philosophy if this principle was observed a lasting revolution could be brought about and the evil of party system, which parliamentary democracy has brought with it, would end. In Roy's philosophy an appeal to the rationality and morality of the people in power was bound to purify politics in many ways. Roy, however, felt that the task of bringing about a revolution of this kind was not very easy. There were certain pre-requisites for such a change namely that of educating the people and wiping out mass illiteracy which was prevalent in India. Not only this, but the people of India will have to be made conscious and careful about their political rights. His another weapon was that of propagation. Roy felt that propaganda was a very effective and powerful check against high-handedness or excessive action of those in power. Propaganda should always be at national and not at local level.

Fascism of Roy. Roy was very much opposed to Fascist philosophy particularly about their contempt for human freedom. For him it meant debasement of human personality and end of man's moral stature. He was also opposed to their concept of racial superiority and inferiority. For him Fascism developed in Italy under certain peculiar circumstances. For him Fascism was nothing else but a point at which counter revolutionary and reactionary forces could rally. It elevates the cult of totalitarianism and provides totalitarian leaders, who are otherwise frustrated, sonic psychological satisfaction. In it whereas on the one hand capitalism receives strength on the other individual becomes socially insecure.

Decolonization of Roy. Roy gave a very novel idea namely that of decolonization which he called as crisis in Imperialism. According to Roy the whole colonial system was based on the principle of exploitation. Basically an imperialist country would try to exploit the colony under its control and shall see to it that there was maximum drainage of resources from the colony. In other words it was an attempt to lower down the living standard of the subject people and at the same time raising up the standard of the imperial country. As however the time passes with that the purchasing power of the people of these colonies to purchase commodities manufactured in the imperial country declines. This means not only slump in the market of the imperial country but also in a way it is also checking drainage on the economic resources of the colony. In order to improve the situation the imperial country would set-up commissions and committees to enquire into the causes of this poverty and finding out solution for raising the living standard of the people to a limited extent so that the people got some purchasing power. This process, he called that of decolonization. In other words in Roy's opinion in an imperial zest for power a stage was bound to come when the people of the imperialist country shall have to check their exploitation and be forced to think in terms of bettering and raising the living standard of the people of the colonies.

Second World War. M.N. Roy had no consistent views about Second World War, which was a major event in world history. As long as Allies and Russia were fighting against Nazism he was in favour of helping the Allies and wanted that these powers should be given unqualified support. It was an international civil war in which conflict was not between the states but between the ideologies. For India's defence in this war agrarian revolution was very necessary. In support of his viewpoint he said that peasants would defend their motherland when they would be sure that the land which they cultivate belonged to them. Industrial growth in India is slow because the people have very limited purchasing power. During war days Indian National Congress had launched Quit India Movement, but Roy condemned it as a movement which had been organised by industrial and financial patrons of Congress party. He supported the formation of people's government but was not in favour of national government, which according to him was fraudulent. He considered Quit India Movement as fantastic attempt by Indian leaders.

During war he even characterised Congress as representative of nascent Indian Fascism. He was opposed to Congress idea and policy of not supporting Allied powers in war efforts. Since Indian National Congress was not supporting war efforts, therefore, he advocated isolation of the party leaders by sending them to jail. He said that these leaders were creating nuisance value and Gandhiji was embodiment of India's backwardness and condemned his action as a mischief.

Achievements and Character of Roy. Roy died almost unknown and unnoticed. He, who struggled so hard for national freedom could not get his due place in our Indian society. Politically and temperamentally he could not remain for long in the fold of any great political organization. Both in the Indian National Congress and Communist Party he could not fit himself. He very boldly championed the cause of individualism. In his philosophy freedom of individual was above everything else. He felt Communist organization simply because it denied individual liberty.

Similarly he had love for democracy. No doubt he criticised the present indirect form of democracy but his alternative was to reform democratic institutions on the basis of decentralization of authority. Basically his ideas about decentralization and Panchayatı Raj have been followed by our national leaders of today. Similarly, he gave the idea of creation of a planning authority to plan our economy and gave that a place in the constitution itself. His ideas have also seen the light of the day and we have also realized the necessity of a Planning Commission to plan our future economy. Not only this but he virtually stood for peaceful revolution or change in our social set-up. This peaceful revolution is the creed of even Gandhian philosophy. But at the same time Roy suffered from certain serious drawbacks. He could not give a proper definition to the term 'education' though in his philosophy that was a solution to many problems. It has, in fact, very rightly been said that he used the term everywhere but without defining as to what that was. Similarly, Roy ignored religion which was not very desirable. In each society religion has got its own role to play and to ignore this important aspect of life is not desirable.

Roy has also stressed on reason which, in his opinion, should be the sole test of judging the validity of an institution. But he has practically nowhere defined the term 'reason' and thus the pivot of his philosophy has been shaken. Roy is also a victim to simplification of many problems, as was the case with Marx. He has not tried to clearly explain the difficulties which were bound to come in the implementation of his organized democracy or economic arrangement, and thus can be charged for misleading the masses. Roy's patriotism is undisputed. Hardly at the age of 15 he went out of his country in search of arms from a foreign country to overthrow a foreign government from Indian soil. Similarly he had to remain in Europe for long to find out ways and means of liberation for the people of India. Even as a Communist he raised a voice against its leadership by suggesting that there should be a separate Communist Party in India to struggle for India's freedom. But in spite of that Roy remained in the background because his philosophy had no mass appeal. Much of that remained ideal and utopian rather than practical and real to life.

BIBLIOGRAPHY

Alfred Rosmer, *Lenin's Moscow*, Pluto Press, London.

B C. Pal, *The Spirit of Indian Nationalism*, London, 1910.

Bampfylde Fuller, *The Empire of India*, London, 1913.

Bipan Chandra, *Communalism in Modern India*, Delhi 1984.

C.R. Das, *India for Indians*, Madras, 1921.

Durga Das : *India From Curzon to Nehru and After*, London, 1969.

Edward Cadogan, *The India We Saw*, London, 1933.

H. Khon, *A History of Nationalism in the East*, London, 1931.

J.M. Kenworthy, *India : A Warning*, London, 1931.

James Camphell Ker, *Political Trouble in India* 1907-1917, Indian edition, Calcutta, 1973.

Jawaharlal Nehru, *An Autobiography*, Bombay, 1962.

———, *Glimpses of World History*, Bombay, 1934.

Jayaprakash Narayan, *Congress Socialist Party (Hindi)*, Patna, Samta Prakashan, 1946.

John Patrick Haithcox, *Communism and Nationalism in India*, Princeton University Press, Princeton, 1971.

John S. Hoyland, *The Case for India*, London. 1929.

Lajpat Rai, *The Political Future of India*, New York, 1919.

Leonard A. Gorden, *Bengal : The Nationalist Movement* 1876-1904, Columbia University Press, New York, 1974.

Lord Meston, *Nationhood for India*, Oxford, 1934.

M.N. Roy, *India in Transition*, Nachiketa Publications, 1971.

———, *India in Transition*, Nachiketa Publications.

———, *Letters from Jail*, Renaissance Publishers, 1965.

———, *Men I Met*, Lalwani Publishing House, Bombay, 1968.

———, *New Orientation*, Renaissance Publishers, Calcutta, 1946.

———, *New Orientation*, Renaissance Publishers, Calcutta.

———, *Our differences*, Saraswaty Library, Calcutta, 1938.

———, *The Future of Indian Politics*, Minerva Associates, Calcutta, 1971.

Margarita Barns, *India Today and Tomorrow*, London, 1937.

Maulana Abul Kalam Azad, *India Wins Freedom*, Bombay, 1959.

Philip Spratt, *Blowing up India*, Prachi Prakashan, Calcutta, 1955.

Prem Bhasin, *Socialism in India*, New Delhi, 1968.

R. Coupland, *The Indian Problem, 1833-1935*, London, 1942.

R.G. Pradhan, *India's Struggle for Swaraj*, Madras, 1930.

Robert C. North and Xenia J. Eudin, *M.N. Roy's Mission to China*, University of California Press, Berkeley.

Ronald Segal, *The Crisis of India*, London, 1965.

S.C. Bose, *The Indian Struggle, 1920-1942*. New York, 1964.

S.K. Vidyarthi, *China in Revolt*, M.N. Roy, Vanguared Publishing Co., Bombay, 1932.

S.R. Bakshi, *Simon Commission and Indian Nationalism*, New Delhi, 1977.

S.R. Mehrotra, *Towards Indian Freedom and Partition*, New Delhi, 1979.

Sankar Ghose, *Political Ideas and Movements in India*, Calcutta, 1975.

Tara Chand, *History of Freedom Movement in India*. Vol. III. New Delhi, 1973.

V.B. Karnik, *Indian Trade Unions – A Survey*, Manaktalas, Bombay.

V.T. Patil, *Nehru and the Freedom Movement*, New Delhi, 1977.

Index